Shooting Arrows and Slinging Mud

SHOOTING ARROWS AND SLINGING MUD

Custer, the Press, and the Little Bighorn

James E. Mueller

University of Oklahoma Press : Norman

Library of Congress Cataloging-in-Publication Data

Mueller, James E., 1960–
  Shooting arrows and slinging mud : Custer, the press, and the Little Bighorn /
James E. Mueller.
      pages   cm
  Includes bibliographical references and index.
  ISBN 978-0-8061-4398-9 (hardcover : alk. paper) 1. Little Bighorn, Battle of
the, Mont., 1876. 2. Dakota Indians—Wars, 1876—Press coverage. 3. Custer,
George A. (George Armstrong), 1839–1876. 4. Dakota Indians—Wars, 1876—
Journalists. 5. War correspondents—United States—History—19th century.
6. Journalism—United States—History—19th century. I. Title.
  E83.876.M85 2013
  973.8'2—dc23
                                                                    2013005670

For Cathy

Contents

List of Illustrations   viii

Preface   ix

1. "So Fit a Death": Custer's Last Stand   3

2. "Horrible!": The News Shocks the Nation   31

3. "The Blood of These Brave Men":
   Assessing the Blame for Defeat   55

4. "A Little Cheap Political Capital":
   The Little Bighorn and the Presidential Campaign   79

5. "The Old Rebel Spirit":
   The Hamburg Massacre Bumps Custer off the Front Page   121

6. "Asses Who Are Braying for Extermination":
   The Indians in Little Bighorn Coverage   146

7. "Custer's Death Was Sioux-icide":
   Humor and the Little Bighorn   169

8. "Duty and Valor":
   The Focus of Little Bighorn Coverage   193

Notes   215

Bibliography   239

Index   247

Illustrations

Unless otherwise noted, all illustrations are courtesy of the Library of Congress, Prints and Photographs Division.

The Custer image, 1864, *Harper's Weekly*	109
George Armstrong Custer, 1865	110
Wesley Merritt, Philip Sheridan, George Crook, James William Forsyth, and Custer, 1865	111
The Newspaper Pavilion at the Centennial Exhibition in Philadelphia	112
Tourists examine a tipi at the Centennial in Philadelphia, *Daily Graphic*	113
Daily Graphic portrayal of Indian rights activist Wendell Phillips	114
Sioux leader Sitting Bull	115
Charity ball organized by southerners to raise money for a monument to former enemy Custer, *Daily Graphic*	116
Columbia mourns the Little Bighorn dead and shames Democratic House Speaker Samuel J. Randall for his party's efforts to cut the size of the army, *Daily Graphic*	117
The Hamburg Massacre, *Harper's Weekly*	118
Rutherford B. Hayes, 1876 Republican presidential nominee	119
Samuel J. Tilden, 1876 Democratic presidential nominee	120

Preface

I first became interested in the Little Bighorn when my uncle and aunt, Donald and Frances Swan, gave me a copy of the Quentin Reynolds book for young readers called *Custer's Last Stand* for my eighth birthday. The poignant drawing of George and Tom Custer dying together at the end of the battle sparked a fascination that deepened when my family visited the battlefield two years later.

Personal interest and professional goals intersected about twenty years ago when I was a doctoral student in journalism at the University of Texas. I chanced upon a picture of Custer on the steps of one of the university's buildings, taken while he was stationed in Austin immediately after the end of the Civil War. I wondered how the Texas press remembered their former enemy when they wrote about the Little Bighorn and started digging at the university library. I found that many Texas journalists reacted emotionally to Custer's death, angry that such a brave, chivalrous man had been killed at the hands of "savages." Custer was a Democrat and an Indian fighter, and in solid Democratic Texas he was a sympathetic character compared to the despised Republican President Grant, the enforcer of Reconstruction. It seemed politics influenced coverage.

But what about other regions of the country? I looked in detail at the Kansas press for a western example, Kentucky for a border region, and Illinois for a northern state. Other surprising patterns of coverage emerged besides partisanship, such as the frequent use of humor in Kentucky papers. I noticed that some newspapers, including those close to the war zone, were sympathetic to the Indian side of the story. As I looked at newspapers published later in 1876 rather than in the immediate aftermath of the battle, I found that other stories quickly pushed the Little Bighorn and the Great Sioux War off the front pages.

I published several articles on my preliminary findings but constantly expanded my research with the idea of eventually writing a book. I studied specific newspapers in the Far West, the South, New York, St. Louis, Hartford, San Francisco, and Baltimore. All were chosen because of their reputation as respected newspapers. Other scholars may disagree with the selection, but it provides a sample of newspaper work from all over the country—a sample that shows the breadth of opinion in 1876 about Custer, Native Americans, and the future of the country.

The original grammar, spelling, and punctuation of quotations from these papers and other archival material are preserved throughout the book, except in cases where an obvious typo would interfere with the understanding of the passage. Headlines in 1876 were often in all-caps. I have changed them to modern capitalization style for the sake of readability, except where it is obvious that the all-caps in the original were used for emphasis rather than design convention. I use the National Park Service spelling of the battlefield—"Little Bighorn"—rather than "Little Big Horn" unless the latter is used in direct quotations.

Depending on the availability of the papers, I examined issues from the time of the political conventions in June until the end of the election in early November. The battle was off most front pages within a month, but I read issues through the election to try to determine how much of an impact the Little Bighorn had on the presidential campaign. Of course, the press covered various aspects of the battle after the election; the Reno court of inquiry renewed interest in the battle in 1879, to cite just one example. However, an assessment of such later coverage is beyond the scope of this book, which focuses on coverage of the battle as a news story.

My main purpose is to shed light on newspaper content about the battle in order to show what was available to ordinary readers in 1876. This book is not a retelling of the battle, although I include a chapter reviewing the history of the Sioux war, Custer, and the Little Bighorn as background for those new to the topic and a refresher for those already familiar with it. Anyone who writes about Custer must include the obligatory phrase "the literature is voluminous." Countless outstanding historians have tackled the subject. I relied most heavily on the works of Robert Utley, James Donovan, and Paul Hedren; the bibliography lists the other works I found very helpful.

Utley and Donovan both touch on press coverage of the battle. Utley devotes a chapter of *Custer and the Great Controversy* to the press's role in stimulating debate about the blame for the army's defeat. Brian Dippie, Richard Slotkin, and Bruce Rosenberg are among those who have written about the role of the press in establishing the myth of the Last Stand. William Huntzicker and Hugh J. Reilly have focused on the frontier press and the Little Bighorn. Journalism historian John Coward has written extensively about the coverage of Indians in relation to the Little Bighorn. Oliver Knight wrote the definitive book on the life of Indian war correspondents, and Sandy Barnard wrote an exceptional biography of Mark Kellogg, the journalist who died with Custer. Sandy talked with me several times about my project and graciously offered me advice and pointed me to useful sources. The excellent work of all of these scholars has informed my own research and understanding of the battle. The work of Ted Smythe and Gerald Baldasty was especially helpful in understanding the Gilded Age press.

I try to address a gap in Little Bighorn literature by approaching press coverage as a news story in the context of the other events of 1876. I focus on the content of the press in an attempt to portray what information, opinion, and even entertainment Americans had available not just in the immediate aftermath of the battle but through the election. During the course of my research, the United States became involved in wars against guerrilla foes not unlike the Great Sioux War in 1876, and the nation held several presidential elections. In comparing the coverage of 1876 to that of our own time, I concluded that 1876 readers were in some ways better informed. Journalists in both eras made mistakes in coverage, but those in 1876 wrote with a passion and transparency that made the issues of the day jump off the pages and slap readers in the face, demanding that they pay attention. At the same time, the research shows that what journalists think is news is not necessarily what will be important to future generations. Custer's Last Stand is the enduring memory of the centennial year for America, whereas the presidential campaign, which dominated news coverage for most of 1876, is now of interest largely only to political scientists and professional historians. I hope this book contributes to examination of the status of the press in our own time as well as to the study of the Battle of the Little Bighorn.

Telling the story of coverage of the battle required the help of many people in addition to the work of the scholars mentioned earlier. I thank Charmaine Wawrzyniec, reference technician and Custer curator at the

Monroe (Michigan) County Library System, for guiding me through the collection and helping me find important articles and documents. When I was on deadline in the copyediting phase, she even looked up the date of an article I had forgotten to write in my notes. I also thank Nan Card, curator of manuscripts at the Rutherford B. Hayes Presidential Center, who helped me find relevant documents among Hayes's papers.

I also owe a debt of gratitude to the great folks at the University of Oklahoma Press. Charles E. Rankin, associate director and editor-in-chief, was consistently encouraging and offered wise advice. Connie Arnold, administrative assistant, was a great help in organizing the photographs. Alice Stanton, special projects editor, has made the editing process flow smoothly. I also appreciate the hard work of Amy Hernandez, marketing assistant.

John Thomas, copyeditor, did a great job catching errors and suggested improvements that made the writing flow better and more clearly. Three anonymous reviewers carefully read the manuscript and made suggestions that tremendously improved the original draft.

Finally, I thank my family for their patience and support during these many years of researching Custer's Last Stand and the press. Parts of several family vacations were spent visiting libraries and historic sites, and our Ford Explorer was a casualty one late night on the road from Hardin to Billings when a deer tried to jump over the car and missed. The car was totaled but no human was injured, and our vacation in Montana was extended three more days as we tried to figure out the best way back to Texas. On our first trip to the battlefield, our oldest daughter Mickey was a teenager who could help supervise her siblings David and Sarah. Now she has three children of her own.

My wife Cathy, who has a demanding job of her own, has helped me in countless ways and in fact came up with the title for the book. Among other things, she diligently read each draft, offered suggestions for improvement, and helped find the photographs. Words cannot express my admiration and love for her, but in gratitude for everything she does I dedicate this book to her.

Shooting Arrows and Slinging Mud

CHAPTER 1

"So Fit a Death"

Custer's Last Stand

On hearing the news of George Armstrong Custer's death in 1876 at the Little Bighorn, a New York theater critic penned an essay claiming that the ideal hero of the frontier had died.[1] Andrew C. Wheeler, a playwright, war correspondent, and novelist as well critic, noted that Custer had a successful Civil War record but that other Union generals like Ulysses S. Grant, William T. Sherman, and Philip H. Sheridan had overshadowed him. Some people were in fact surprised when reading the extensive Civil War achievements listed in Custer's obituary. Nevertheless, the erstwhile "boy general"—he had reached that rank at age twenty-three during the war—was unquestionably the leading hero of the plains Indian wars.

Custer's frontier reputation was based in part on his memoir, *My Life on the Plains*, which had remained popular since its release in 1874 and was, according to Wheeler, sold out in New York the day after the battle was reported in the city. Wheeler explained that Custer wrote only "good newspaper English" and his memoir was full of dime novel clichés, "but it is precisely these defects which attest the genuineness of the work and constitute its charm." *My Life on the Plains* was an excellent nonfiction complement to the frontier-themed novels devoured by a public seeking romance and adventure.

"What happier combination of circumstances! Thanks to Cooper and Beadle's dime series we are all Indian-mad, and, through the progress of settlement in the Far West, and the presence there of the army recruited from every section of the country, almost all of us have a personal interest in the ceaseless struggle with the Indians. Romance and

3

intense personal feeling are thus blent as they, perhaps, never have been." It was, Wheeler wrote, as if Sir Walter Scott had been writing his popular romantic medieval novels during the Crusades, and every English family at that time was reading them.

It was an apt comparison. Custer, who had read such romances as a boy, was often compared to a knight in newspaper stories about his cavalry charges. According to Wheeler, Custer was the perfect fit for this idealized image transplanted to the American West:

> Not till the sun falls dead from the signs [skies] will such a niche be so filled. Custer had the presence of a popular hero, and flashed through the history of a prosaic age resplendent and romantic, with the locks of a Cavalier or hero of a Norse saga; the dress and fiery enthusiasm of Rupert; the luck of a favorite of the fairies. On the plains he becomes the ideal hunter and warrior, with his fringed buckskin suit, his gay arms and trappings, his thoroughbred horse, his grayhounds and staghounds by his side. Such a character takes and retains the public eye. . . . And when at last he fell in battle fighting against the odds and surrounded by his comrades he crowned the story of his life with so fit a death that it will be many years ere his name fades from its place in history and literature—if it ever fades and does not rather become enduring in popular tradition like that of Carson or of Boone.

Wheeler was certainly correct about Custer's image as a frontiersmen, but he downplayed too much the public's appreciation of his Civil War record. No newspaper sketch artists were on hand at the Little Bighorn in 1876 to record what would become known as Custer's Last Stand. But readers could easily imagine what it looked like without any help from a picture. Custer's image as the *beau sabreur* of the Civil War—the very epitome of a cavalryman—had been embedded in the public's mind since his appearance on the cover of *Harper's Weekly* in March 1864. That drawing shows Custer leading a charge in a nameless battle. The youthful officer, shaven except for flowing mustache, is hatless, sword upraised to urge forward a group of bearded, grizzled veterans, blurry in the background. Custer's horse, wild-eyed and champing at the bit, is bounding toward the unseen enemy. The sketch might have been from a fight on the Rapidan River in Virginia—the magazine was not specific in its story—but it clearly illustrates Custer's Civil War record—a series of usually victorious, furious charges, including one at Gettysburg that some historians argue saved the battle and thus the war.[2]

The press noticed Custer for more than his combat leadership. When he was promoted to general—the youngest in the Union army at the time—he designed his own outfit of a dark blue velveteen jacket with gold braid curling up the sleeves, a light blue large-collared navy shirt, a wide-brimmed hat, and a red necktie. His clothing and long, golden hair and flowing mustache gave him a look that was easy to remember. It was a look that inspired hero worship in men and crushes in girls.

A decade of press coverage followed Custer to the frontier, where he traded Union blue for buckskins and created a new look for a new era. He hobnobbed with visiting Russian royalty, led exploratory expeditions, and helped grow his own legend by writing numerous magazine and newspaper articles as well as *My Life on the Plains*. He even found time to lead a victorious yet controversial campaign against the Cheyennes in what is now Oklahoma.

Is it any wonder that, when the *New York Herald* solicited money for a monument to Custer after the Little Bighorn, it received donations from everyone from waiters to Broadway actors, and from both Union *and* Confederate veterans? A wagon driver who could afford to give only 25 cents wrote that he would also give his life if the government called for volunteers to avenge Custer. An office boy named Philip Hoffman said he would be rejected if he tried to enlist, but he was contributing 10 cents and would collect more donations at work. "I am of German parents, but as an American by birth my heart swells with indignation over the death of our gallant General and soldiers at the hands of the brutal Indians." An anonymous school girl sent 10 cents after reading the *Herald* story to her mother, who presumably was illiterate. "We girls admire brave men, because, I suppose, and as mother says, we are such cowards ourselves. I would give the world to have had one look at the fearless General Custer; and then he was so young and, as the papers say, so handsome. I could cry tears over his sad fate. All the girls and women, I fancy, must feel as I do, for such heroes as General Custer are what they most admire, and then, you know, they are scarce. Leave it to the school girls and a monument will soon be raised to the gallant General Custer, for he was a man."[3]

Uniquely charismatic men like Custer, who always seem to be in the right place at the right time, are indeed rare, which is why he was always good copy, as journalists are wont to say. If it is true that he led himself and his men to their deaths at the Little Bighorn in a mad dash for glory, then he was only doing what the press and its voracious readers expected him to do. At least that was the take of a *Louisville Courier-Journal* correspondent who had attended West Point with Custer. The reporter, identified only as J.M.W., wrote that twenty-five or thirty years earlier an officer would have hurt his reputation by trying to draw attention to himself like Custer did, but that the Civil War "changed all that feeling."[4]

The country had eagerly followed the exploits of its soldiers during the War of the Rebellion, as it was fondly characterized by the North. Officers learned quickly that press coverage, though not more important than battlefield success, could nevertheless help make or break careers. George Gordon Meade, the hero of Gettysburg, feuded with the press, and the resulting bad publicity may have kept the ambitious general from running for president after the war. Custer was not that ambitious, but he knew good press could help get promotions in the small, competitive peacetime army.[5]

The *Courier-Journal* writer thought Custer's image would remain intact despite his leadership in a defeat in which he and all the men under his immediate command perished:

The old Indian fighters, judged by the modern standard, were slow, but it was because they had little to gain in reputation by dash, and so they went at the Indian cautiously, with no other motive than to punish him. The country now demands that our Indian fighters shall be dashing fellows, who shall sweep over the plains with their whirling squadrons and ride down the ruthless savage. Custer was only meeting the demand of the country when he met his fate. His fault was the fault of his times and people. He fulfilled to the letter, from the golden locks floating in the wind down to the jingling spurs that impelled his fiery steed to the charge, all the popular conditions prescribed for the dashing Indian fighter of the frontier. His memory will go down to posterity as surely as it should go as a hero, and even now criticism on his military operations sinks back abashed in the thronging crowd of tender and glorious memories that cluster about the life of this dead young soldier.[6]

The tender memories thronged because of Custer's tragic yet heroic death, but before the shock of the Little Bighorn Indian fighting on the frontier was just one of many issues to think about in a time the *Hartford Daily Courant* called "the condensed age." The *Courant* worried that the popularity of abridged books in 1876 was a sign people were too busy to read seriously and think about big ideas. Book sales were hurt by large public libraries, where readers were "borrowing [books], galloping through them and returning them" instead of purchasing copies to keep for continual reflection. "The age is active, restless beyond all precedent," the *Courant* harrumphed.[7]

Perhaps people were extraordinarily restless because it was an era of unprecedented change. It was, after all, also the "Gilded Age," named after the 1873 novel by Mark Twain and Charles Dudley Warner that spoofed American greed, materialism, and corruption during the rapid and unsettling period of postwar industrialization. In 1876 the country was still suffering the effects of the Panic of 1873, a depression that would last until 1879. It would cause widespread bankruptcies, bank closings, deflation, violent strikes, and unemployment as high as 14 percent.[8]

Amid this economic turmoil, always in the background like a chain-rattling ghost, was the vivid memory of a horrific war that had killed or maimed hundreds of thousands of Americans and laid waste to one region of the country. The great contest had begun as a call to save the Union, but after four years of devastation and slaughter it had taken on the more spiritual meaning of "a new birth of freedom." Now, a little more than ten years later, the new freedom seemed closer to death than birth. Reconstruction was going poorly in the South. Groups like the Ku Klux Klan were terrorizing blacks, who were desperately clinging to the right to vote. Northerners were getting tired of funding an army to police the violence in the South.

Politicians violently disagreed over how to handle the country's problems. A resurgent Democratic Party had won the midterm elections in 1874 and appeared ready to ride public anger over Republican scandals to take the White House in 1876, which would mean the end of Reconstruction. Republicans, on the other hand, had vilified the Democratic Party for ten years as rebels and traitors. Republicans promised to "wave the bloody shirt" to try to win just one more presidential election. People on both sides feared that a close election might be disputed and prompt a return to civil war.

Yet there was still a sense of optimism over the country's growth that was manifested in the Centennial Exhibition in Philadelphia. Almost 10 million people—about one-fifth of the population—attended the fair.[9] The exhibition contained an amazing sampling of artistic, scientific, and industrial displays celebrating the nation's one-hundredth year of progress. It included new inventions like the typewriter, which visitors could use for 50 cents to write a souvenir letter, and a gizmo called the telephone, which so shocked the Brazilian emperor Dom Pedro II that he dropped the receiver when he tried it, saying, "My God! It talks!" One of the stars of the exhibition was the Corliss steam engine, a 1,500-horsepower behemoth that was the largest and most powerful machine of its type in the world.[10]

Such scientific marvels were a stark contrast to a large display of various American Indian tools, pottery, tipis, and weapons. A 65-foot canoe and life-size papier-mâché and wax figures modeling Indian clothes gave fairgoers a thrilling illustration of what was considered a rapidly dying race. Charles Rau, a Smithsonian curator who organized the display, said in a speech called "The Happy Age" that Americans should "glory" in having surpassed their primitive ancestors and in knowing that progress "governs the development of mankind."[11]

While the fairgoers were gawking at Indian mannequins, across the continent the army was marching against flesh-and-blood warriors who were not ready to accept the idea that their time was past. On May 17, one week after President Ulysses S. Grant had opened the Centennial Exhibition by starting the Corliss engine, a column of infantry and cavalry under the command of Brig. Gen. Alfred H. Terry marched out of Fort Abraham Lincoln in Dakota Territory to converge with two other columns to force Sioux, Cheyenne, and Arapaho bands onto reservations. In charge of the Seventh Cavalry regiment under Terry's command was Lt. Col. George Armstrong Custer. Despite Custer's celebrity, what would come to be called the Great Sioux War got comparatively little attention in newspapers back East. Since the founding of the country, Americans had opposed a large peacetime army for fear it would infringe on their civil liberties, and they considered Indian conflicts to be police actions instead of real wars.[12] The current war, or police action, was not widely popular because many saw it as merely a pretext for seizing the Black Hills, where gold had been discovered two years earlier during a surveying expedition led by Custer. The *Courant,* for example, on May 19 castigated Custer for "his rose-colored reports of the Black Hills" that led miners to invade the Indian territory. "They [the miners] are being killed and scalped by the score, and in their behalf the nation is obliged to incur the expense of a military campaign for the slaughter of the Indians who are only defending their lands from lawless depredators. So much for Custer."[13]

And so much for the Great Sioux War. The Gilded Age crowds at the Centennial were more concerned with wonders like a two-ton silver nugget pulled out of a mine in Virginia City, Nevada. The nugget's popularity bothered George P. Rowell, a pioneering ad man who had organized the Centennial's Newspaper Pavilion, where fairgoers could read just about every newspaper in the country but often passed it by for shinier objects. "Thousands of curious men and women are drawn about it, and look wonderingly and wistfully at its huge form," Rowell said of the nugget, admitting that it was a better draw than his newspaper building. "It represents to man's cupidity just so much of life's happiness. But thieves may break through and steal such treasures. Who thinks of the toiling thousands of earnest literary men and women, scattered over our states and territories, who waste midnight oil in preparing that mental food which, enduring when silver and gold have taken to them wings and departed never to return, proves to be a lasting comfort!"[14]

Rowell, the founder of the industry journal *Printer's Ink* and a namesake newspaper directory that was one of the first annuals to provide circulation statistics, believed fervently in the power of journalism to improve lives. "Track the globe around, and those lands will be found most highly civilized and forward in catering to their people's comfort where the press is most plentiful, free and powerful," he wrote. Rowell was bullish about the future of newspapers despite the economic depression. He claimed that more than eight thousand newspapers were published in the United States, more than all the titles in all the other countries of the world combined.[15] In fact, growth in the number of newspapers in the United States—10 percent a year—was greater in the 1870s than in any previous decade in the nation's history. Why the growth in an economic downturn? Newspapers were the main medium of news, and they provided cheap entertainment to boot. Most of these newspapers were started in small towns or new industrial cities, and many of them practiced the "new journalism" that emphasized topics of interest to the ordinary reader, things like crime, sports, and features rather than what had long been the staple of the news business—partisan political coverage. After all, people needed a break from the standard ten-hour day, six-day work week, and they needed information they could use; few wanted stories about political wrangling unless they were told with humor. Editors were beginning to see readers not just as voters in elections but as consumers of goods in a market society.[16]

"Americans are a nation of newspaper readers," Rowell declared. "There are papers for girls and boys, for teachers and taught, for trades, arts and sciences, for the lovers of the wonderful, the religious, the agriculturists, the metallurgists—in a word, the physician, as he rides to the birthplace of some young patient, and the undertaker, as he drives to the house of mourning, must each have his paper to while away his time."[17]

The editors who produced those papers were just the sort of people who would be excited by the futuristic gadgets and optimism of the Centennial Exhibition. They were "early adopters of new technology and innovators" in business practices who eagerly took advantage of the changes in America, according to one historian.[18] Like Rowell, these editors believed that their profession wedded to modern technology could change the world for the better. An editorial in the *Alta California* on June 26 reminded readers that the telegraph had been invented only a little over thirty years earlier, and it had made rapid communication possible between their city of San Francisco and the rest of the world: "It has linked all civilized nations together, annihilated space and time, and, we really believe, done much toward annihilating their misunderstandings, and so making wars less likely to occur. The telegraph brings the different Governments face to face, and misunderstandings can be explained before the people at large know anything about it; and so national antagonisms are prevented by seasonable telegraphic correspondence."[19]

But on the very day that editorial appeared, and almost a month after the Centennial Exhibition opened, antagonisms between several American Indian tribes and the U.S. government were in full force on the Little Bighorn River. The remote battlefield, located in what is now southern

Montana, was so far removed from the nearest telegraph that most Americans would not learn of the disaster for ten days. As San Francisco journalists dreamed of a future without war and Philadelphia fairgoers contemplated the passing of the Indian, warriors were besieging the demoralized survivors of the Seventh Cavalry after killing Custer and about 265 of his troopers the day before.[20] The war, which had been so distant in both miles and imagination, would shortly become very real to the public, because the Little Bighorn made it sensational front-page news. It was, as one journalism historian called it, "one of the great news stories of the nineteenth century."[21]

The Little Bighorn was a great story for two main reasons: the magnitude of the defeat and the death of Custer. Furthermore, the circumstances of the battle and Custer's career were controversial, a main characteristic of any good story. As the great western historian Robert Utley noted, the country almost immediately engaged in what he called "the Custer Controversy" over who was to blame for the defeat.[22] It is a debate that is still unresolved today. To some, Custer and the Little Bighorn represent white arrogance and the imperialistic conquest of the American Indians, a point of view summed up in the title of a book by activist Vine Deloria: *Custer Died for Your Sins*.[23] Others see him merely as an idiot who led his men to death in one of the most ill-planned battles in American history. Indeed, Custer's Last Stand is frequently listed in compilations of historical disasters or epic military defeats.[24] On the other hand, historians with a thorough knowledge of Indian warfare, like Utley, note that Custer was following the standard tactics of the time and had some justification for the decisions he made. Paul Hedren, in an exhaustive study of the Great Sioux War, writes that, although Custer's decision to attack was driven in part by his impulsive nature, "his decisions as the battle unfolded were all logical."[25] Like many of those with outsized personalities, Custer attracted devoted friends but equally bitter enemies in his lifetime, and the fantastic nature of his death has carried the same debate forward among historians and Custer buffs who are sometimes called Custerphiles or Custerphobes, depending on their perspective.[26] Both camps find his life endlessly fascinating, and with good reason, for it includes the highs and lows of a real American character.

Custer was the son of a village blacksmith in New Rumley, Ohio, where he lived until he was fourteen. His parents sent him to Monroe,

Michigan, to attend Stebbins Academy while he lived with his sister and her husband. He did not excel at the school and came back to finish his education in Cadiz, Ohio, where he taught in a one-room schoolhouse while he applied to West Point. Despite being a Republican, the local congressman awarded the Democrat Custer a place at the military academy, perhaps in part because the congressman was trying to help a constituent who wanted to end Custer's pursuit of his daughter by sending him to New York state.[27]

Custer himself later wrote that his record at West Point was best used as an example of what not to do. He frequently earned demerits for various infractions related to studies, dress, and general behavior. He once asked his Spanish instructor to translate the phrase "Class dismissed," and when the clueless prof spoke the words Custer led the rest of the students out of the room. But Custer was able to control his behavior well enough to graduate, and that was no small feat in an era when few people graduated from high school, let alone college.[28]

Custer graduated in an accelerated program created so he and his classmates could fight in the looming Civil War. As a fresh second lieutenant Custer arrived at the front just in time to fight in the war's first major battle in the east, Bull Run. He got there through what would become known in the army as "Custer's luck." When he arrived at the War Department in Washington, D.C., to get his first military assignment, Custer by chance was introduced to Gen. Winfield Scott, the head of the entire army. Scott gave Custer a choice of assignments, and when Custer said he wanted to go to the front, Scott assigned him to a combat unit and gave him dispatches to take to the field commander, Irvin McDowell. Custer delivered the dispatches, joined the fight, and led his cavalry company safely back to Washington while the rest of the army was routed. He was mentioned for bravery in an official report of the battle.[29]

Fearless and eager to tackle all opportunities, including flying in an observation balloon, Custer drew the attention of superiors and rose quickly through the ranks. By the end of the war he was leading a division and was the favorite of Phil Sheridan, commander of the Army of the Potomac's cavalry. Sheridan bought the table on which Lee and Grant signed the surrender of the Confederate army and gave it to Custer's wife, Libbie, with a note celebrating Custer's role in winning the war.[30]

Custer's postwar service was marked by controversy as well as success. While serving in frontier Kansas, he was court-martialed and sentenced to a one-year suspension without pay for a series of charges that included leaving his post without permission to visit his wife and ordering deserters shot without trial. However, Sheridan realized he needed Custer to fight the warring tribes, got the suspension shortened, and had Custer lead the campaign that resulted in victory at the Washita. Unlike Custer's Civil War triumphs, the Washita was tarnished by charges that the Seventh Cavalry wantonly killed civilians and that Custer had abandoned Maj. Joel Elliott and eighteen troopers who disappeared during the fight. Their bodies, horribly mutilated, were later discovered in a mini-version of Custer's own last stand.[31]

One of Custer's top subordinates, Capt. Frederick Benteen, wrote a letter blaming Custer for Elliott's death that was published anonymously in the *Missouri Democrat*. When Custer heard of the letter, he called his officers together to tell them he would "cowhide" the man who had accused him of knowingly abandoning Elliott and his men. Benteen put his hand on his pistol and said he had written the letter. Custer, stunned by the admission, left the meeting saying he would deal with Benteen later. He never did.[32]

Unlike Custer, Benteen was not a West Pointer and had risen through the ranks during the Civil War, fighting for the North although his family sided with the South. His father told young Fred when he enlisted that he hoped the "first bullet gets you!"[33] Historian James Donovan notes that Benteen had been Custer's enemy almost from the beginning of their relationship in the frontier army, but that the Washita cemented his animosity toward Custer. According to Donovan, "New officers assigned to the regiment realized quickly that there was a Custer 'family' and a small but active anti-Custer faction led by the cantankerous Captain." Most new officers tried to remain neutral, but Benteen's loathing of Custer guaranteed that the regiment's officers would be split in their loyalty to Custer, even beyond his death.[34]

Also standing outside Custer's inner circle was his other top subordinate, Maj. Marcus Reno, who like Benteen was a decorated Civil War veteran older than Custer. Reno was a cheerless, luckless man who had few close friends and seemed to antagonize people just by his personality. He was also a belligerent drinker, which got him into trouble on several occasions. Reno's main source of happiness was his wife, but she died unexpectedly in 1874, leaving him with one son whom he turned over to relatives to raise. Such a man would not be a natural friend for the tee-totaling, fun-loving Custer.[35]

Custer created his regimental "family" in part by getting assignments for his close friends and relatives. Such behavior was not unusual in the nineteenth-century army, but Utley notes that Custer was "one of the most accomplished nepotists in an army full of assiduous nepotists."[36] In any case, the nepotism did not mean that Custer was stocking the regiment with incompetents. His inner circle included his brother Capt. Tom Custer, his brother-in-law 1st Lt. James Calhoun, and his good friend 1st. Lt. William W. Cooke. All were combat veterans of the Civil War, and Tom had earned not one but two Medals of Honor during the Civil War. For one of the citations, Tom had been shot in the face while taking a flag from a rebel soldier.[37]

Calhoun, a bit of a card-playing rogue like Tom, had married the Custer brothers' sister Maggie and was so good-looking he was nick-named Adonis. The Canadian-born Cooke had lied about his age to join the Union Army and had been wounded and awarded three brevet promotions for distinctive service. Cooke was also the officer Custer chose to accompany him to ride alone into a Indian village in Texas to negotiate the release of white captives.[38]

Myles Keogh, however, had led the most interesting life. Keogh was an Irishman who had been decorated for bravery while fighting with the Battalion of St. Patrick, a volunteer group of his countrymen protecting the Papal States and Pope Pius IX from Napoleon II and the Piedmontese. After that war ended, the adventurous Keogh joined the Union Army during the Civil War, fighting in more than thirty battles, including a botched raid on the notorious rebel prison camp at Andersonville, Georgia. The rebels instead captured Keogh's unit, but he was exchanged for rebel prisoners after two months and completed his service with distinction. Despite his binge drinking, Keogh became a Custer favorite and is likely the soldier who introduced Custer to the Irish drinking song "Gary Owen," which became the regiment's anthem.[39]

The Seventh also had inexperienced officers, like 2nd Lt. Jack Sturgis, who was only about a year out of West Point at the time of the Little Bighorn. His father was Col. Samuel D. Sturgis, the titular head of the

Seventh Cavalry. The elder Sturgis had a mixed Civil War record. He had led the charge that carried Burnside's Bridge at the Battle of Antietam, but he suffered such an embarrassing defeat when in command at the battle of Brice's Crossroads that he was relieved of active command for the rest of the war. Colonel Sturgis and Custer did not get along when they both wound up in the Seventh Cavalry, but Sturgis was assigned desk work while Custer got the field command at the front.[40]

The conflicting personalities and wide range of talent in the Seventh Cavalry's officer corps in the 1870s were matched by a group of enlisted men who were in many cases inexperienced, ill trained, and unmotivated. About a quarter of the troops had joined the regiment in the past year, and many had received only rudimentary training in horsemanship and weaponry. Some had joined because of the high unemployment rate.[41] About 40 percent were foreign born. Trumpeter John Martin, for example, was from Italy, and his name was an Anglicized version of Giovanni Martini. He spoke English so poorly that when during the Little Bighorn Cooke sent him to order Benteen forward, Cooke wrote the message rather than trust Martin to deliver it verbally.[42] On the other hand, one recent study of the frontier army argues that the popular historical criticism of the typical soldier is overblown, pointing out that noncommissioned officers were usually promoted from the ranks. "They were typically older, steady, and thoroughly experienced soldiers, often Civil War veterans, and as a group invariably reflected their company's and regiment's reputation and esprit de corps and instilled it in the ranks."[43]

The "Fighting Seventh" had that spirit and a reputation as the best and most experienced Indian-fighting cavalry regiment in the army. Custer and many of his men took justified pride in their unit. Custer on several occasions said the Seventh could whip any number of Indians it encountered. Pvt. Charles Windolph, a German immigrant in the regiment, wrote in his memoir that riding on good horse with a carbine and pistol made him feel proud and "ready for a fight or a frolic."[44]

Custer knew he would have a fight as early as 1874 when he led a government survey of the Sioux's Black Hills. He told a New York reporter that the Indians were "quiet" because they believed the government would keep its word to protect their treaty rights. "But the moment they think it is not acting in good faith, there will be a rising of every tribe between the Missouri River and the Rocky Mountains."[45]

The continuing poor economy caused the government to act in desperation, if not exactly bad faith, in 1876, although the cause of the Little Bighorn could best be traced to events ten years earlier. Increasing western migration after the Civil War led the government to construct three forts through Sioux territory to protect the Bozeman Trail. This infuriated the Sioux, who, under the famous chief Red Cloud, harassed the forts. On December 21, 1866, Capt. William J. Fetterman, a Civil War veteran new to Indian warfare, led eighty men out of Fort Phil Kearny to rescue a woodcutting detail that was under attack. Sioux warriors acted as decoys, pretending to be injured or worn out from the fight, walking and leading their horses just out of reach of the soldiers. They lured Fetterman's detail beyond sight of the fort into an ambush in which every man was killed. Soldiers recovered the frozen, fearfully mutilated corpses, and the undermanned garrison, including the families, spent a grim Christmas wondering whether they would survive. They did, but news of the fight, which up to that time had been the army's worst defeat at the hands of the plains Indians, shocked the country. Although the army won a few subsequent fights against the Sioux, the tribes kept up the harassment until the federal government negotiated a peace settlement in the Fort Laramie Treaty of 1868. The government abandoned the three forts, which the Indians burned. On the one hand, the treaty could be seen as a victory for the tribes because the government abandoned the posts. But as one historian noted, "the victory proved illusory," because the government also established the Great Sioux Reservation in all of what is now South Dakota west of the Missouri River. Various agencies were established on the reservations where the tribes could draw rations and supplies. The government also established an "unceded territory" from the reservation west to the Big Horn mountains that was to be free of whites and where the Indians could roam to hunt game. The "victors" were now largely dependent on the government.[46]

Most of the bands, including those led by Red Cloud and another prominent chief, Spotted Tail, went to live on the reservations. The reservation Indians totaled about 15,000 people. However, about 3,500—what Utley called "holdouts"—refused to move to the reservations and abide by the treaty. These roamers would often visit the agencies in winter, where they drew rations, stirred up their more peaceful brethren, and threatened the white agents. They would then return to the unceded territory in better weather to hunt, and sometimes agency Indians joined them.[47]

One of the main threats to the tribes' way of life was the construction of railroads through the territory. The Fort Laramie treaty actually permitted the construction of railroads anywhere on the plains, even in the reservation itself provided the Indians were consulted about the route and then paid for it. But the fine print of the treaty meant nothing to the roaming bands. They were outraged when the Northern Pacific Railway began surveying a route through the territory that would connect St. Paul, Minnesota, with Seattle. The Northern Pacific, with military escort, first began surveying the route in Sioux country in 1871, and expeditions for the railroad or other purposes followed every year through 1875. The Sioux resisted with harassing raids and small fights.[48]

Custer commanded the Seventh Cavalry as part of the escort during the 1873 expedition, and his shoulder-length curls drew the attention of the Indians, who at this time began calling him "Long Hair." Long Hair was almost lured into a trap by a small decoy party, much like the tactic that had done in Fetterman. But Custer realized the danger of the situation before it was too late and was able to retreat to a defensive position until he was rescued by the rest of the expedition. The Panic of 1873 stopped construction of the railroad, but not the exploration of Sioux country. In 1874, Custer led an expedition into the Black Hills to scout for a fort to supervise the Indian agencies, but he also brought along miners to investigate reports of gold. Newspaper reporters who accompanied the expedition exaggerated the discovery of gold, one story claiming, "From the grass roots down it was 'pay dirt.'"[49]

The news prompted a gold rush, made more intense by the ongoing depression. The army tried to keep out the prospectors, but it was spread too thin. Many prospectors who were chased out just went back in, and some soldiers deserted and joined them. And the army was even drawn into fights between warring tribes. According to Utley, Sioux leader Sitting Bull was more concerned with the Crows than the railroads, and the two tribes had been raiding each other's reservations since the Fort Laramie treaty was signed. The violence spilled over into attacks by Sioux warriors on whites in the area. The Sioux also attacked the Crow agency, killing and stealing the facility's animals. The agent asked the army for help, but there were too few troops at nearby Fort Ellis to prevent the depredations.[50]

After the gold rush, the government sent a commission led by Iowa senator William B. Allison to buy the Black Hills. The negotiations went nowhere. Red Cloud and Spotted Tail were open to the idea, but just about everyone else was intimidated by the non-agency Indians. Little Big Man, one of Crazy Horse's band, led a charge of painted and screaming warriors, firing guns into the air, to the commission's negotiations held at the Red Cloud Agency. He said he was sent by Sitting Bull and would shoot anyone who signed a treaty.[51]

The Allison commission left without a treaty and recommended that Congress give the Sioux a fair price for the Black Hills. If they declined, no more rations would be provided to them, and the government could do this because the time limit on rations to be provided under the Fort Laramie treaty had expired. Utley wrote that Grant faced "an impossible dilemma" when the negotiations failed, and he and other government officials agreed that war was the best solution. At a meeting in November 1875, Grant ordered the army to quit interdicting prospectors invading the Black Hills, and the non-agency tribes were ordered to report to the reservation or be declared hostile and forced there by the army. The deadline for reporting to the reservation was January 31, 1876. Since this edict was served in the dead of winter, it would have been dangerous for the Indians to move their camps even if they had wanted to. But as Utley noted, they likely misunderstood the ultimatum, thinking there was no reason for it because they had been peaceful and did not intend war against the government.[52]

The government, however, intended war on the tribes. The responsibility fell to Sheridan, who was head of the Military Division of the Missouri, headquartered in Chicago but overseeing the vast area of the Great Plains. Sheridan planned a winter campaign—like the Washita—in order to find and fight Indians when they were hunkered down in the harsh plains weather. The plan called for three columns totaling about 2,500 men to converge on the hostile bands. One column of about eight hundred men was commanded by Brig. Gen. George Crook, forty-nine, a Civil War veteran who had led successful Indian war campaigns in the Northwest and Arizona. Crook, head of the Military Department of the Platte, was to proceed north from Fort Fetterman, in the Wyoming Territory.[53]

Brig. Gen. Alfred H. Terry, head of the Department of the Dakota in St. Paul, would be overall commander of two columns. Col. John Gibbon, forty-nine, would lead about 450 men east from Fort Ellis in western Montana Territory.[54] Terry had planned for Custer to lead a column of almost a thousand soldiers and three Gatling guns (an early machine gun mounted on a carriage like a cannon) west from Fort Abraham Lincoln in Dakota Territory.

It was a solid plan led by experienced officers. The competency of the troops was not that of the Civil War army, which by the end of the war was so well equipped, trained, and battle-hardened that it was among the finest in the world. Still, the frontier army was trained in military tactics, which in theory allowed the soldiers to fight as a team and increase their firepower and effectiveness, particularly against native warriors, who usually fought as collections of individuals in hit-and-run raids. The Indian Bureau reported to the army that it would face no more than eight hundred warriors in camps scattered throughout the unceded territory.[55]

On the other hand, the tribes also had military advantages, not the least of which was that they were fighting for their homes on familiar ground. On an individual basis, although the soldiers were trained in military tactics, their training was often minimal, and target practice was infrequent. In reality, a typical recently enlisted soldier from an eastern city was a poor match for a plains warrior who had grown up in a culture steeped in horsemanship and close-combat fighting.[56]

Nevertheless, the Seventh Cavalry was led by a cadre of experienced officers and noncommissioned officers, many of whom were combat veterans of the Civil War. Even though the regiment continually absorbed new recruits as replacements, at the beginning of the Little Bighorn campaign less than 2 percent of those listed ready for duty had been in the army for less than four months—a period of time inadequate for thorough training. But the overall composition of the regiment included a substantial number of experienced and capable soldiers.[57] The Seventh was ready for its part in Sheridan's plan.

The army's plan was put to the test almost immediately. Crook started his column in early March, and one of his detachments captured a village on the seventeenth. But the Indians counterattacked and recaptured the village, forcing Crook back to Fort Fetterman, which he would not leave again until May 29.[58] Preparations for Terry's columns were slowed by winter storms both literal and figurative. Gibbon's column was not able to leave Fort Ellis until April, and plans for the Dakota column were thrown in turmoil when Custer was summoned by Congress to testify in hearings investigating corruption in the awarding of post traderships, lucrative businesses that were distributed in many cases after kickbacks were paid to government officials. Secretary of War William Belknap, a friend of Grant, and Orvil Grant, the president's brother, were both involved in the scandal. Custer, who was angry that the system cheated troops and Indians with shoddy, overpriced goods, provided mostly hearsay testimony on March 29 and April 4. He did not personally implicate Orvil Grant, who admitted that the president had given him license to four posts, for which he acted as middleman. Nevertheless, Grant was furious with Custer and ordered him removed from the upcoming campaign.[59]

After the committee released Custer, he tried to see Grant several times, on May 1 waiting outside his office for five hours before an aide told him the president would not see him. Custer then got permission from the inspector general to return to Fort Lincoln, but on May 4 Grant ordered him detained in Chicago for leaving without seeing himself or Sherman. Custer appealed to Sherman, who agreed to let him go to St. Paul, where on May 6 Custer tearfully begged Terry to help get him reinstated. Terry was a combat veteran of the Civil War but had limited experience fighting Indians and knew he needed Custer. Terry, who had practiced law before the Civil War, also knew how to write a persuasive appeal to Grant. He helped Custer write a telegram that included this line: "I appeal to you as a soldier to spare me the humiliation of seeing my regiment march to meet the enemy and I not share in its danger." Either from the sentiment of the appeal from one veteran to another or the public pressure from newspapers urging Grant to let Custer go, the president finally relented, and on May 8 Custer received word he could go on the expedition but would not be in command of the Dakota column. Sherman gave the news to Terry and told him, "Advise Custer to be prudent, not to take along any newspaper men, who always make mischief, and to abstain from personalities in the future."[60]

Meanwhile, the tribes had been unifying for war. The failed attack by Crook had persuaded various Sioux and Northern Cheyenne bands to gather together for self-defense. As spring came, their numbers were also strengthened by the annual migration of agency Indians to join their roaming relatives for hunting. In 1876, resentment over the government's threats and the continuing gold rush swelled their numbers more than usual. In early June, Sitting Bull, a key spiritual leader of the Sioux, organized the Sun Dance, a religious "ceremony of tribal renewal and spiritual rededication." During the ceremony, Jumping Bull, Sitting Bull's adopted brother, cut fifty matchhead-size pieces of flesh from each of the chief's arms as a sacrifice. Sitting Bull, bleeding profusely, then danced for hours around the Sun Dance pole while staring at the blinding sun. He fainted, and when he opened his eyes he revealed a vision of soldiers riding upside down into an Indian village. A voice proclaimed in the vision that the soldiers had no ears and would die, but the Indians should take no spoils from them. The stirring vision, which forecast a great victory, gave the Indians a feeling of invincibility.[61]

Crook was the first to feel the sting of this invincibility. After refitting his column at Fort Fetterman, the veteran Indian fighter marched northward again on May 29. By June 17, Crook had made it to the upper Rosebud Creek. Hundreds of warriors surprised the column that morning as the soldiers brewed their coffee. The two sides fought for six hours before the Indians withdrew. Crook claimed he won the fight because he held the battlefield, but he withdrew to refit and called for reinforcements for his command, which already totaled about 1,300 men. During the next few weeks, Crook made only feeble attempts to track the hostiles. Five reporters accompanied Crook's column, and news of the Rosebud had reached Chicago by June 23—two days before Custer attacked at the Little Bighorn.[62]

Historians disagree whether Crook could have communicated the news of the battle to Terry and thus Custer. Hedren concluded that Crook had "faithfully" fulfilled his orders by sending word to Chicago and claimed Terry was beyond direct contact. Certainly, communication among the various columns in the field was difficult and potentially hazardous for the scouts who carried messages. Yet, as Donovan points out, after the battle scouts had traveled 300 miles from Crook's column through dangerous territory to the Crow Agency and returned safely.

But Crook made no attempt to send news to Terry, even though Crook himself had complained about lack of information from the other generals. Whether Crook deserves any blame or not, the fact remains that Terry's Dakota column proceeded without intelligence about the increasing strength and aggressiveness of the hostile tribes.[63]

Gibbon, who had left Fort Ellis on April 1, was scarcely much more help than Crook. A Sioux war party had stolen the ponies of Gibbon's Crow scouts, and, although a reconnaissance had located the Indian village on May 16, Gibbon could not get his troops across the flooded Yellowstone River to attack it. The Indians moved the village, but Gibbon's scouts found it again on the twenty-seventh. Terry and Custer, who had marched from Fort Abraham Lincoln on the seventeenth, were also searching for the village, but Gibbon did not pass word to Terry of the exact location until he met him on June 8 aboard the riverboat *Far West,* a boat contracted to carry supplies and troops for the expedition.[64]

Terry dispatched Reno on a final scouting mission to ensure that the Indians had not moved away and established a base camp at the mouth of the Powder River, where the cavalrymen stored their sabers, which were not needed in the long-range combat that typified Indian fighting. Terry also drew up plans for an attack in a June 21 meeting that included both Gibbon and Custer. Terry's plan called for Custer's regiment to be a mobile, fast-moving force that would drive the Indians toward Gibbon's troops. Reno's scout had not found the village itself, but the campsites suggested that the warriors numbered about eight hundred. No one at the meeting seemed concerned about agency Indians joining the hostiles. The main concern of the officers, reflecting military experience in fighting Indians, was not defeating them in battle but rather catching them, because they invariably scattered when threatened or attacked. Terry offered Custer the Gatling guns and a battalion of the Second Cavalry, since Custer's column was to be the main attack force. But Custer concluded that the Gatling guns would slow the march of his command, which was, after all, supposed to be the strike force, and that the cavalry battalion would not add that much firepower.[65]

The next morning, June 22, Terry sent Custer written orders based on the previous day's discussion. The meaning of the orders has been so controversial that many scholars reproduce them in full. Space precludes that here, but the general outlines of the debate concern how much freedom Terry intended to give Custer in pursuing and attacking the village. Were the instructions meant to be followed explicitly, or were they "advisory"?[66] Utley wrote that Terry's orders to Custer were "discretionary" because none of the officers knew for sure where the village was, so Custer's actions would be governed by circumstance. Terry's order admitted that it was "of course impossible" to give Custer explicit directions and that in any case he had too much confidence in his ability to give him orders that "might hamper your action when nearly in contact with the enemy." It was clear to all that Custer was to ride hard after the hostiles and use his best judgment when he found them.[67] Custer's own attitude was apparent when he told his officers that they needed fifteen days' rations on their pack mules. When some officers complained that the mules were too worn out from Reno's scout to carry that much, Custer was not sympathetic. They could carry what they wanted, he said, but they would be responsible for their companies. "You had better carry along an extra supply of salt. We may have to live on horse meat before we get through," Custer added.[68]

At noon on June 22, the Seventh Cavalry paraded through camp in front of Terry and Gibbon. When the last trooper had passed, Custer shook hands with the two officers. "Now Custer, don't be greedy, but wait for us," Gibbon said. "No, I will not," Custer replied and rode off to join his soldiers.[69]

Custer drove himself and the men hard, even considering his reputation for tirelessness, which led his suffering men to call him "Hard Ass."[70] They rode twelve miles that first day and thirty miles the next, when they struck the trail Reno had found. On the twenty-fourth they rode another thirty miles, reaching the end of Reno's patrol. They examined the Sioux Sun Dance site, which contained enough powerful medicine—including the scalp of a white man—to make Custer's Indian scouts nervous. They also found signs of fresh trails mixing with the old trail. The agency Indians were continually joining Sitting Bull's village, which had more than doubled to almost one thousand lodges, a number that would house about seven thousand people, including about two thousand warriors.[71]

Custer might have thought the converging trails were diverging trails, meaning that the village was scattering and he would not be able to catch it. At any rate, he felt a sense of urgency and gathered his officers that night, telling them he would conduct a night march to follow the trail, then rest the command while scouts located the village, which he knew was close.[72] Recalling the meeting later, some officers were struck by Custer's attitude. Instead of his usual brusque recitation of orders, Custer explained his decisions, such as his reasons for not taking the Gatling guns. He told the officers that he relied on their judgment and loyalty. Custer's unusual manner made a deep impression on everyone. After the meeting, Lt. George Wallace told Godfrey he believed Custer would be killed in the coming battle because he had never heard him talk like that.[73]

The officers rousted the men at midnight, and they covered another six miles in darkness until halting at 2 A.M. A scouting party went up a lookout known as the Crow's Nest, from which they were able to spot smoke from the village and a huge pony herd. Custer's favorite scout, Bloody Knife, said they would find enough Indians to keep them fighting for two or three days. Custer smiled and said, "I guess we'll get through with them in one day."[74]

Custer's plan to rest before attacking was ruined when he received word that the command had been spotted by at least two parties of Indians. The village would surely scatter, so Custer decided to march immediately and attack as soon as he found the exact location. After marching toward the village, Custer called a halt at noon and divided the Seventh into four commands. Reno took three companies of about 140 men and Custer took five with about 225 as they marched on either side of what is now called Reno Creek. Custer assigned Benteen three companies of about 125 men to scout the hills to the left to catch any Indians who might be escaping that way. Capt. Thomas McDougall was assigned about 135 men—one company, plus duty men from the other companies—to guard the pack train, which trailed to the rear.[75]

After a march of about ten miles, Custer and Reno found an abandoned Indian campsite containing a single tipi with the body of a warrior killed in the battle of the Rosebud (although no one in Custer's command at that time even knew of Crook's defeat). They spotted about forty warriors riding toward the Little Bighorn and dust clouds beyond the hills that hid the Little Bighorn valley. Fred Gerard, an interpreter riding with the command, yelled that the Indians were "running like devils."[76]

Custer evidently believed Gerard's assessment, for he ordered Reno to chase the Indians into the valley and charge the village, promising that he would "support him" with the whole outfit. Custer did not tell Reno about any overall plan for the battle, and Reno had only a vague notion of Benteen's mission.[77] Custer meanwhile took his command along Reno Creek and halted at the junction of its two forks to water his horses. He received word that the Indians were in fact not running away but storming out of the village to meet Reno. Although Custer had told Reno he would support his attack, he instead turned north away from Reno Creek.[78] Custer's plan remains a mystery, for it died with him, but the likely theory is that he planned to attack the other end of the village, which would have been similar to his many-sided attack on Black Kettle's village at the Washita. Such a move would support Reno's attack, as Custer had promised.

Reno certainly could have used more immediate support. When he reached the valley floor, growing numbers of mounted warriors appeared in his front. Fearing his command would be destroyed, Reno dismounted his men in a skirmish line, then moved them into a grove of cottonwoods when it appeared he would be outflanked. But the pressure continued to worsen. Reno's orders from Custer had been based on an enemy running away and included the notion that the rest of the Seventh would engage in support of Reno's command. But the situation Reno found himself in was quite different, and he had received no word from Custer on an updated plan.[79] Reno, who several sources claimed had been drinking that day, ordered the men to mount preparatory to breaking out of the cottonwoods. When Bloody Knife was shot in the head so close to Reno that blood and gore splashed his face, Reno seemed to lose his senses. He ordered a dismount, then a mount, and "led" a mad, panicked retreat out of the woods to the safety of the hills beyond the Little Bighorn.[80]

Some men did not hear the order or were wounded and could not escape. The rest provided what the Indians described later as a buffalo hunt. Little resistance was offered as the warriors shot or clubbed any hapless troopers who were too slow to make it up the steep banks of the Little Bighorn to the relative safety of a hill where the stunned survivors gathered. Benteen, who had received an urgent message from Custer—"Come on. Big Village. Be Quick. Bring Packs. P.S. Bring

Pacs."—arrived at the battlefield in time to see Reno's men staggering up the hill. The hatless, bedraggled Reno exclaimed, "For God's sake, Benteen, halt your command and help me. I've lost half my men."[81]

From their hilltop position, many troopers claimed to hear heavy firing, including two distinct volleys, but neither of the senior officers ordered a march toward where Custer was presumably engaged. They could have been waiting for the pack train; Custer had ordered Benteen to bring the packs with him. They also were bogged down by wounded and demoralized men from Reno's valley fight. Nevertheless, their inaction remains controversial to the present day because Benteen had explicit orders to join Custer. Furthermore, as historian Edgar I. Stewart points out, a general military principle dictates marching to the sound of gunfire.[82]

Eventually some junior officers on their own initiative moved their companies toward the firing. They saw a large number of Indians riding horses and shooting at the ground. The warriors then turned their attention to the approaching troopers and quickly drove them back to Reno's position. Joined by McDougall's pack train, the troopers prepared a defensive position as best they could given that they had no shovels or entrenching tools.

The Indians besieged the demoralized troopers, picking them off with long-range sniping until night fell. As the cavalrymen heard dancing and singing from the village below them, they used whatever tools they had to scoop out shallow entrenchments and built barriers with packing boxes, saddles, and dead horses and mules. A few survivors from the valley fight who had been left behind and hid all day from the Indians straggled in.

The sniping started again the next day. The troopers quickly ran out of water, and the hot June weather tormented the shelterless men, especially the wounded. Benteen, although junior in rank to Reno, took effective command, since Reno still had not recovered from the shock of the valley disaster. Benteen supervised the defense, led a foot charge to drive away Indians who had gotten too close to the perimeter, and organized a foray of volunteers to go to the river to get water. Nineteen men earned the Medal of Honor for participating in the dangerous expeditions to the river.[83] It looked like the command might be able to hold out, but all wondered what had happened to Custer. Some veterans thought of the Washita, where Custer's critics accused him of abandoning Joel Elliott's command. Had he done the same thing at the Little Bighorn?[84]

Custer's movements are still a mystery, although archaeological evidence and Indian accounts provide good clues. What seems certain is that he rode off to attack the village from another direction. When he reached a bluff, he halted and got his first clear view of the village. He sent a courier to McDougall to bring up the pack train. After a ride of a half mile or so, he sent Benteen the urgent message to join him with the ammunition packs.[85]

Custer sent two companies under Capt. George Yates down a coulee toward a ford in the river, perhaps as a feint to draw pressure from Reno and to hold the ford for a full-scale attack on the village when Benteen arrived with reinforcements. He ordered Keogh's companies to take position on a ridge, probably to cover Benteen's approach while the remaining companies under Keogh headed north. Indian fire drove Yates's command back, and warriors under Gall, fresh from defeating Reno, attacked Keogh's command. The troops dismounted to form more effective firing lines, but the Indian numbers overwhelmed them, breaking their lines and forcing about forty survivors to gather on what became known as Last Stand Hill. The soldiers, including Custer, shot horses for a primitive breastwork and fought until most were killed. A group of about ten apparently tried to escape by running toward the river but were cut down. Others tried to escape individually, but no soldier survived to tell the cavalry's version of the battle.[86]

No one can say who was the last to die; in reality there were several small "last stands" around the battlefield. How Custer died is uncertain, because the Indians did not know at the time that they were fighting him, and even if they had it is doubtful anyone would have recognized him in the dust and smoke of the battle. Many theories have been advanced over the years, including the idea that Custer was shot at the ford trying to cross the river, and that troopers carried his lifeless or fatally wounded body to Last Stand Hill. Spent shells from his rifle were, however, found near his body, indicating that he had been fighting to the end.[87]

White journalists, historians, and soldiers constantly quizzed Indian veterans about who killed Custer, and several men were identified by

other Indians or claimed the honor for themselves. Wooden Leg, a Cheyenne veteran, called such claims boasting and said the Indians who knew
Custer did not see him that day, and most of the others had never heard
of him until the white people began to ask about him.[88] None of the
accounts can be proved.

Stephen Ambrose, the great World War II historian, wrote a dual
biography of Crazy Horse and Custer early in his career. Ambrose's book
includes the most moving account of Custer's death, based on a newspaper interview done with Sitting Bull a year after the battle. Sitting Bull
admitted in the interview that he did not participate in the combat, but
as a respected leader he got what modern soldiers would call a debriefing
from warriors who had just returned from the fight. Sitting Bull said that
on Last Stand Hill, "the Long Hair stood like a sheaf of corn with all the
ears fallen around him." He said that Custer killed a man right before
he died and then laughed. The reporter, incredulous, suggested that Sitting Bull meant Custer had cried out. No, Sitting Bull insisted, Custer
laughed because he had fired his last shot.

Ambrose argues that this version sounds right because of Custer's
larger-than-life-personality. He had achieved much in his thirty-six
years, often by gambling against the odds. "He had lived big, thought
big, had only big ambitions. He had nothing to regret," Ambrose wrote,
even on his last day. "Like all confirmed gamblers, however, he knew
someday he would have to lose. At least, when he lost, all the chips were
on the table. It was a winner-take-all game, and Custer would have
played it again if given the chance. He laughed. Then he died."[89]

The white survivors were all entrenched about four miles from Last
Stand Hill. In the early evening of June 26, the day after Custer's command was destroyed, the surviving cavalrymen saw a huge gathering of
Indians—the packed-up village—proceed deliberately to the southwest
toward the Big Horn mountains. The valley below appeared deserted.
Still, the survivors remained alert on the hilltop, fearing a renewed
attack and wondering what happened to Custer.

They found out the next morning when Terry's column arrived. Lt.
James H. Bradley had discovered the Custer battlefield and counted 197
bodies. The fact that not all of the 210 men with Custer were found
left an opening for tales of a lone survivor. Over the years, many have
claimed that title, but none have been authenticated.[90] More likely the

bodies were destroyed by the Indians, who mutilated most of the corpses frightfully, many beyond recognition.

The soldiers were never able to identify the body of Sturgis, the son of the Seventh Cavalry's official commander, although some of his clothing was found in the abandoned Indian camp. One soldier claimed that one of several scorched heads found in the same area was that of the young lieutenant. A photograph taken in 1879 depicts a marker for Sturgis, but this was apparently a fictitious gravesite set up to assuage his grieving mother, who had visited the battlefield the previous year.[91]

Calhoun and Keogh were both found among their men southeast of Last Stand Hill. The groupings of the bodies indicated where their units had held defensive positions. Calhoun's body was stripped and scalped. Keogh's body although stripped was not mutilated, perhaps because he wore a Catholic medallion, which was found on his corpse.[92]

Cooke, Custer's adjutant who had written the last message to Benteen for Custer, was butchered. Indians had removed the hair from his head and from one side of his face to get his flowing "dundreary" whiskers. Tom Custer's corpse was one of the most brutally mutilated on the field, with his head crushed flat. He was recognized only by the tattooed initials on his body. Some speculated that the mutilation was the revenge of Rain-in-the-Face, a warrior who had been arrested a few years earlier for killing two men attached to the 1873 military exploration of the Yellowstone area. Rain-in-the-Face subsequently escaped from the guard house and, according to some sources, vowed revenge against Tom Custer. Most historians, however, discount that tale. Rain-in-the-Face, who learned to write his name and sell autographs years after the battle, told several different versions of his role in the Little Bighorn, sometimes claiming he killed Tom and other times not.[93]

Most observers gave a consistent account of Custer's body. Custer was found sitting upright against a horse in a pose that looked like he was sleeping. His body was stripped but not scalped. One fingertip was cut off, one thigh was slashed and an arrow had been shoved up his penis. He was shot twice, in the left temple and the left side of the chest beneath the heart. Either wound could have been fatal, but the headshot might have been done by another officer, perhaps even Tom, who would not have wanted his brother taken alive. It was probably not suicide because there were no powder burns on the body, and Custer, who was right-handed, would not have naturally shot himself in the left temple. Furthermore, the chest wound was bloody but the head wound was clean, indicating it was a done after death.[94]

Benteen had initially refused to believe the news that Custer was dead, saying he thought Custer had abandoned the survivors like he did Elliott at the Washita. Terry ordered Benteen to search the battlefield and see for himself.[95]

There are at least two versions of what Benteen said when he recognized Custer's corpse. In one, Benteen merely identifies Custer's body to his satisfaction and rides off. The quote that sounds right, given Benteen's hatred of Custer and the raw emotion of the moment is, "There he is, God damn him, he will never fight again."[96]

In the literal sense, Benteen was right. He would no longer have to serve under a younger man he despised and considered incompetent. But if Benteen thought Custer's death meant Custer would be forgotten, he could not have been more wrong.

CHAPTER 2

"Horrible!"

The News Shocks the Nation

While Benteen was cursing Custer and the grieving, stunned troopers were burying their dead comrades, the rest of the country thought Custer was alive, if they thought of him at all. Journalists and their readers were caught in the time warp of nineteenth-century communication. Although the telegraph made communication nearly instantaneous where there were telegraph lines, the battlefield was so remote that it seemed to be in another world. News could travel from the Little Bighorn only as fast as a man and horse could carry it to the nearest telegraph line, which was a ride of several days.

The day Custer died, the *New York Herald* was still digesting news of Crook's June 17 defeat at the Rosebud, which the *Herald* had not reported until June 24. The *Herald*, a Democratic paper that had long supported Custer's career, editorialized on June 25 that it would not rush to judge Crook until all the facts were in, while between the lines the paper implied that another general (read Custer) would have done better. The *Herald* remained confident in the overall plan for the campaign: "If Crook cannot find the Sioux and whip them, other commanders will be more successful."[1]

The widespread expectation of success and the perception that the war was unnecessary—brought about by broken promises to the Indians and botched negotiations over the Black Hills—were two of the main reasons most newspapers gave relatively little coverage to the Sioux war before the Little Bighorn was fought. The *New York World*, for example, sounded bored when commenting on news of the first skirmish of the war back in May: "The general order published elsewhere announcing the purpose of the Government to force those Sioux who have left their reservations, back into their lawful limits, and congratulating the troops engaged in the recent assault on the village of 'Crazy Horse,' brings a most dismal subject once more to the front. Is there no possible method of keeping the peace on our frontiers without destroying the remnants of the Indian race?"[2]

The dismal subject of an Indian war was less important to journalists than other news like the fall election and Reconstruction. As an example of how closely the newspapers followed violence in the South, the *New York World* on May 29 published two full columns on the lynching of six men in South Carolina suspected of the murder of an elderly couple in their home in Edgefield County. The Democratic *World* editorialized sympathetically with the vigilantes, who it claimed had acted "with unusual deliberation" in front of the whole population of the town, which approved the action. The lynching, the *World* claimed, was not political but the result of "lax administration of justice" under the Reconstruction government. In contrast, the *World* ran only one paragraph on Crook's expedition leaving Fort Fetterman. The story was sandwiched between the lynching piece and a story about a foiled robbery on Fifth Avenue.[3]

Unlike the Civil War, which had been covered by hundreds of correspondents from papers around the country, the Indian wars were covered haphazardly by a small group sent from newspapers that were willing and able to hire reporters to cover the fighting. Only two major newspapers, the *Chicago Times* and the *New York Herald,* regularly covered the Indian campaigns between 1867 and 1881. The majority of newspapers were content to rely on wire reports or "exchanges" of stories with the newspapers that had correspondents at the front. Many newspapers also used freelancers and sometimes army officers. Custer himself actually contributed stories to the *New York Herald.*[4]

But even a celebrity soldier like Custer could not get major coverage of the Great Sioux War. Custer tried to get the *New York Tribune* to cover the campaign, writing on February 26 to publisher Whitelaw Reid, who had been a friend of his since the Civil War. Custer told Reid that it would be the biggest expedition since the war. But Reid did not think it was worth a full-time reporter and instead hired a young man named Dick Roberts, a family friend of the Custers, to send occasional dispatches while he was working as a herder on the campaign. Roberts's horse gave out during the campaign, so he was left at the Powder River depot before the battle.[5] John F. Finerty, a *Chicago Times* war correspondent, wanted to accompany Custer, but his boss, publisher Wilbur Storey, told him to go with Crook. "Terry commands over Custer, and Crook, who knows more about the Indians, is likely to do the hard work," said Storey, explaining that Crook had more success in Arizona than Custer did in Dakota.[6]

So the only reporter to accompany Custer was Mark Kellogg, a forty-three-year-old widower with two young daughters. Kellogg had bounced around the upper Midwest before settling on journalism as a career. He was working for C. A. Lounsberry at the *Bismarck Tribune* when he got what he thought was his big break to ride with Custer. Lounsberry, who had been a colonel in the Union Army, greatly admired Custer and in fact gave away pictures of him with subscriptions. Part of Little Bighorn lore is that Lounsberry wanted to accompany the expedition but could not go because he had to stay home to take care of his sick wife. It makes for a good story that Kellogg, the journeyman reporter, died trying to earn his big scoop in a fight he was never supposed to cover. But Kellogg biographer Sandy Barnard argues convincingly that Lounsberry probably flirted with the idea of going himself but never seriously considered it because of his extensive business and political interests and because his Civil War wound would have made the campaign too difficult for him. Kellogg, on the other hand, was still vigorous and could ride and shoot, having served in the militia. In addition, everyone involved expected the campaign to be a routine roundup of northern Indians. Lounsberry in his own subsequent writings created the tale, perhaps to claim a share of the Little Bighorn story, that he was saved from death at the Last Stand by a timely family illness.[7]

The *New York Herald* and *Chicago Tribune* also both later claimed Kellogg as their reporter because they had helped fund his trip, but Lounsberry wrote more than thirty-five years later that he had paid all of Kellogg's expenses, and that the ill-fated scribe had ridden off on Lounsberry's horse and wearing Lounsberry's belt from the Civil War. By virtually all other accounts, Kellogg rode a mule, and one of Lounsberry's children recalled that the belt was too small for Kellogg.[8]

New York Herald publisher James Gordon Bennett, Jr., like his name-sake father, was never shy about promoting his newspaper, and he praised Kellogg's work for the paper and the profession and sent $500 to Kellogg's orphaned girls after the Little Bighorn.[9]

But if the *Herald* was bearing part of Kellogg's expenses, it did not really take advantage of his services. The *Bismarck Tribune* published four of his stories before the battle and may have used part of a fifth. The *Herald,* on the other hand, published only two by Kellogg and two others that were apparently written by Lounsberry based on Kellogg's notes.[10] The Great Sioux War was not a dominant news story, even for a New York newspaper claiming to fund a war correspondent. For one thing, newspapers in 1876, as for most of U.S. history, focused on local news like crime, government, weather, and even sports, includ-ing baseball. (The National League was founded in 1876.) International news was also of interest, and wars and preparations for possible wars at that time involved Turkey, Serbia, Greece, England, and other powers. The Centennial Exposition going on in Philadelphia generated a steady supply of news about displays and the celebrities who visited them, and most towns were planning local celebrations as well. Finally, 1876 was a presidential election year with the main issue being the thorny topic of Reconstruction. If and when should federal troops be pulled from the South? Riots, murders, and assaults were a frequent occurrence in the South as the region's people struggled to adjust to a post-slavery society.

The Indian war seemed much easier to solve and thus less newswor-thy. Troubling signs from the campaign were ignored. A reporter with Crook interviewed some miners who passed the command, fleeing the Black Hills in terror of the Indians. The soldiers taunted the miners as "tenderfeet." When one soldier asked a miner if he had found gold, the miner said, "Yes; but a darned sight too many Indians." The miners pre-dicted a long, fierce war, but the reporter predicted success because the army had "maturely planned and organized" the campaign.[11]

Stories from Terry's command were confident, too; everyone's con-cern was only finding the Indians, not defeating them. "The where-abouts of Sitting Bull is now as much of a conundrum to the military as is the hiding place of Boss Tweed to the New York police," a *Herald* story noted. The anonymous reporter wrote that the command hoped Sitting Bull would attack them. The story explained that Sitting Bull could dodge one or two of the advancing columns but it was hoped he would likely then be caught by the third.[12]

Some newspapers were shaken out of their overconfidence by news of the battle of the Rosebud, which the *Herald* reported with screaming headlines including "Almost a Savage Victory" and "The Sioux Warriors Magnificently Led."[13] The ferocity of the Rosebud fight surprised the editors: "The fact that we are really at war comes like a shock in this centennial season, which was according to the poets, to be a season of peace and reconciliation. . . . While we are preparing to celebrate with becoming fitness the hundredth year of our independence there comes upon us suddenly the announcement that we have a war, a battle, and if not a defeat, certainly not a victory. It is hard to understand the exact position of affairs in our Indian country." But a few days later the *Herald* was optimistic again, concluding that "the net is gradually being thrown around the swarthy Sitting Bull." The only worry was whether the chief would "sit long enough" for the army to catch him.[14]

Like the *Herald,* the *World* also temporarily moved the war coverage to the front page with the news of the Rosebud, but it thought the scope of battle had been exaggerated in dispatches from the front. The *World* was optimistic because Custer was on the scene. A subsequent story about Terry's column praised Custer's "frontier" skill and predicted that he would face fewer warriors than he did during the 1873 Yellowstone expedition. Custer was "doing good service, and will probably do something to put his enemies to the blush before he returns."[15]

Other papers ignored the Rosebud battle. The *Hartford Daily Courant,* for example, devoted only one paragraph to the battle in its list of brief page 2 wire stories that included the news that the German leader Bismarck was being treated for "chronic inflammation of the veins of the legs." The *St. Louis Globe-Democrat,* one of the premier papers in the Midwest, put its seven-paragraph story about the Rosebud on page 4 between a story about a rape and a tale of a lawsuit over an old land claim. The *Globe* gave almost equal space to a story about a woman who tried to drive mosquitoes out of her house by igniting gunpowder in a frying pan. The result blew powder and bits of the pan into her face, hands, and body. This "war on the mosquitoes" as the *Globe* called it, was a failure, and "it is safe to say that the device will not become generally popular."[16]

Real war became news the next day when the *Globe* reported the Battle of the Little Bighorn under the headline "The Scalping Knife!" with a second headline explaining "General Custer and His Command Annihilated." Like most newspapers, the *Globe* first ran a story based on a pair of dispatches datelined July 5 from Salt Lake City, but that dateline hardly explained the drama of getting the first news out. Since Kellogg had died with Custer, the first stories were based on the account of Muggins Taylor, a scout who Terry had ordered on June 28 to carry a brief report of the battle to Fort Ellis, in Bozeman, Montana Territory. Warriors chased Taylor during a harrowing nighttime ride, but he managed to escape to the *Far West,* the army's supply boat that was moored on the Bighorn River. After a brief stay on the boat, Taylor set off on the 175-mile ride to Fort Ellis, but he became so exhausted that he stopped at Stillwater, Montana. W. H. Norton, a Stillwater correspondent for the *Helena Herald,* interviewed Taylor, wrote a story, and gave it to a courier, who arrived in Helena at about noon on July 4. The editor of the *Herald*, Andrew Fisk, put out an extra late that night and telegraphed it to Salt Lake City, from where it was transmitted to papers across the country.[17]

Meanwhile, Taylor had ridden into Bozeman on July 3, where he was interviewed by the *Bozeman Times,* which put out an extra that night and became the first newspaper to report the battle. Taylor also gave Terry's official report to Capt. D. W. Benham, who carried the report to the telegraph office with instructions to send it to division headquarters in Chicago. However, neither the report nor the *Times* story went out from Bozeman until July 5, and the official report was mailed instead of telegraphed. Benham, who said the lines were working, called it "criminal negligence." The telegraph operator called it equipment failure, claiming the telegraph lines were down. The *Chicago Times* had reported on July 1 that telegraph communication between Chicago and Fort Ellis had been out for several weeks.[18] Custer historian W. A. Graham wrote cheekily that the telegraph operator might already have started celebrating the Fourth when many people "absorbed their patriotism from a bottle."[19] Whatever the facts were, it created a serious controversy later on because Terry wrote a second confidential dispatch to Sheridan that was more critical of Custer than the official dispatch, which merely gave the details of the battle. But the second confidential dispatch was inadvertently released to the public first, making it appear that Terry was trying to protect himself by blaming Custer.[20]

The very first stories for most newspapers did not assign blame but rather combined the *Bozeman Times* and *Helena Herald* accounts under a series of subheads. Most editors had the same story to work with, but there was no uniform reaction to how the story should be played. Some newspapers indicated through their layout that they thought their readers were interested in other things. In 1876, newspapers used multiple headlines for stories, often telling much of the story in a series of descriptive phrases. The more headlines the paper used, the more important its editors thought the story was. For example, in St. Louis, the *Globe* gave more space to a story about a tornado and flooding in Iowa under the headline "Grim Death." About fifty people were killed, but the story got six headlines at the top of the page compared to three headlines for the Little Bighorn in the middle of the page. A few papers, like the *Austin Daily Democratic Statesman,* did not get the story in time for the July 6 issue and downplayed it on the seventh. The *Statesman* did not even give the battle its own headline but instead published a few paragraphs under its regular column of news by telegraph.

Nevertheless, for the majority of papers the Little Bighorn dominated the news. The first story was sometimes accompanied by a disclaimer that it was not confirmed and was too horrific to be true. The *Baltimore American and Commercial Advertiser* coverage was typical. It emphasized the carnage, its second headline calling the battlefield "a veritable 'slaughter pen.'" The *American* published five paragraphs on the battle, including the details that Custer, two of his brothers, his brother-in-law, and nephew were all killed among an estimated loss of about three hundred. The story noted that Indian casualties could not be estimated because "they bore off and cached most of their dead." The story included the sense of mystery that has followed the battle ever since: "Nothing is known of the operation of [Custer's] detachment, only as they trace it by the dead." The story was remarkably accurate considering that it was not based on any eyewitness testimony. The estimate of army casualties was close to the actual total, and estimates of Indian casualties are still in dispute to this day because they kept no written records, and they had removed their dead before the troopers examined the battlefield. The story reported that Reno attacked one end of the village with seven companies while Custer attacked the other end with five companies. In reality, of course, Custer had divided the Seventh Cavalry into four separate units. McDougall and Benteen did not join Reno until after his attack was repulsed. Still, the story's sparse details of the battle—that the men often were dragged from their horses by the Indians, who "poured in a murderous fire from all directions"—were true. The story also noted accurately that the dead were horribly mutilated.[21]

The subhead in the *American* over the second dispatch noted that the story was "partially confirmed" by the report from the *Times*. However, the *American,* one of the oldest and most prestigious newspapers in the country,[22] remained skeptical and ran an editorial doubting the story's veracity: "Until further advices are received we shall refuse to believe the story told the correspondent of the Montana *Herald* by a demoralized scout. Nevertheless, it seems certain that our troops have met with a serious defeat on the Little Horn, but we cannot believe that so experienced an officer as Gen. Custer could be led into a slaughter pen such as described by the couriers who brought the dismal news to the Montana settlements."[23]

The *New York Times* was particularly horrified by the news, perhaps because its editors had been devoting scant space to the war. On June 26, the day the Seventh Cavalry survivors were fighting for their lives, most of the news in the *Times* was about the Democratic convention meeting in St. Louis. A two-paragraph dispatch about the Battle of the Rosebud was relegated to page 7. The *Times* also carried a brief editorial about the battle, criticizing the army's Indian allies and deploring the thirty casualties the army suffered. It concluded that the Rosebud defeat occurred in an area that was no longer "the heart of Indian country," implying that the Sioux were not much of a threat because immigrants could move safely in most of the rest of that area.[24]

When the *Times* finally learned of the Little Bighorn, it screamed in a front-page headline, "Massacre of Our Troops." Subheadlines used the word "butchered" to describe Custer's death and said he had attacked "an overwhelmingly large camp of savages." On the editorial page, the *Times* opined that most people would be shocked by the Little Bighorn because they had forgotten there was a war on. "So few newspaper readers have followed the course of the Indian warfare in the North-west that the overwhelming defeat of Custer's command and the butchery of the gallant commander and his men, will produce both astonishment and alarm," the *Times* admitted. "We have latterly fallen into the habit of regarding the Indians yet remaining in a wild or semi-subdued state as practically of very little account. It is only now and then when some such outburst as that of the Modocs, which resulted in the slaying of Gen. Canby, Commissioner Thomas, and others, or that which we now record with so much sorrow, comes like a shock, that we realize the character of the Indian and the difficulties of the situation."[25]

Kansas was home to several army posts, which from time to time had garrisoned Seventh Cavalry troopers, so newspaper readers in that state were more attuned to the war. But the defeat of Custer was perhaps more shocking to Kansans because they believed in the superiority of the U.S. Army. J. H. Downing, publisher of the *Ellis County Star* in Hays, Kansas, was friends with a telegrapher at Fort Wallace, Kansas, and got the news before local army officers saw it. He quickly remade his front page to accommodate a one-paragraph story with the headline "War! Our Troops Surprised by the Sioux. General Custer and His Entire Command Killed." Downing's *Star* was the first paper in Kansas to publish the news; it had arrived too late for other papers to get the story in that day's edition.[26]

Downing wrote later that the officers at Fort Hays were so upset that they "came galloping over to town and crowded in the Star office. They said they didn't believe our story; that it couldn't be true, else the post commander would have received word direct from Fort Leavenworth."[27] The news created an equal sensation when it was published in Leavenworth the next day. A page 4 story described the reaction in town, where people gathered in groups to discuss the news in hushed tones. "Some endeavored to disbelieve the report, because of the suddenness of its arrival and the enormity of the result, but a seeming straightforward story had been told, and it was with sad hearts that it was taken to be too true."[28]

Most editors used similar language to describe the calamity. Some variation of "butcher," "slaughter," or "massacre" appeared in headlines around the country. In New England, the *Hartford Courant* called the battle in its headline "An Awful Slaughter" and "The Worst Indian Battle in Years." In Kansas, the *Topeka Commonwealth* on July 7 headlined that "Over 300 United States Troops Butchered by Indians" and called the battle "The Most Disastrous Defeat that has Ever Befallen Our Troops while Fighting Indians." In Kentucky, the *Flemensburg Democrat,* a weekly, was not able to print the news until July 13 but nevertheless screamed in a front-page headline, "Terrible Slaughter!" reporting that "General Custer and Five Companies of Cavalry Annihilated in Montana."[29]

Bennett's *New York Herald,* never one to be outdone in sensationalism, used the word "slaughter" in two of eight headlines on July 6. Under the main headline, which screamed "A Bloody Battle" in type twice the size of the other headlines, the *Herald* reported "General Custer Killed," "The Entire Detachment Under His Command Slaughtered." After noting "Seventeen Officers Slain," and the "Narrow Escape of Colonel Reno's Command," the *Herald* described the battlefield as "A Horrible Slaughter Pen."[30]

Most newspapers emphasized that Custer was killed, and newspapers often described him as "gallant" or "dashing" in their headlines. For example, the *Galveston News,* which claimed the largest circulation in Texas, emphasized in its series of headlines that "Sitting Bull's Lodges Charged by Gen. Custer and Five Companies with Great Carnage," explaining that "The Gallant Custer and Several kinsmen Fall at the Head of their Column." The first *New York World* headline was "Custer Killed," with the subhead explaining, "A Whole Family of Heroes Swept Away." The main *Louisville Courier-Journal* headline was simply "Custer."[31]

Other major southern newspapers noted the battle but did not emphasize it as much as other stories. The *Courier-Journal*'s cross-town rival, the *Louisville Commercial,* gave the story only three headlines under the label "The Indian War." The *Commercial* took a local angle, headlining that "Lieutenant Crittenden, Son of Thomas L. Crittenden, Among the Slain." The elder Crittenden had been a major general in the Union Army during the Civil War and had served as Kentucky state treasurer after the war. The *New Orleans Picayune* published three front-page stories on July 7, one of which was from its Washington correspondent. The headline noted "Excitement over the Little Horn Massacre," but three of the six headlines referred to news for the South, such as the appointment of a new marshal in Louisiana. The second story was headlined "Another Account of the Little Horn Fight" with the carelessly misspelled subhead "Gen. Cusert and His Entire Force Massacred." The story got closer to the correct spelling of the general's name, calling him "Custar" in the lead and then finally getting the name right in the list of officer casualties. The story's last headline noted "Col. Reno's Gallant Fight."[32]

In Chicago, home of Sheridan's headquarters and a vibrant newspaper market, journalists wrote some of the most dramatic headlines for the story. The *Chicago Times* wrung every detail out of the dispatches with a series of evocative headlines starting with "Butchered Boys." The second headline compared Custer to the Revolutionary War hero Mad Anthony Wayne. The *Times* described the attack as "A Tiger-Like Assault by the Dashing Cavalryman on Five Thousand Sioux." One headline described Custer's end, although anything known about his death at that time was mere speculation based on the location of the bodies: "Custer and His Brothers Meet Death at the Head of Their Columns Unflinchingly." The most dramatic front page belonged to the *Chicago Daily News* on July 6, which included a two-column map of the Montana and Wyoming territories and a headline twice the size of most newspaper headlines screaming "Custer Slain." The subheads explained "Desperate Battle with the Sioux," "A Fatal Sunday Fight on the Little Horn," and "Custer, with Five Companies, All Killed."[33]

After reporting the bare details that Custer and his detachment were killed in an attack on Sitting Bull's village, based on the Bozeman and Helena reports, the press around the country began getting much more information based on stories compiled by Lounsberry from interviews with survivors, military reports, military experts, and Kellogg's last dispatch. These reports were supplemented by local interviews with army officers, veterans, frontiersmen, and anyone who might have known Custer at any time in his life. Large newspapers added much of their own material; small newspapers sometimes printed only edited-down versions of the copy generated by Lounsberry.

Lounsberry, who was roused out of bed when the *Far West* docked in Bismarck at 11 P.M. on July 5, went to work immediately. In the kind of extraordinary fit of newswriting that journalists produce when in the midst of a big story, Lounsberry for the next twenty-four hours dictated information to the Bismarck telegrapher John M. Carnahan and his assistant, S. B. Rogers. When Lounsberry paused to organize the material, Carnahan kept the line open by using the standard telegrapher's trick of relaying the New Testament. The telegraph toll was $3,000 for the

50,000 word story. Bennett gladly paid the price because it gave him the most comprehensive coverage of the battle.[34]

The July 7 *Herald* story was a traditional version of what journalists call the second-day story—more detail, more background, and a beginning stab at trying to answer the "why" question. Despite the sensationalism of the top headline, "The Massacre," the coverage was a professional compilation of the information known at the time presented in a way to interest the reader. The subsequent eleven headlines let the readers know what was in the story without sensationalizing. The second headline, for example, dispelled any doubts about the story: "The Gallant Cavalry Leader's Death Officially Confirmed." (Custer was so famous that his name was not needed in any of the second-day headlines.) Other headlines promised comments from Sheridan, Sherman, and Grant and noted that the story would include background on the current Indian war as well as previous Indian campaigns. One headline quoted Terry on Custer: "A Mistake for Which He Paid the Penalty of His Life." In modern newspaper design, this headline would have been set within the text of the story as a "pull quote" to draw the reader into the story, but in 1876 it acted in the same way, a device to attract attention.[35]

The story itself was not a coherent narrative but rather a series of dispatches from around the country. The first paragraph summarized Terry's confidential report and what was known about the battle. It was generally accurate and included the oft-repeated facts that Custer had declined offers of additional troops and Gatling guns because he thought the guns would impede his movements, and that he believed he had adequate force for the job. "General Terry visits no censure on Custer, simply saying in his report that he gave his life for his fault. All the evidence shows that he was surprised, defeated and destroyed." The battlefield, in contrast to the description in the story, was not in a canyon but rather a river valley, and the Indians did not lure Custer into an ambush. Most Indian accounts say they were as surprised by the attack as Custer was by the size of the village and the fact that the Indians did not scatter when attacked. Nevertheless, "surprised, defeated and destroyed," summed up the Little Bighorn from the U.S. Army standpoint pretty well.

The most interesting dispatches in this issue were interviews with Sherman and Sheridan, both of whom doubted that the initial reports were true. The *Herald* reporter described Sheridan, who was attending a Civil War reunion in Philadelphia, as very courteous and acknowledged having "read the painful narrative" of the battle in the newspapers. But Sheridan, who was speaking in the morning, said he could not believe the news because it was too incredible and had come from a scout, not a reporter. "These scouts on the frontier have a way of spreading news, and all frontier stories, especially about Indian wars, are to be carefully considered," he said.

Unlike the modern practice of the inverted pyramid, where the most important news comes first, the anonymous Sheridan interviewer strung the story out over two more meetings with Sheridan during the day as the general received more reports. When the reporter interviewed Sheridan and several other officers in Sheridan's hotel room that afternoon, the mood was much different. Sheridan spoke "with sorrowful feeling" about Custer and stressed that it was too soon to pass judgment on what caused the defeat, although he quoted Terry's report and said Custer had paid with his life.

Emotions started to run high when the conversation turned to federal Indian policy. Sheridan said he had sent every available man to the war zone but that he did not have enough troops to do what the government wanted. Another officer then "said with some fervor that this was one of the results of the policy of the democratic House, which invited Indian defeats by cutting down the army." Sheridan, apparently not liking the turn in the conversation, said his business was military, not politics, and he did not want to be understood to be criticizing any branch of government. The question of the size of the army was not one of politics, he said, but one "that should interest democrats as well as republicans."

Sheridan left to go to the reunion, and the reporter then quoted at length from an interview with "an officer of distinction" who wanted to remain anonymous. The officer voiced in memorable terms what the reporter said was a common sentiment among the veterans at the reunion—"that Custer threw his command away by an act of bravado." The unnamed officer said—in a quote that is often repeated in Custer biographies—"The truth about Custer is that he was a pet soldier who had risen not above his merit but higher than men of equal merit. He fought with Phil Sheridan and through the patronage of Sheridan he rose, but while Sheridan liked his valor and his dash he never trusted his judgment."

Sherman, who was also interviewed in a Philadelphia hotel room, was even more incredulous than Sheridan at the news. Sherman had taken off his coat and boots and was fanning himself by a window when the reporter entered. He greeted the reporter with several questions: "Is it true? What news have you got? What about Custer?" When the reporter said he did not know anything more than had been in the paper that morning, Sherman said the story must be exaggerated. "I cannot believe that Custer and his whole command would be swept away. I don't think there were enough Indians there to do it like this."

After a discussion about the campaign, Sherman again insisted the report was exaggerated when, mid-sentence, a knock on the door brought a telegram from Sheridan confirming Custer's death. Sherman thought the fact that Terry was transporting Custer's wounded meant the full story would soon be obtained from eyewitnesses.

When the *Herald* reporter asked him why Terry had sent Custer off on "a detour" up the Rosebud, Sherman said that the best way to find Indian camps was to divide and search different areas, trying to take them by surprise. "There were good reasons for Custer making this detour," Sherman said. "He probably had his own good reasons for weakening his force by sending Major Reno around the Indian camp with seven companies. That was probably intended to cut off their retreat after the attack had been made."

The reporter asked Sherman for the reasons for the campaign—another indication of how fuzzy the whole war was to the general public—and was told the military was forcing the hostiles onto the reservations at the request of the government. "That is something I am very anxious you should say in the Herald, because I want it understood," Sherman said. "We are doing this at the request of the Indian Department. It does not originate with the War Department."

The *Herald*, like many newspapers, published local reaction stories. In New York, according to the *Herald*, people were angry and felt they knew Custer through his popular magazine articles. "To hundreds who knew nothing of his military record General Custer was a brilliant cavalryman, who delighted to scout the broad prairie in search of wild adventure. To these, as well as to those familiar with his remarkable war record, or personally acquainted with him, the news was depressing. The magnetism of the man discovered for him a warm sympathy among the people, so that in his cruel end thousands recognized a personal loss as well as a national disaster."

The *Globe-Democrat,* although it did not have a correspondent on the campaign, bragged about its coverage, noting that interviews with local experts threw "a vast amount of light on the subject." The paper reported that many St. Louisans initially did not believe the news, especially given "the somewhat incoherent dispatches" that made up the first stories. "On every side expressions of doubt were heard, and men more or less posted in the methods of Indian warfare were to be heard on every side declaring their disbelief in the report, while some were no[t] slow to assert that the whole affair was a canard gotten up for some nefarious purpose."[36]

The Seventh's titular commander, Samuel D. Sturgis, was stationed in St. Louis at the time of the battle. When a *Globe* reporter learned Sturgis's son was among the dead, he jumped on a streetcar and hurried to Sturgis's quarters, where he found the family "in deep grief" because they had just received an official telegram from Terry's adjutant informing them of their loss. Another story based on interviews with local officers summed up the feeling that Custer rushed into battle to restore his reputation. Sturgis was quoted as saying that the success of the Indians "would in all probability rouse them to a general sense of fearlessness."[37]

In the same issue, a *Globe* reporter also interviewed former Missouri governor Thomas Fletcher, who had visited the Indian agencies the year before and described the nonagency Indians as "utterly untamed." A former clerk at the Standing Rock Agency, J. D. Keller, told the *Globe* that he knew Sitting Bull quite well, but his description called that assertion into question since he said Sitting Bull was five feet tall and had one leg shorter than another from a wound to the knee. Sitting Bull was actually about five foot ten,[38] and his wound was to his foot.

But strict accuracy was not as important as getting *something* in the paper. As the *Galveston News* wrote on July 16 when explaining why it was publishing a letter written by Custer in 1874, "Everything pertaining to the late Gen. Custer is at this time interesting." One of the attitudes of the press in the nineteenth century was that of *Chicago Times* publisher Storey, who, during the Civil War, told a correspondent, "Telegraph fully all the news, and when there is no news, send rumors."[39]

Speculation, if not downright rumor, started in earnest on July 8, which for many papers was the third day of coverage. The *New York Herald*'s main story emphasized the tragic romance of the battle. Its set of twelve headlines started with "Custer's Death" and included dramatic descriptions like "Where the Yellow-Haired Leader Lay in the Embrace of Death," "Friends and Comrades Around Him," and "The Savages Respect the Body of Him They Knew So Well." The headlines even lionized Maj. Marcus Reno, who later would be cast as a villain: "Reno's Desperate Fight Against Overwhelming Odds," "Deeds That Shall Go Sounding Down Through the Ages." The set of headlines concluded by quoting the last four lines of Theodore O'Hara's poem, "The Bivouac of the Dead," which is featured on memorials around the country: "On Fame's eternal camping ground Their silent tents are spread; And glory guards with solemn round The bivouac of the dead."[40]

The story under the headline, which historian Oliver Knight called "the major story of the battle," was the bulk of Lounsberry's all-night effort and covered about three pages of the newspaper (including a four-column map).[41] It was a tremendous amount of copy for a paper in 1876, even one of the largest in the country like the *Herald*. The beginning was written in the first person and described the battlefield, so it was probably based on the account of Maj. James Brisbin, who was commander of the battalion of the Second Cavalry that Custer had refused to take with him to the Little Bighorn. Brisbin, a former newspaper editor, was known as "Grasshopper Jim" because of his interest in agriculture and the articles he wrote praising the value of the land in Montana and the Northwest.[42] His writing skills did not fail him in his description of the battlefield:

> Couriers are about to leave with General Terry's despatches, and I take advantage of the opportunity to send a hasty and necessarily imperfect account of the battle. I write from the scene of Custer's magnificent but terribly fatal charge, from a plateau on which, but a few hours since, I saw at a glance 115 heroic soldiers of the Seventh United States cavalry lying where they fell at the hands of a savage foe, cold and dead. Near the top of a little knoll in the centre of this plateau lay Custer himself and it touched my heart to see that the savages, in a kind of human recognition of heroic clay, had respected the corpse of the man they knew so well. Other bodies were mutilated; Custer's was untouched—a tribute of respect from such an enemy more real than a title of nobility. He lay as asleep, his face calm and a smile on his lips.[43]

The description conformed to most other accounts, although it left out what at that time was considered the too graphic details of the arrow in Custer's body, and the horrible mutilation of Tom Custer was not mentioned at all. Brisbin tugged at the reader's heartstrings by noting the placement of the bodies of Custer's family: "Almost at Custer's feet lay a fair, beautiful boy of nineteen. This was young Reed, Custer's nephew. He was visiting the General at the time he was ordered on this expedition, and insisted upon coming with him. In the field, a little way off, lay Boston Custer, another of the General's brothers. Within a few feet of each other the three brothers had fallen, and on the skirmish line was the body of Lieutenant Calhoun, the husband of Custer's sister. Mrs. Calhoun lost here a husband, three brothers and a nephew."

The Reno battlefield, Brisbin wrote, "was a dreadful place" with dead Indians, troopers, and horses all "mingled as if they had died where they fought in all the wild confusion of the melee. The stench was awful, and the bodies were covered with flies. One officer recognized the body of 1st Lt. Donald McIntosh among the many littering the field. "McIntosh was himself part Indian, a highly educated gentleman and a fine officer. He has fallen in battle with his face toward the enemy and it is hoped the government will remember his widow and his little children at Fort Lincoln."

The story then outlined the three-pronged plan for the campaign, but Brisbin admitted he knew nothing of Crook's column other than "common rumors," reinforcing the fact that everyone, including the participants, was operating in the dark. Under such conditions, it is surprising that the press accounts were as accurate as they were. It also showed that everyone, including the readers, knew the reports might contain rumor or as yet unconfirmed facts—it was what was expected.

Brisbin's account of the last conference at the mouth of the Rosebud with Custer, Terry, and Gibbon did not include the standard Little Bighorn lore that Gibbon told Custer not to be greedy, foreshadowing the disaster as caused by Custer's ambition. Instead, Brisbin described Custer as sad and worried as he shook Terry's hand for the last time and later said, "God bless you." Brisbin speculated that Custer was still upset about Grant's anger toward him. On the other hand, Kellogg was upbeat the night before the command left. Brisbin chatted with him after midnight when Kellogg had finished his dispatches. The reporter, unlike Custer, was not burdened with command and instead hoped the troopers would "overhaul the Indians and have a good fight." Kellogg was the last man Brisbin saw from the Seventh Cavalry the next morning. The reporter trotted off after Custer, riding on a mule carrying two saddlebags bulging with paper and pencil and enough bacon, sugar, and coffee to last fifteen days.

The account of the action of Reno's command was accurate in the broad outlines of the battle, although it portrayed Reno as acting more in command than later accounts indicated and hardly mentioned the actions of Benteen at all. The story did not speculate on Custer's part of the battle other than to state that he had evidently planned to attack the other end of the village. "As he dashed forward he raised his hat, and the soldiers cheered lustily. This was the last seen of Custer or his men until they were found dead and horribly mutilated."

The second main account, from George Herendeen, a scout with Reno, was much more dramatic. Herendeen, along with about a dozen other soldiers, was left behind in the woods when Reno made his precipitate retreat to the bluffs. After several harrowing hours, the men cautiously made their way to Reno when the Indians turned their attention to Custer. Herendeen's story at one point referred to the scout Mitch Bouyer as Nuch Bayer, and he added several fanciful details, claiming the Indian chiefs were using flags to rally their men as if they were a cavalry unit. The story claimed that, although the Indians fought splendidly, they lost as many men as Custer did. Most historians, however, claim that Indian casualties were probably light compared to those of the cavalry.[44]

Herendeen, quoting the scout Curley, who had ridden with Custer and then escaped, helped create the lore of the Last Stand. "He [Curley] says the fight lasted over one hour, Custer contending against 10 times his number. They fought splendidly until the Big Chief Custer fell, and then many became somewhat demoralized. Most of the officers and men had been killed before Custer." Herendeen added that Curley was trustworthy, although for years historians have debated his account, and he remains one of the most controversial figures of the battle.[45]

Herendeen's account also provided some of the first details about the mutilation of the dead—sensational but true information that created some of the battle's mystique: heroes fighting a desperate battle against a savage foe who took no prisoners. "I think some of our men were captured alive and tortured," said Herendeen, who was hidden in the woods when some of the mutilations were being done. "I know the colored scout Isaiah [Dorman] was, for he had small pistil balls in his legs from the knees down, and I believe they were shot into him while alive. Another man had strips of skin cut out of his body. Hordes of squaws and old gray-haired Indians were roaming over the battlefield howling like mad. The squaws had stone mallets and mashed in the skulls of the dead and wounded. Many were gashed with knives and some had their noses and other members cut off."

The story also included a list of casualties under the headline "The Roll of Honor." Other stories included information about plans to honor Custer's memory and a brief profile of Kellogg. Overall, the *New York Herald* provided readers with a lot of information that they could use to sort through the disaster. Certainly Sherman and other government officials thought so. When asked for more details about the battle, Sherman told the *Herald* Washington correspondent that the public was "fully informed" and any future plans must remain secret out of military necessity. Grant held a dinner that night with Secretary of War James Cameron, Sherman, and others but did not include the press. The *Herald* reporter tried to get another interview by ambushing Sherman. "It was near midnight when General Sherman returned to his hotel, where he immediately locked himself up, and no information could be had of what the army is to do." The reporter noted Sheridan would be in town the next day, evidently to discuss war plans, but he would likely not talk to the press, either: "Some strictures have been passed upon General Sheridan in military circles for giving so freely, at Chicago and elsewhere, a free explanation of what is being done, and it was said that, as he was a subordinate officer, he had no right to give out any information without the consent of his superior officer."[46]

A critic could fault the *Herald* coverage for inaccuracy or sensationalism, or as the military did for divulging secrets, but the truth of journalism is that the first accounts often contain errors; it cannot be otherwise in a deadline business. What is more amazing is the overall accuracy of the account, particularly given the confusion and shock of the participants and the fact that no reporter was on the site. The details and lists of causalty figures were no more sensational than the details published of

brutal crime stories or the torture and beheadings committed by terror-
ists in the twenty-first century.

At any rate, neither Sherman nor anyone else could stop the press
from publishing more information about the battle. On July 9, the day
after the *New York Herald* reported that the general of the army had
locked himself in his room, the paper published Terry's official report
and a story about Sitting Bull's autobiography, including a drawing from
the chief's pictographic record of his life. The paper also published an
account of Curley's escape from the battlefield; he claimed that he threw
a Sioux blanket over his head—not a good disguise in the June heat—
and rode in a charge with the hostiles until he could race to freedom.[47]
Curley had in fact simply left before Custer's command was surrounded
and had watched the end from a distance. But this early press version
helped create the idea that he had slunk off the battlefield in elaborate disguise, much like the stories that Lincoln had traveled through Baltimore
in ridiculous disguise in 1861 and Jefferson Davis had been captured in
1865 in women's clothing.

Other stories warned that the war was spreading as heretofore friendly
Indians left the agencies to join Sitting Bull, who had plans for "A Grand
Red Confederacy" of "renegades and desperadoes," including white
men. Veterans of the Reno fight told the *Herald* reporter that "the Indians were led in their attacks by whites. Men also who have been engaged
where attacks have been made on the Black Hills trains inform me that in
every instance they heard English voices urging the Indians to the attack.
The Indians are desperate and are goaded forward by desperate men, and
the government must either surrender the frontier to these savages or
fight it out." Such breathless copy of wild rumors would seem irresponsible, but on the other hand Terry's official report included the detail that
Reno himself was "very confident" that white men were fighting with
the Indians at the Little Bighorn.[48]

On July 11 the *Herald* reported Custer's supposed last words before
the fight: "An officer informs your correspondent when Custer came in
sight of the 1,800 lodges, a village of upward of 7,000 Indians, he swung
his hat and said: 'Hurrah! Custer's luck. The biggest Indian village on
the American continent.'"[49] The quote sounds fake because Custer was
not known to speak of himself in the third person. "Custer's luck" was
a popular phrase in the army, and not always of admiration but rather

often of jealously for Custer's ability to get out of scrapes and find himself in the right place at the right time. What Custer most likely said,
based on the testimony of Trumpeter John Martin, the last survivor to
see Custer alive, was "We've caught them napping." Custer based this
on his observation of the village, which at that time appeared devoid
of warriors because they were on Reno's side of the field. Nevertheless,
the quote fits the stereotype of Custer as a reckless fool, and versions
of it were repeated in other newspapers and indeed in modern times in
the tone of movies like *Little Big Man*. In 1876 the *Dallas Daily Herald*,
for example, embellished the anecdote by contrasting Custer's misplaced
optimism with his supposed fate: "When the head of Custer's column
came in sight of the four thousand Sioux, he rose in his stirrups, swung
his hat in the air and shouted: 'Hurrah, Custer's luck; the biggest Indian
village on the continent!' An hour later Rain-in-the-Face had cut out
his heart."[50]

The Rain-in-the-Face anecdote made good newspaper copy because
of his revenge motive against the Custer brothers, and many newspapers
repeated some version of the story. The *New York World* put the story on
the front page with two headline decks screaming "Horrible Treatment
of the Bodies of the Big Horn Victims" and "Custer's Heart Cut from
His Body and Raised Upon a Pole." The story, based on reports from
Sioux City, claimed that "Rain-in-the-Face cut the heart from Custer's
dead body, put it on a pole, and a grand war-dance was held around it.
The Indians were jubilant, boastful and sanguine of making better terms
on account of their success."[51]

Descriptions of mutilations were repeated in many stories and became
ever more graphic as witnesses either were interviewed or sent their own
stories to different newspapers. For example, the diary of an anonymous
officer with Gibbon's command described the battlefield as "horrible in
the extreme" in a *New York Herald* story published on July 13: "It is sick-
ening to look at the bodies stripped. Here a hand gone, here a foot or a
head, ghastly gashes cut in all parts of the body, eyes gouged out, noses
and ears cut off and skulls crushed in."[52]

The next day the *Herald* published an account from 1st Lt. John Car-
land, who was serving escort duty on the steamboat *Far West*. "It makes
one's heart sick to look over the battle ground and see the poor fellows,
some of them with the entrails cut out, others with their eyes dug out

and hearts laid across their face. They even stopped to cut their pockets to get their money and watches. The most fearful sight was Colonel Cook. He was a splendid looking man with long dark whiskers. They dug his face all out so as to get at his fine beard, it is supposed. They did not disfigure General Custer in any way but his brother Tom Custer was opened and his heart taken out."[53]

Bradley was so upset by the repeated stories about the mutilations that he wrote a letter to the *Helena Herald* about a month after the battle denying that George Custer's heart had been cut out and downplaying desecrations of the other bodies: "Many of the bodies were not even scalped, and in the comparatively few cases of disfiguration, it appeared to me the result rather of a blow with a knife, hatchet, or war club to finish a wounded man, than deliberate mutilation." Bradley's discounting of widespread mutilation is, however, refuted by dozens of accounts, including those of some Indians who described the aftermath of the battle. A clue to Bradley's motivation is found in the letter itself, where he states that "the bare truth is painful enough to the relatives and friends of these unfortunate men without the cruel and gratuitous exaggeration of their grief that must come from the belief that they had been horribly mutilated after death."[54]

Gruesome details of horrific events have been a staple of publishing since the first printing presses in England cranked out ballads about murders in the 1600s. In the case of the Little Bighorn, they no doubt fueled a feeling of vengeance toward the tribes and led newspapers to eagerly publish rumors about the demise of Indian leaders and inflated reports of Indian casualties. In the second week of July most papers started carrying a report that Sitting Bull had been killed in the battle. For example, the *Baltimore American* on July 11 reported not only that Sitting Bull was killed in the battle but that the chief collected $20,000 from the dead troopers.[55] Some stories would add that a man named Milburn, supposedly Sitting Bull's white advisor, was killed with him.[56] On July 21, the *American* published a brief story confirming that not only Sitting Bull but Crazy Horse had been killed in the battle. Yet more "confirmation" was printed three days later, including the details that a scout had seen the body. Sherman was asked about the rumor and said it did not matter whether it was true or not because the Indians had at least twenty other capable war leaders.[57] The *Dallas Daily Herald* picked up the story late and on July 26 reported it with undisguised relish, combining it with the report that Sitting Bull spoke French: "General S. Bull scorned to speak English, but conversed in very fair French. His impassioned oratory in his native tongue was wonderfully effective on his savage cohorts. But Custer's men sent the General and Crazy Horse to their happy hunting grounds, and there is no further need for French interpreters in future Pow Wows."[58]

Newspapers also initially inflated the casualty figures for Indians. One officer estimated that several hundred Indians were killed, although he admitted that it was hard to tell because of their practice of removing the dead from the field. He also addressed the rumor of Sitting Bull's death and said an Indian who looked like the chief was found on the field, "but no doubt this is false because they would have tried to carry him along."[59]

Eventually both Sitting Bull and Crazy Horse turned up alive and delivering quotes, at least through intermediaries, to the press. Sitting Bull gave his side of the story through a widely published interview with Bear Stands Up, an Indian at the Spotted Tail Agency who said he had come from Sitting Bull's camp. Sitting Bull told Bear Stands Up that he did not want to fight the white man but that he would defend the Black Hills. "Sitting Bull says that if troops come out to him he must fight them, but if they do not come he intends to visit the agency, and he will consult his people for peace." The same story gave reports of discussions among the agency Indians about selling the Black Hills. The story portrayed them as cooperative and wanting peace.[60]

>>→

As Sitting Bull debated coming in to the reservation and Terry and Crook could not catch the Indians, it appeared that the war was winding down. A widely published story from the *Chicago Times* in late August that noted the troops were going into winter quarters drew mostly negative reactions. The *Globe-Democrat* headlined the story in bold type "At an End" and in subheads editorialized "Virtual Failure of the Indian Campaign" because "The Red Skins Nowhere to be Found."[61]

The *New York World* was even more scathing in its criticism of the campaign, declaring that it had ended "in an ignominious fizzle. The United States troops have been out-marched, out-maneuvered and out-fought; Sitting Bull and his hostiles have gone in to winter quarters, and their families are surrendering to the Government, which will have to feed them all winter." The *World* sarcastically suggested that Terry, who had characterized the Indians as starving, go South to edit a campaign newspaper, presumably because his statement was as trustworthy as a political opinion sheet.[62]

In the space of two months newspapers had gone from blithely predicting a quick victory to despairing over the magnitude of, not just Custer's defeat, but the failure of the entire campaign. Someone was to blame. Journalists were eager to help the public figure out who deserved it.

CHAPTER 3

"The Blood of These Brave Men"

Assessing the Blame for Defeat

Some newspapers, like the *St. Louis Globe-Democrat,* did not wait to analyze the battle before fixing blame for the disaster. It was obvious, the *Globe* wrote, that Custer had blundered. "In connection with many military officers on the subject of the disaster, there seemed to be but one opinion as to the causes which led to the slaughter," the *Globe* claimed in a story published the day after the news was first reported, although the only officer quoted in the story was Sturgis, the commander of the Seventh who had feuded with Custer and whose son died in the battle. "Of course, it is impossible now to say what motives impelled the dead hero, but the army officers here seem to think that in a rash desire to re-establish a fame somewhat beclouded by the misfortunes of the last campaign, he purposely rushed into the fight in the hope of winning victory against overwhelming odds before any of the forces of Gen. Terry could come up and share the coveted honors. His wild determination cost him his own life, and his country the lives of numbers of gallant officers and men who were determined to obey orders, though they might know that 'somebody blundered.'"[1] The quoted phrase from the Alfred Tennyson poem *The Charge of the Light Brigade*—about the tragic charge of the British army's Light Brigade during the Crimean War, only twenty-one years earlier—neatly connected the Little Bighorn to another military catastrophe brought about by poor generalship.

The *Globe* later criticized the Custer "admirers and partisans [who] rushed into print at once to throw the blame of his defeat and of the loss of so many brave soldiers upon some one else" like Terry or Reno.

Custer made two major mistakes: not waiting for Terry before attack-ing, and dividing the Seventh Cavalry when he decided to attack on his own. Reno and Benteen managed to save their own commands despite Custer's faulty plan. "These are facts which prove that Custer, for the sake of reaping the honor of a conspicuous victory, threw aside both pru-dence and obedience." In Custer's defense, the *Globe* noted that no one in the whole expedition knew the numbers of the Indians they were fac-ing. Nevertheless, the *Globe* concluded that Custer's attack was "a terrible blunder, an unexcusable blunder, and one which is certain to cost the country more lives than were lost on the 25th of June."[2]

But the *Globe,* like the Custer partisans it decried, and in fact most newspapers in 1876, was itself partisan. Custer was a Democrat who had testified in Congress to corruption within the Republican Grant administration. The *Globe,* despite its hyphenated name, was a Repub-lican newspaper that was vigorous in its support of the party. Although the facts cited by the *Globe* can be used to support its argument about the Little Bighorn, other newspapers and military experts at the time disagreed, and those disagreements often, but not always, fell along par-tisan lines. Republican newspapers like the *Globe* tended to emphasize Custer's mistakes while ignoring the culpability of other players, espe-cially the Grant administration. Democratic newspapers usually blamed the administration for providing inadequate numbers of troops for the frontier and for the Indian peace policy that supplied the tribes with food and weapons. Although these papers often admitted that Custer's charge was reckless, they focused on the ineptness of his superiors, including Grant, for putting him in a hopeless situation. They tended to portray Custer as a heroic cavalryman defeated by forces beyond his control.

This split in the way the battle was interpreted held throughout the country. Because the South in 1876 was solidly Democratic, most southern newspapers excused Custer and blamed Grant. Northern and western Democratic newspapers usually joined their southern breth-ren in castigating the administration, whereas Republican newspapers in those regions blamed Custer. As the weeks wore on and the govern-ment debated how to respond to the enlarging Indian war and the racial violence in the South that intensified as the election drew near, Custer dropped from the debate and the two sides blamed either Grant or the Democrat-controlled House of Representatives, which Republicans often called the "Rebel House" or "Confederate House" to attack the Democrats' connection to the wrong side of the Civil War.

Initially, however, the focus on press coverage centered on Custer, whose celebrity as an author, Civil War hero, and frontiersman would have made him the emphasis of most stories even had he not been the officer in command on the field. In addition, Custer had important friends in the newspaper industry. Whenever he visited New York, Custer had often mingled with Democratic movers and shakers like August Belmont, publisher of the *New York World,* and James Gordon Bennett, Jr., publisher of the *New York Herald.*[3] The *Herald* was among the most important and widely quoted papers of the day,[4] and it was especially emotional in defending the reputation of the dead cavalryman.

When Custer died, Bennett's paper reacted with emotional editorials that indicated more than a journalistic interest in the battle. On July 7, in one of four Little Bighorn editorials that covered about half of the opinion page—an extraordinary amount of space to devote to one topic—the *Herald* admitted that Custer's charge "may have been rash" but argued that Grant's insult to his honor by removing him from command led to his behavior. Civilians, the *Herald* intoned, could not understand the extreme sensitiveness professional soldiers feel from such a public hurt. "If the intense, excruciating smart of soldiers under disgrace be a fault it is a 'failing which leans to virtue's side.' General Custer was a man whose mental organization made him peculiarly vulnerable to the sting of disgrace. It is only an impetuous man of quick and almost boiling sensibilities that can make such a bold dashing cavalry officer as General Custer had shown himself to be. It is in the nature of such a man to be elated by marks of honor and appreciation, and to be plunged into desperation and despair by a public stigma fixed upon him by a superior whose acts it is not permitted him to question."[5]

Had Custer been in overall command of the expedition, the *Herald* continued, the campaign would have been better planned and Custer's impulsive nature would have been restrained by the responsibility. Instead, Terry had split his forces, leaving Custer with insufficient troops. Grant, as an experienced soldier, should have known better how to organize the campaign but had degraded Custer for political reasons. The *Herald,* like the *Globe* and many others, quoted Tennyson's poem: "Some one may have blundered at the Little Horn; but this was merely one consequence of the parent blunder perpetrated by President Grant. . . . It would hardly be too severe to say to President Grant, 'Behold your hands! they are red with the blood of Custer and his brave three hundred.'"

The *Herald* sought the opinion of prominent experts on the cause of the defeat. Joseph E. Johnston, the widely respected Confederate commander of the Army of the Tennessee, refused to be drawn into the debate, even when the reporter made leading statements like "General Custer seems to have been rather hasty in his operations." Johnston replied, "Of that I can't say." Confederate cavalry general John McCausland did state his opinion when asked if he thought Custer was rash at the Little Bighorn. "No. By ___ he was not," McCausland said. "He did the very thing a cavalry commander should have done. I would have done the same thing myself. He found the Indian trail, was close upon them, and was he to turn back? Certainly not. The only way to fight with cavalry is to dash—to charge."[6]

Custer's Civil War fights were revisited in several feature stories. The *Herald* on July 10 published almost a page of such stories under the headline "The Dead Cavalryman," with nine mostly eulogizing subheadlines like "Le Chevalier sans Peur et sans Reproche," which translated from French is "the knight without fear and beyond reproach." The phrase was typically used to describe Bayard, a medieval French knight. Other headlines referred to reminiscences of his Army of the Potomac comrades. "I Wish to God Old Custer Was Here!" one headline screamed. The story included a widely reprinted piece from the *Chicago Tribune,* which had interviewed three local veterans, all of whom concluded that Custer was not to blame for the Little Bighorn. "Some call him rash, and they are saying now that Custer ought to have known better than to have charged when he did," said one veteran, identified as Colonel Birge. "But that is all bosh. He had just as much judgment as any man."[7]

A veteran identified as Major Dean said he had witnessed Custer perform the bravest act he had seen during the war when a stone fence had broken up a charge Custer was leading. "Custer got twenty yards ahead with his color bearer right in among the rebel infantry. The color bearer's horse was shot, but the man was not hurt. "Custer jumped off his horse, picked up the man by the jacket collar and his breeches, swung him on his own horse, gave him a slap with his sabre, and sent him off to the rear, and was left there alone among the rebel infantry; but you bet that we got in there in about half a minute."[8]

The *Herald* also honored Custer with poetry. An unsigned piece set off a series of stories about the "Golden-Haired Leader" and the reasons for the defeat:

> Foremost of those dead heroes,
> Who showed them how to die,
> Shall any shame him
> Now or blame him?
> We who claim him will then know why.[9]

The Virginia poet James Barron Hope, who the *Richmond Whig* claimed was "next to Tennyson, if not better than him," wrote that Custer's charge was just as heroic as that of the Light Brigade, but British troops had more to motivate them because they knew they were charging in front of the major European armies, so "if they saw death before them, they also saw History with her pen and Fame with her trumpet. But Custer and his men had none of these inspirations. In a wild and savage country, in the solitude of a wilderness and against a barbarous foe, they [rode] to an awful death, with nothing to animate them save a sense of duty; and the men who fell on the Little Horn will take up the right of the line of shadowy heroes who died in the Balaklava Valley."[10]

The *Indianapolis Journal* portrayed Custer as a martyr in the congressional debate over the size of the army. An army officer wrote a letter to the paper describing a conversation he had had with Custer in January. Custer "used this expression:—'It will take another Phil Kearney massacre to bring Congress up to a generous support of the army.' His disaster comes home to me with fearful force," the officer wrote.[11]

People around the country expressed their sorrow. In Washington a group of Custer's Civil War comrades formed a committee to adopt resolutions in his honor and arrange a memorial service. Apparently the same group, although it was not identified by name, made plans to organize a Custer Monument Association. The *Herald,* daily raising money for its own fund, encouraged the creation of such associations all over the country: "This is a work in which the humblest can join, for no one is so poor that he cannot do homage to valor and self-sacrifice."[12]

No encouragement was needed to remember Custer in his hometown of Monroe, Michigan, where the main hotel was decorated with two American flags, bordered with crepe. Two blocks down from the hotel was a display of photographs of George, Tom, and Boston Custer, Autie Reed, and James Calhoun. The photos were set among a background of flags entwined with black crepe. "Women stop before that window and weep. Men halt there, brush away a tear, and sigh, 'Poor Custer—poor boys!'" The anonymous writer of this article, who had served with Custer in the Civil War, interviewed Custer's father on his front porch while Custer's mother sat inside the house "hugging her great sorrow in the darkness." Custer's father, Emmanuel, was about seventy, white-haired and stooped. He was grieving so intensely that he had trouble speaking when he told the reporter that "they were all good boys" and called his home their "headquarters" when they would come to visit.[13]

The reporter told Emmanuel that some newspapers had praised his son but others had called him reckless. "'They should not have said so,' he replied. 'I am his father, and shouldn't a father know the characteristics of his own son? He was neither proud nor vain. He fought to whip and not for praise. He was not reckless. He had much to live for, and he would not throw his life away. No, no. They wrong my dead boy. They shouldn't say so.'"

The reporter broke the news to a farmer he met who was harvesting a field outside of town. The farmer turned pale and his hand shook as he brushed away a tear. The farmer had been wounded in the leg while serving with Custer, and the general had taken his arm and helped him to the rear. "I would have given my right arm to save his life—aye, I would have died in his place!" he told the reporter.

The story noted that Custer loved music and was always jolly. During one hot battle, he ordered the band to stand by the artillery to give the gunners "something lively" to raise their spirits. Confederate fire forced the musicians to dive to the ground, and one shell went clear through a drum. "That beat was out of time," Custer said with a laugh and let the bandsmen return to the rear.

The reporter concluded that "General Custer's military life was a wild romance, developing some interesting incident every day, and what could be truthfully written of his most daring exploits in the saddle would fill a hundred Herald columns." Lost in remembering the Civil

War, the reporter had forgotten for a moment that Custer was dead, and the realization made his heart ache: "It would have been glorious for him to have died as the head of his old Third division, his sabre gleaming and his long hair floating out behind—it was so terrible for him to die with the desperation of despair in his soul. Men have dared to whisper that it was a blunder. Let no man whisper it again. The general who made no blunder through four years of almost daily fighting would not be apt to blunder in a skirmish. . . . If he is to sleep in a grave among the sterile hills, may some soft voiced bird carry a flower to blossom above his noble breast, and it will console our grieving hearts to know that the bitter winter blasts sweep another way."

Custer's most passionate defenders were the southern newspapers, especially those in Kentucky and Texas, where Custer had served on Reconstruction duty. The *Louisville Courier-Journal* was published by Henry Watterson, who had befriended Custer when he served in Kentucky after the war. The paper angrily rebutted charges in Republican newspapers that Custer was rash: "We knew him intimately, and were familiar with his motives, purposes and feelings. He chafed under departmental injustice, and was goaded to his death by the miserable system which Grant and [Secretary of War William] Belknap have established. There is no use mincing words about it. The man was hounded like a dog. He was not given a dog's chance. The president is an accomplice to his murder and the immolation of his command. The Republican party is responsible for the disaster. The whole affair was, more or less, a setup job, because Custer was not a thief. All this talk about 'reckless courage' is a mere blind to cover up the villainy."[14]

Kentucky was a border state during the Civil War, so its press could be expected to show some sympathy for a former Union general. But newspapers in states that were officially part of the old Confederacy and still under Reconstruction rule not only forgave Custer his role in their defeat but praised him as a brave foe. The *Dallas Daily Herald* recounted an 1864 battle between forces under Custer and Confederate general Thomas Rosser, who was identified by the paper as the brother of Dallas resident Robert S. Rosser. The *Herald* wrote that Custer and Thomas Rosser "were true and marked types of the Northern and Southern soldier, and had blended together all that fierce, stubborn, unyielding courage which has characterized the fights of the American soldier from Valley Forge to the capital of the Montezumas. We feel persuaded that no one will regret the gallant Custer's death more than the brave young Virginian [Rosser] who opposed him so well along the banks of the Rapidan."[15]

The *Galveston News* praised Custer's frontier skills, publishing a first-person account of the writer's conversations with Custer and various Indian chiefs in the Indian Territory in 1871: Custer "was truly a picture of chivalry and conscious manhood, and the stoical Red Cloud and Spotted Tail appeared to keep their eyes directed upon him continually. The latter told me afterwards that he looked upon Custer as the greatest of the white chiefs, who understood his race—the Indian—better than all the others combined.[16]

The response was similar throughout the South. The *News* in Raleigh, North Carolina, reported that southerners were enthusiastically in favor of a monument to Custer in Washington. "Nowhere in the world is bravery more admired than in our country," the *News* reported, emphasizing that the South was a different country from the North. "The men of the Southern States are ever ready to do honor to the memory of a gallant soldier. The South will sustain it representatives in an appropriation for a monument to Custer."[17]

In New Orleans, the *Picayune* noted that the U.S. Army was smaller than that of any major power "but in point of discipline and courage is second to no other" because it featured leaders like Custer. "Gen. Custer was one of the most efficient and gallant officers in the service. During the late war of secession he distinguished himself on many hard fought fields, and since its close he has been almost constantly engaged in the protection of the settlements of the far Northwest against the constantly recurring raids of the savage tribes. As a successful Indian fighter no man in the army had a better record. His intimate acquaintance with the tactics of that system of warfare and his thorough understanding of the Indian character eminently qualified him for the command which he held at the time of his death, and will render it all but impossible for the War Department to supply his place."[18] The *Atlanta Constitution* compared the Little Bighorn to the great battles of history: "The fate of Custer and his brave, devoted followers, reads like the story of a renewed Thermopylae, and furnishes to American history a sad but glorified page."[19]

Southerners gathering at White Sulphur Springs, West Virginia, planned a Grand Custer Memorial Ball to raise money for the *New York*

Herald monument fund. A *Herald* reporter there found Confederate veterans who fought against Custer and remembered him fondly. The man who was organizing the ball, Col. George L. Peyton, was a prisoner of Custer's during the war. Peyton told the reporter that his cousin, identified as Major Fariah, had dressed in civilian garb to go home through Union lines to visit his family. "He was conducted into his own parlor, where Custer was seated in slippers and dressing gown. Upon learning who the intruder was, Custer, with the genuine instincts of a gentleman remarked, 'Major Fariah, I don't know whether it is my duty to ask you to take a seat or yours to ask me, under these very peculiar circumstances of war.'" Sheridan, who was Custer's commanding officer at the time, ordered Fariah executed as a spy since he was caught in civilian clothes. Custer, however, revoked the order because he didn't think a man should be shot for trying to visit his family.[20]

Custer apparently also endeared himself to the future editor of the *Wheeling Register,* who recalled that Custer had once held his fire so as not to kill a Confederate general who was recklessly exposing himself in an attempt to rally his troops after a "gallant but unsuccessful charge upon Custer's brigade." The editor, Captain Moffit, compared Custer's death at the Little Bighorn to the biblical story of David and Uriah, in which David ordered Uriah to the front to be killed so that he could have Uriah's wife. Grant, who was playing the role of David in the Little Bighorn story, nevertheless could still be a hero if he would get behind the monument and thus "inaugurate the great centennial event of '76—a thorough reconciliation of the North and the South."[21]

Although Democratic papers in both regions praised Custer's bravery, some either ignored addressing his leadership at the Little Bighorn or admitted, hesitatingly, that he might have been to blame. In Kentucky, the *Owensboro Examiner* conceded that Custer might have been rash, "but the latest accounts from the gory field show that he gave the redskins the best turn he had in his shop after he did get in." In Kansas, the *Leavenworth Daily Appeal* discounted Custer's critics while avoiding discussing his tactics: "The daring deeds that have marked the military career of the gallant Custar would fill a volume, for he never hesitated when duty called for or his native valor prompted action. The love Custar's officers and men bore to their leader was the natural outgrowth of the confidence in his skill and admiration for his courage. He never failed to be in the front rank of the battle, where the bullets flew thickest, and never ordered even a squadron into action without being willing and anxious to lead it. The memory of Custar will live in the hearts of the American people when that of his ungenerous persecutors will have faded into a shadowy recollection."[22]

The Democratic paper in the Illinois capital of Springfield, the *Illinois Daily State Register,* argued that the Little Bighorn was just one of those mistakes that happen in war. Although some Custer critics argue that he should have delayed his attack, he probably had "military reasons" for ordering the assault, the paper wrote. In any case, "he proved by his gallant conduct how undeserved was the censure of Grant, and it is quite certain that but for the political strategy of the administration he would have been in command of a force which, instead of suffering a murderous defeat, would have gained a glorious victory."[23]

The *Chicago Daily News,* on the other hand, stated on its news page that the defeat was Custer's fault because he did not follow Terry's plan. The paper emphasized Custer's mistakes in its subheads for its battle analysis stories: "Disobedience of Orders—A Fatal Blunder" and "Custer's Blunder." Yet the *News* had nothing but praise for Custer's bravery on its editorial page in the same issue. Grant's insult to his honor prompted Custer's fatal attack against overwhelming odds, the *News* opined. "It was a desperate act and done in violation of orders, but who shall blame him? He went into the valley to win death or, by a feat of gallantry, win back the fair fame of which Grant so unjustly robbed him. He won death, and took it as we might expect, in the foremost of the fray, sword in hand."[24]

The positions of some Democratic papers evolved as the story developed. The first editorial about the battle in the *New York World,* for example, called Custer "one of the bravest and most distinguished generals of our army" and mourned the fact that he was killed because of the administration's poor Indian policy. A later editorial criticized Grant and a "partisan press" for blaming Custer for the disaster when he had been relegated to a subordinate role in the expedition. "There's nothing in the scanty intelligence which has been received concerning the massacre to show that Custer was in any way blamable," the paper argued.[25]

As more details emerged, the *World* admitted that Custer might share some blame, although it still defended his aggressiveness when on the trail of the enemy: "It may be that Custer, over-greedy of glory, charged the Indians rashly without waiting for the cooperation of his comrades; but the best test of his conduct is to suppose the consequences had he acted differently. If he had been a day behindhand, if he had retreated and allowed the Indians to escape, if he had delayed an attack while Gibbon was engaged—in any of these contingencies would he not have been pronounced a poltroon?"[26]

The *Chicago Times,* nominally independent but usually supporting the Democrats, published on its news pages Terry's report that Custer had not followed his plan but stressed in a subhead that this was "An Opinion that Custer Disobeyed Orders in His Zeal to Achieve Victory." Another subhead emphasized Custer's courage: "The Remains of Their Brave Commander Alone Escaping the Scalping Knife." But on the editorial page, the *Times* called the whole campaign "A Terrible Blunder," caused by either sending in the troops piecemeal or mishandling the troops in combat. Custer might have been motivated by overconfidence or ambition, but in any case he should have waited for reinforcements before making his "ill-advised" attack. "There is a dreadful blunder somewhere, which only later and more complete developments can locate. The *Times* fears that it may be placed on the gallant, ill-fated Custer, for the reason that it cannot believe that he was ordered to attempt the insane movement in which he perished."[27]

Three days later, however, the *Times* defended Custer and castigated Terry for being timid and trying to shift the responsibility of the disaster to Custer. The paper also unequivocally blamed Sheridan and Sherman for not providing enough troops and putting a frontier neophyte like Terry in charge of the expedition. "There is now all the light that will probably ever break through the . . . wall of military red tape, on the Custer massacre," a *Times* editorial declared under the headline "Too Much Courage," excusing Custer for his decision to attack. "Custer may have been overzealous, rashly impetuous, overdaring, but, his daring and impetuosity, his countrymen call to mind, have before now won hopeless fields and saved us in the moment of desperate disaster."[28]

About two weeks later, after publishing several survivor stories critical of Custer, the *Times* finally made up its mind, blaming Custer alone for the defeat, even though it obviously pained the editors to do that to a loyal Democrat. The campaign as a whole was well planned, the *Times* wrote in its analysis piece that covered much of the front page. "It may as well be understood—and as unpleasant as may be the conclusion—that the failure in Terry's movements, with all its afflicting consequences, is not the fault of Grant, or Sherman, or of the peace policy, or of anything else in the world save CUSTER'S RASHNESS and inexcusable disobedience of orders. The Times does not wish to say an unkind thing of the dead cavalryman, but the truth of history and justice to the living imperatively demand that the responsibility of this disaster be placed where it belongs." The *Times* dismissed the arguments of much of the country's Democratic press that Custer was goaded in the attack by Grant's insult: "It may be that he was soured by his treatment at Washington; but this is absolutely no excuse for leading other men to certain death. It was not punishing Grant to lead 300 men into a slaughter-pen." The personal bravery of Custer also did not mitigate his decision and could not be compared to the charge of the Light Brigade, because the Crimean War attack was made in obedience to orders. "The country may as well reach a just conclusion in this case, however much it may reflect unfavorably upon the dead. There was no 'massacre.' Custer fell in a fair fight which he himself invited and inaugurated; and which resulted as it did wholly from his rashness, his desire to distinguish himself, to his personal and entirely unwarranted ambition."[29]

In its ultimate criticism of Custer, the *Times* demonstrated true party independence and sounded more like a Republican newspaper that would reflexively blame Custer. For example, the main Republican rival of the *Times*, the *Chicago Tribune*, praised Custer's courage but blamed him for the defeat: "He was a brave, brilliant soldier, handsome and dashing, with all the attributes to make him beloved of women and admired of men, but these qualities, however admirable they may be, should not blind our eyes to the fact that it was his own madcap haste, rashness, and love of fame that cost him his own life, and cost the service the loss of many brave officers and gallant men."[30] In a similar manner, the Republican *Chicago Inter-Ocean* attributed the disaster to Custer's overconfidence. On July 10, most of its front page consisted of a profile of Custer written by William Curtis, who had accompanied Custer's 1874 Black Hills expedition and thus knew Custer and the Seventh Cavalry quite well. Curtis wrote that Custer was brave and had great knowledge of the Indians. "But why, the reader will ask, did Custer not apply this knowledge in the battle of the Little Horn? No one will ever know. But the most reasonable inference is that he was betrayed by his own self-confidence." Terry had developed a plan of cooperation among the columns, but Custer did not wait for the other columns. "The supposition of those familiar with Custer's character is, that he arrived first in the enemy's country—Custer was never behind-hand in his life; HE WAS ALWAYS AHEAD OF TIME—and when he saw the enemy before him, with his confidence in himself and his men, he dashed upon them, without waiting for co-operation, and was destroyed by superior numbers in a position that was disadvantageous to him and advantageous to his foes. Custer loved a fight; and was jealous of opportunities. And this led to his fearful mistake."[31]

Small-town Republican Illinois papers agreed with their big-city brethren. The *Galena Gazette*, Grant's hometown newspaper, cited Custer's incaution: "The total annihilation of G. Custer and his brave command is the Indian event of the year, as a horror. It ranks with the Modoc ambuscades in California. Such daring of our soldiers as this lacks that 'better part of valor'—'discretion.'" The *Ottawa Republican* similarly blamed Custer even though it admitted that little information was available other than "conjectures." Custer lost the battle because he wanted a great victory and attacked before waiting for the other columns. "It was a mistake for which he paid full dear, and his death will prevent the criticism which would otherwise be severe."[32]

Kansas Republican newspapers used the same arguments as those in Illinois. For example, the *Chanute Times* blamed the general's defeat on his reliance on "Custer's luck," which it claimed led him to believe he could win against overwhelming odds: "Custar knew from his scouts that the Indians far out-numbered the troops, yet he attacks them with the odds greatly against him, and suffered the terrible defeat which might have been predicted by the merest tyro in such matters." *The Commonwealth,* in the state capital of Topeka, recalled the Civil War in a July 7 article that compared Custer's arrogance toward the Indians to that of Southerners toward Yankees: "He adopted the 'one to five' theory fashionable in the South at the outbreak of the Rebellion, and paid the penalty of his mistake by the loss of his own life, and the lives of his kinsmen and of three hundred of his men."[33]

In the East, far removed from the battlefield, Republican editors also unequivocally blamed Custer. The *New York Times* argued that there was "an evident understanding" that Custer should wait for Gibbon's command before attacking. "Had he waited for the co-operation of that body, he need not have weakened his attacking force so fatally as he did, and, in all probability, the sad issue of that day's fighting would have been reversed," the *Times* opined a few days after the battle was first reported.[34]

In New England, the Republican *Hartford Daily Courant* editorialized that Custer was reckless and that Crook would never have made the same sort of mistake. "This is the way the affair looks, and as General Custer knew that General Terry was approaching with the main army, his rashness seems explainable only on the theory that he hoped by a brilliant dash to gain a decisive victory, and to secure to himself the honors of the expedition, the leadership of which had been taken from him." The *Courant* even blamed Custer for the suffering of the widows and orphans of the Seventh Cavalry dead: "The poor women with their children are not only left friendless but almost penniless. Their condition is thoroughly pitiable. Congress, however, with its usual philosophy, have voted to Custer's father, mother and widow each a pension of fifty dollars a month, but to these poor people suffering because their husbands obeyed Custer's orders nothing is given. Apparently it is better to act without orders than to obey."[35]

The *Baltimore American and Commercial Advertiser* was equally direct in its criticism, speculating in its first editorial about the battle that Custer had been lured into a trap through overconfidence: "Probably he had been so long accustomed to merely charging the savages and scattering them like sheep that he rushed into his fight with the expectation of repeating what he had so often done before." Like many other Custer critics, the *American* wrote that respect for the dead made the paper refrain from making "harsh comments" about him, but the editorial proceeded harshly to urge that Custer serve as an example for other officers: "The profound sorrow with which the news of this gallant soldier's misfortune is received is mingled with the feeling that it should teach caution to the officers in command of the forces operating against the hostile Indians. There must be less rashness and more of cool carefulness in entering into future engagements with them . . . and his heedless intrepidity ought to find no imitation during the remainder of the war."[36]

Most papers, including the *American,* published some version of a brief profile of Custer. The way the papers crafted the biography, selecting some quotes and deleting some facts, often revealed the politics of the editors. No more blatant example could be found than in comparing two small-town Kansas papers that doubtless did not have the time or staff to do a lot of news gathering or editing of Little Bighorn stories. The *Wathena Reporter* and the *Wyandotte Herald* published similar profiles of Custer based on information they had gotten from other papers or wire services. The stories were almost identical until they discussed Custer's Indian-fighting career. Both noted that he had been in numerous fights with "uniform success." But the Republican *Reporter* in its July 15 story added that "perhaps his previous successes as an Indian fighter might have rendered him liable to underrate the foe at whose hands he finally met his death." The Democratic *Herald* did not mention the Little Bighorn at all but instead concluded its July 20 biography with a list of Custer's newspaper and magazine articles.[37]

Nevertheless, a variety of Republican newspapers went against what we now call the "talking points" of their party and defended Custer. In Illinois, the *Bloomington Pantagraph* argued that an attack was Custer's only option at the Little Bighorn because he could not halt or retreat without being defeated. The *Pantagraph* concluded that the disaster was, "in truth, one of those overwhelming calamities which occasionally fall on the most brave and most skillful officers, and which in the present case, could not reasonably be foreseen."[38]

The Republican *New York Tribune,* published by Custer friend Whitelaw Reid, in its first editorial about the battle suggested that Custer's attack was rash. But it added that, because there were no survivors from the Seventh Cavalry, "the fatal mistake and its resulting horrors of slaughter can therefore never be fully explained." A few days later the *Tribune* argued that neither Custer nor Terry was to blame because they did not know the number of Indians they would face. "Why he attacked we do not know. There may have been good reason. It seems difficult to believe that a soldier of Custer's experience and merit engaged in a conflict which he did not have reason to suppose would not be serious, under such circumstances. It is more rational to suppose that circumstances not now fully known led him to believe that the force before him was small, would be easily routed, and if he delayed for rest or reinforcements, would get away altogether. If he erred in judgment, we cannot say how far the circumstances caused that error."[39]

For newspapers in the Far West, basically in the war zone, the responsibility for the military defeat did not much matter compared to getting more troops to the front and stopping the policy of arming the Indians. The *Laramie Daily Sentinel* in Wyoming wrote that "with the very meagre report we have of the affair it is useless to criticise or speculate over it. . . . It may be this awful disaster will rouse the government to a sense of the magnitude of the job it has on hand, and result in a future vigorous prosecution of the war against the savages."[40]

The *Helena Daily Herald* quoted at length from a story in the *Salt Lake Tribune* that it claimed "handsomely and effectually vindicates" the officers involved in the Little Bighorn, and especially the charges of rashness against Custer. "We confess that we feel more keenly these indirect charges against Custer, and it grates harshly on our feelings to hear it said the loss of the Indians was relatively greater; that our disaster after all is not one over which the nation need take alarm. The loss of such a man as Custer is a national loss of the first magnitude. No officer of our little army had so brilliant a record. . . . To think that such a hero should go through so many perils, achieve so much to deserve the loving admiration and gratitude of a nation, and then be slaughtered by the vile savages, is terrible to think of."[41]

The Republican *Bismarck Tribune,* published by Custer fan Lounsberry, wrote carefully to suggest that Custer made a mistake but had reasons for his actions: "While we do not desire to criticise General Custer, or characterize his charge as a rash one, it seems he was too anxious for glory for his regiment, if not for himself. . . . Still it is believed that Custer had reason to suppose the Indians were in full retreat; and as he had troops that none would hesitate to pit against three times their number, those in authority are not inclined to censure. Gen. Sheridan insists no mistakes have been made, and that the Indians shall be made to pay dearly for the death of Custer's brave band." Lounsberry, ever the good journalist, took care of his news source, praising Terry as a "true gentleman and brave soldier" whose plans were good but were not carried out by his subordinates, including Custer, who attacked before Terry had intended.[42]

In an unusual twist in Denver, the Democratic-leaning (although claiming to be independent) *Rocky Mountain Herald* and the Republican *Rocky Mountain News* each took the opinion of the opposing political party. The *Herald* republished the lengthy Republican *Chicago Tribune* editorial blaming the defeat on Custer's rashness.[43] The *News,* on the other hand, wrote that Custer had too few troops and "would never have met with his disaster had he been properly supported."[44] But both papers could agree that the disaster was created in large part by the peace policy of supplying the Indians with arms and necessities. Force was the only thing Indians understood, opined the *Herald.* "We are told that a number of Quakers and members of the 'Peace Commission' have already put in an appearance in Washington for the purpose of obtruding their 'peace policy' upon the government in its dealings with the Sioux. But we apprehend that, under the present rather unpromising state of affairs in the Black Hills, very little attention will be paid to their appeal in behalf of the poor savage."[45] Although the Republican *News* did not mention Grant by name, it too condemned his peace policy, in even stronger language: "Custer and his men have been murdered, not by Indians, who were only the instruments of their death, but by the sleek, smooth talking, Quaker advocates of the peace policy, who have always insisted that the Indian was a man and a brother, and an older brother at that, with all the rights of primogeniture."[46]

Republican newspapers were in a difficult spot because they often wanted to criticize the unpopular peace policy—it seemed obvious to everyone at the time that it didn't work—yet they wanted to support their party in an election year and avoid blaming Grant. Most handled it the way the *Rocky Mountain News* did, by criticizing the policy and simply ignoring the president. Republican newspapers almost always blamed the policy on "the government" or the "Quakers" or nameless citizens who "loved Indians." Newspapers in largely Republican Kansas, which was on the frontier, were particularly adept at this tactic. The *Newton Kansan* on July 21 urged the transfer of the Indian Bureau to the War Department and asserted that the current policy had "utterly failed." But it did not mention who had implemented the policy. The *Saline County Journal* on July 20 argued, "It behooves the government and all its citizens to 'love' the Indian no longer and settle down in a policy which will not only definitely dispose of the Indian problem, but fully avenge the deaths of those gallant men who fell on the 25th of June." Neither paper mentioned Grant or the administration.[47]

The *New York Tribune* initially scolded papers representing both parties for trying to use the Little Bighorn for politics: "It would be decent to wait a while till the nation has recovered from its grief before attempting to utilize so sad an occurrence for party purposes," the *Tribune* editorialized on July 8. It waited nine days before criticizing what it called "our incomprehensible Indian policy" in a lengthy editorial that acknowledged that foreign governments must be astonished to think the United States arms its enemies. The country's only explanation, the *Tribune* explained, is that foreigners just do not understand the problem. Grant and his administration's contributions to the problem were not mentioned.[48]

The *Chicago Tribune* also treated Grant as the invisible man in its ferocious editorial condemning the peace policy: "The best use to make of an Indian who will not stay upon a reservation is to kill him. It is time that the dawdling, maudlin peace-policy was abandoned." The *St. Louis Globe-Democrat* said it had "all along deprecated the unfortunate Indian Policy" that led to the Little Bighorn. "It is useless now to lament the violation of the Sioux treaty. Whatever may be thought of the act, the consequences are at hand, and the sole duty of the Government is to see that they are made as light as possible both for ourselves and for the Indian tribes." The *Globe* did not mention Grant as the author of the policy and mentioned "the president" only in the context that Congress should provide enough troops to defeat the hostiles.[49]

If Grant was mentioned, it was to defend him. The *Leavenworth Daily Times* on July 14 quoted a story that it emphasized it was reprinting from a Democratic paper that said the Indian war was caused by "rascally traders," not by the president or "the excellent people who are trying to Christianize the Indians." On July 12 the *Commonwealth* in Topeka noted that some "mean and thin" Democratic papers were trying to blame the Little Bighorn on Grant instead of Custer, but no "sensible" person would believe it. No one would know why Custer attacked, but he did it for his own reasons. "Gen. Grant was no more responsible for it than Gen. Washington. After all the fuss that was made prior to the march of the expedition, about Gen. Custer's being deprived of his command, he appears to have been at the head of all the command he wanted. He fought that command to win or lose, and he lost. That man who would fasten the responsibility on innocent people thousands of miles away, merely as an electioneering dodge, is less of a man than any Indian who ever murdered a baby or scalped a woman."[50]

The Republican *Chicago Inter-Ocean* not only wholeheartedly supported Grant but castigated any Republican newspaper that criticized him. A lengthy editorial attributed Grant's failures to associates who betrayed him. After listing his accomplishments in prosecuting scandals and starting civil service reform, the *Inter-Ocean* concluded, "Talk of reform! He is the father of it."[51]

Perhaps the strongest defense of Grant came from the *New York Times,* which argued that Grant himself could not undo a treaty system that had been set by Congress and had been subject to corruption for years. The policy was not a complete failure and in fact had helped civilize some tribes, the *Times* argued. The Indians were fighting because they had been cheated and whites had invaded their lands. "Had the peace policy never been heard of, we do not see that this collision would have been prevented. It belongs to no party or President; it is one of the fruits of a long course of rapacity and injustice by the nation."[52]

Many Republican newspapers, instead of defending Grant, went on the attack against the Democratic House of Representatives for wanting to reduce the size of the army. The opinion of the *Baltimore American and Commercial Advertiser* was typical. It accused Democrats of wanting to shrink the army "to the merest skeleton" so there would not be enough troops to fight outbreaks of violence against blacks in the South. "With migratory tribes of Indians on our Northwestern frontier capable of mustering such a band of warriors as Custer and Reno encountered on the 'Little Big Horn,' it would be more than folly to talk of reducing the army. On the contrary, a loud demand will come from the *plain* people of the country for such an enlargement of the regular army as will admit of an active and effective campaign against the Sioux, and all other savages who take the war path."[53]

Republican papers in Kansas, which was near the war zone, were particularly vehement in their criticism of the Democrats' idea to keep the army small. The *Oskaloosa Independent* on July 8 wrote that the Little Bighorn proved the "folly of the rebels and Democrats in Congress." The *Independent*, which despite its name was a Republican paper, wrote: "All the frontiers are exposed, but that is nothing so the army can be got out of the way, should the rebels desire to enact any unlawful deeds. It is all very well for them to play the role of political demagogues, but it is death to the exposed settlers and troops, too few in number to meet the savage foe. O shame, thy name is modern Democracy." Another small-town Kansas paper, the *Washington Republican,* agreed and on July 21 asserted that brave troops were slaughtered for lack of support and that "to leave the nation crippled and defenseless appears to be the policy of Democracy."[54]

The *Republican* of San Antonio, Texas, also condemned congressional Democrats for trying to cut military appropriations and suggested that charges of corruption against the administration were mere politics. A July 15 editorial claimed, "This Congress is spending millions in investigations for political effect; and they have actually found but one victim—Belknap. Reduce the army in the face of recent events if it dare, and the people will execrate it for poltroonery; the blood of Custer and his slaughtered command protests against the democratic folly. Our army is ridiculously small compared to other nations . . . incapable of performing the work assigned to it over such a vast country, flanked by foreign nations and girdled by an immense frontier inhabited by hostile savages."[55]

The San Antonio paper was a rare Republican organ in the South, but its use of hyperbolic language was typical of the region's newspapers, most of which were Democratic and used their evocative prose on Grant. Many southern newspapers were so strident that a reader would be left with the impression that the president had led a dark conspiracy to have Custer killed. In publishing such harsh attacks, the editors were often following the sentiment of local politicians. In Kentucky, J. C. S. Blackburn, who had been a member of the House of Representatives' committee that took Custer's testimony on the post tradership scandal, told a reporter "that the blood of Custer was upon the head of Grant."[56]

Nevertheless, the editors used their skill in writing to cut even deeper than the politicians did. One of the most vivid passages appeared in the *Dallas Daily Herald* on July 7 when it wrote that "the Grant administration, dripping with the blood of Custar and his men, will now probably attempt to make a little cheap campaign capital by plunging the country into an expensive Indian war." The *Herald* blamed the administration for ignoring signs that the Indians were organizing and wrote that the administration was "directly responsible for this massacre. The blood of these brave men is upon the hands of Grant, Sherman and the Secretary of War." A subsequent piece suggested that the Republican Party should not have honored Grant in its election platform because he had Custer "butchered."[57]

Many southern papers promoted a conspiracy theory that Grant arranged to have Custer killed by sending him West with a greatly outnumbered command. Grant's motive, so the theory went, was to silence Custer from exposing corruption on the frontier: "Grant and his friends were anxious to get rid of Custar, and in order to prevent his testimony being given before the investigating committee, he was sent to the front to fight the Indians," intoned the *Fort Worth Daily Democrat*. "His death will relieve him of his testimony against the Post-traderships. What a sad commentary on our government that the chief magistrate and his cabinet should rejoice in the death of one of its gallant generals." The *Democrat* repeated the theory in even stronger language in a later editorial, describing Custer's death as if it were an organized crime hit: "Custar knew too much about the sale of Post-traderships to suit the fastidious feeling of Grant and Belknap. His untimely death will be a great relief to them."[58]

The *West Texas Free Press* of San Marcos, a town between San Antonio and Austin, agreed with the Fort Worth paper: "The Indians left the battle ground, which looked like a slaughter house. I suppose Grant and his friends are satisfied. Their miserable management of the Indian bureau has produced this state of affairs."[59]

The theory was not confined to Texas. On July 7, the first day the *Constitution* in Atlanta reported the Little Bighorn, the paper ran a frontpage brief blaming Custer's death on Grant: "When Grant ordered General Custer to the west in order to get the general out of the way of the investigating committees of congress, he little imagined how successfully he was about to dispose of Custer. The dead general was a brave and able officer, and his death will be greatly regretted." The paper repeated the point the next day, asserting that Grant had put Custer on "this highway of death" and that the Republican Party "has another awful crime to answer for before the people."[60]

Two small-town Kentucky papers sounded like they were writing a pirate story when they explained Grant's supposed motives. The *Mayfield Monitor* claimed: "Dead men tell no tales. Custer will make no further revelations of crookedness in the War Office. Grant sent him West, and the Sioux have effectually closed his mouth." The *Owensboro Examiner* similarly wrote: "Nobody will ever doubt again that the president isn't a far-seeing man. He knew when he ordered Custer to go out among the Indians that they would close his mouth against 'crookedness.' No, indeed; 'dead men never tell tales!'"[61]

Watterson's *Courier-Journal,* reflecting the publisher's friendship with Custer, was emotional in its denunciation of Grant, calling him "the grim chieftain who, refusing to see his young comrade because that comrade was not a thief, ordered him to his grave." The *Courier-Journal* not only blamed the administration for supplying weapons to the enemy but suggested that the president himself gave Custer's murder weapon to Sitting Bull: "The *New York Herald* in one of its anti-Administration moods the other day declared that the Indian Bureau killed Custer. The fact, indeed, is demonstrable. The arms, ammunition and other supplies in the hands of Sitting Bull and his men were obtained at the agencies. The government of the United States supplies its enemies with material wherewith to kill our soldiers. General Grant himself presented Sitting Bull with a magnificent rifle when he was in Washington last year. A shot from that weapon might have killed Custer."[62]

The problem with the story was that there were two Indians named Sitting Bull, but the famous one did not go with Red Cloud and other chiefs to visit the White House and meet Grant. Republican papers like the *Hartford Daily Courant* tried to clear up the confusion: "The other chief of the same name belongs to the friendly Ogallala tribe, and is living peacefully on the reservation. A year ago, for bravery in saving the life of an Indian agent, he was presented with a handsome rifle in the name of the President, a fact which has led to the mistaken report that 'the President probably furnished the gun which killed Custer.' The story shows how easy it is for false and malicious rumors to obtain general circulation."[63]

It was not rumor but fact that federal troops were stationed in the South on Reconstruction duty while Custer was fighting in the West. How people interpreted that fact usually depended on their politics. Democratic newspapers, particularly those in the South, countered the Republican argument that Democrats wanted to reduce the army by claiming that there were plenty of "idle" troops in the South. The *Galveston News* urged Grant in a popular phrase to "take his heavy hand off the South" by transferring soldiers to the West. The editorial, which was run on the front page, asked, "Why should Mississippi be strongly garrisoned while troops are wanted to fight Sitting Bull in Dakota and all that region which is now threatened with a long, cruel and possibly a disastrous war?"[64]

Watterson's *Courier-Journal* regularly attacked Republicans over the troop issue. Like many newspapers, the *Courier-Journal* published a state-by-state list of where federal troops were stationed, ranging from forty-two soldiers in Maine to 3,718 in Texas. The total for twelve southern states was 7,052 compared to 2,817 in the northern states, prompting the *Courier-Journal* to assert that 4,000 soldiers could "very easily" be spared for the Indian war.[65]

The *Dallas Daily Herald* once again provided some of the most vehement and frequent examples of this type of argument. On July 7, the same day it first reported the battle, it wrote: "By a miserable, niggardly, partisan policy General Custer and his family, officers and three or four hundred of his men have been sacrificed. If the troops now loafing and idling in the South to influence the Presidential election in the interest of the Radical nominees and the Grants, Mortons, Blaines and Babcocks had been where they belong, with Custar, this horrible and unprecedented massacre of brave men would not have disgraced us in this Centennial year." The next day it reported that "the all absorbing topic is the massacre of Gen. Custar and his men. The greatest feeling of indignation is against Grant for not having kept enough men in the Indian country to do the work."[66]

The *Herald* was just getting wound up. The paper saved its most passionate writing for the July 9 issue, when the editor ranted for seven paragraphs—a huge editorial for the *Herald*—in a piece headlined "Custar's Murder." The editorial contrasted the "brave," "lamented," and "gallant" Custer with the "venal" and "imbecile, corrupt and fast falling to pieces" Grant administration. It asserted that just the troops stationed in Louisiana would have made the difference in the Indian campaign but were kept in the South to force people to vote Republican. "Why have the troops been used for political purposes instead of being sent to subdue the warlike red-men? It is a crying shame. Humanity sickens at this monstrous indifference of the Republican party managers to sustain the cause of justice and right." After emotionally appealing to sympathy for Custer, his family and his men, the editorial reminded readers that the deaths were caused by the administration sending troops to Mississippi and Louisiana instead of to the West: "The blood fairly curdles at the picture. Every family in the land should promptly resent this outrage on common decency, on national honor, and on the lives and blood of the murdered Custar and his band. The Indians were not voters, otherwise Custar would have had all the force necessary."[67]

Newspapers from both parties were gearing up for what they expected would be a bitter election campaign. Editors were quick to interpret the Little Bighorn through the prism of politics and the interests of their regions. In some cases that was reflected in their early opinion pieces assessing blame for the Little Bighorn. But by fall, the military campaign was cooling down as the election campaign was heating up. By September the battle was two months old and the bulk of the presidential campaign was yet to come. Party leaders and journalists had a decision to make. Was the Little Bighorn still a campaign issue, or had the country moved on?

CHAPTER 4

"A Little Cheap Political Capital"

The Little Bighorn and the Presidential Campaign

Rutherford B. Hayes, the Republican presidential nominee in 1876, had been invited by Custer a few years earlier to visit him in the West. Custer and Hayes knew each other from their Civil War days, and in 1873 they spent some time together at a Union Army reunion in Toledo, near Hayes's Fremont, Ohio, home and Custer's adopted hometown of Monroe, Michigan. The reunion featured Grant and several other famous generals.[1] Hayes described the reunion fondly in his diary, noting that the president asked him to join him on a stand to review the troops and receive the ladies. Custer, Hayes wrote, invited him to "tour the plains next season at any time."[2] Although Hayes had twice been governor, it was likely that Custer outshone him, wearing his full dress uniform and placed fourth in order in a receiving line behind Grant, Sheridan, and Sherman. At any rate, there was enough attention to go around; journalists estimated that two thousand ladies shook their hands and about a quarter of them kissed the celebrities.[3]

Hayes never made it to the plains to visit Custer, and two years later when Custer died he was absorbed in his own campaign for the presidency. The Republican Party had nominated Hayes only less than two weeks before the Little Bighorn, choosing him as a compromise candidate acceptable to the supporters of the four frontrunners, all of whom had significant flaws of one sort or another. Although Hayes went into the convention as a long-shot "favorite son candidate" of Ohio, the party leaders ultimately chose him because he had a distinguished war record, a reputation for personal integrity, and a proven ability to win tough elections in a battleground state.

Every vote would be important for the Republicans because 1876 looked like a Democratic year. The country had experienced hard times since the Panic of 1873; many voters were tired of Republican government and especially the party's Reconstruction policy of supporting carpetbag rule in the South with federal troops. Additionally, the numerous graft and kickback scandals of the Grant administration made the reform of civil service one of the main issues. The Democrats had trounced the Republicans in the midterm elections of 1874, and their expected presidential nominee, New York governor Samuel J. Tilden, was a proven vote getter with a reputation for attacking corruption and reforming government.

Although the enormity of the Little Bighorn debacle suggests that it would have been a major campaign issue, at least in terms of reforming corruption in the Indian Bureau, Hayes's supporters rarely mentioned it, other than in passing, in letters to him about the campaign. For example, a man named H. Capehart wrote Hayes on July 7 to congratulate him on his nomination and tell him that he "would not cease to exert [his] best efforts" to get Hayes elected. "Amid our rejoicing at your good fortune we have to pause to . . . drop a tear for our gallant but fallen Custar, who we all admired and loved. History records no braver name than his." But Capehart never suggested that the brave man's demise was relevant to the campaign.[4]

P. W. Hitchcock, U.S. senator from Nebraska, wrote Hayes that he was anxious for the safety of their mutual friend George Crook, who Hitchcock believed was in danger of being attacked by the hostiles who had wiped out Custer. Crook needed reinforcements and supplies, he wrote. "Your position now before the country would of course give weight to any suggestion you choose to make. I write thinking you might wish in a friendly off-hand way to communicate with Sheridan Sherman or Grant. Crook I know now wants help more than Terry. Excuse this hasty volunteer advice."[5]

Benjamin F. Potts, governor of the Montana Territory and a fellow Ohio Civil War veteran, wrote Hayes about the battle on July 5—a day before it was reported in the East. Potts predicted a long and bloody war and that the miners in the Black Hills had better leave before the Indians killed them "to the last man." He told Hayes that he had offered Sherman a thousand volunteers, which he hoped would be accepted "for I am anxious to take the field again." Potts wrote that Hayes's nomination was popular in Montana, and he hoped to be able to visit Ohio in September to help with the campaign, although it was difficult to arrange. "I have a Secretary that acts as Gov. in my absence that [is] a drunken little Scrub & I cant well leave the Territory." Despite Potts's interest in the presidential election, he never mentioned the role the Little Bighorn might play in the campaign.[6]

Another Hayes supporter, W. G. Deshler, optimistically called Hayes the next president of the United States but warned that the campaign would be difficult. "We must not fail to carry Indiana—of course as to Ohio, it is only a question of how large the majority should be—But we must not do as poor Custar did—leave our Gattling Guns behind or refuse to take them in to action, from over confidence, it's to be a fight to the hilt—we must go in to win."[7]

Hayes never recorded his thoughts about the Little Bighorn and Custer's death in his voluminous diary. But he must have thought associating with Custer's memory was a political liability, because he declined an offer to participate actively in the Custer National Monument Association, which was created almost as soon as the news of the battle was reported. Sheridan was the president of the organization, and Michigan senator Thomas W. Ferry was the first vice president of the group. One of the secretaries, J. M. Bulkley, a Monroe attorney and boyhood friend of Custer, wrote Hayes that he had been elected as one of the vice presidents and they hoped Hayes would help gain subscriptions for the fund.[8]

Hayes's reply is not to be found in his presidential library, but it could not have been positive because Bulkley sent another letter sounding aggrieved at Hayes's answer, which apparently suggested that he was too busy to deal with fundraising: "The managers of the association are not insensible to the facts stated in your letter, and fully appreciate the multiplicity of your public duties, yet we hoped that the endorsement you could give the movement with such other material support as you deemed proper would have some weight and influence with others." He concluded by thanking Hayes for suggesting someone else to help with the fundraising.[9]

If Hayes had thought Custer or the Little Bighorn was a solid campaign issue, he doubtless would have been active in the fund, for he was an astute politician. At fifty-three, he had been governor of Ohio three times and served two terms in the House of Representatives; he had even been elected to one term while he was still in the army and did not actively campaign for it. But despite his long acquaintance with Custer and his deep friendship with George Crook—he had named his fourth son George Crook Hayes—he did not make the Indian campaign in which Crook and Custer fought an issue in the political campaign.

The 1876 election has always held a certain fascination for political scientists and historians because it was the closest presidential election in U.S. history and the only one decided by one electoral college vote. A lesser known fact is that it had the highest turnout—82 percent—of any election in U.S. history, dwarfing modern figures. The turnout for the 2008 election, for example, was 57 percent, and the turnout for the controversial 2000 election was 51 percent.[10] The 2000 election generated a brief uptick in interest among the press and public in the 1876 campaign because of their similarities. In both elections the loser of the popular vote won the electoral college vote, the votes from the state of Florida were crucial to the outcome and were challenged by both sides, and the final result was decided by outside agencies. In 2000 the U.S. Supreme Court ended the recounting of ballots in Florida, and in 1876 Congress set up a special commission, including some Supreme Court members, to rule on the disputed electoral ballots.[11]

Historians have not, however, reached a consensus on the role of the Little Bighorn in the election. Historians who write about Custer and the Little Bighorn tend to emphasize that the battle was a tremendous campaign issue, whereas historians who focus on the Hayes presidency or 1876 election tend to mention it only in passing or ignore it completely. Michael Holt, in a relatively recent book about the election, does not mention the Little Bighorn and instead focuses on the voting patterns of the election. Hayes biographer H. J. Eckenrode likewise did not mention the Montana disaster in his account of the election, instead describing what he saw as the most important issues: "The Democrats found, readymade, an abundance of campaign material," especially hard times and the "hundred and one scandals of Grant's administration."[12]

The Republicans, too, had a ready-made issue—the "bloody shirt" of rebellion and abuse of blacks and white southern Republicans by southern Democrats. Republicans waved the bloody shirt in 1876— even though it was becoming tattered from being overused in previous elections—to point out that Tilden had not served in the Union Army and that racial violence in the South should remind northern voters why they had fought the war. Republican campaign materials in 1876 accused Tilden of being a traitor, a swindler, and a wrecker of railroad companies but did not mention the current Indian war being waged by the Republican administration of U.S. Grant.[13]

One Georgia Republican said at the time that southerners did not care about any number of national issues, including Grant's Indian policy. They did not care about foreign policy or civil service reform; they considered themselves Republicans or Democrats based only on the final three amendments of the Constitution adopted to ensure black equality.[14] In fact, many historians who studied the 1876 election suggest that the campaign was based more on personal attacks—what we today would call the "politics of personal destruction"—than on policy issues like the prosecution of the Indian war.

Kerwin Swint lists the election as number sixteen in a ranking of "the 25 dirtiest political campaigns of all time." He writes that the main issues were government corruption, the Panic of 1873, unemployment in the cities, and falling crop prices and does not mention the Indian war. Although the parties had serious issues to debate, the campaign degenerated into personal attack: "The campaigns of the 1870s and 1880s were intensely personal and nasty. The Hayes-Tilden campaign set a new standard for nastiness, maybe because the campaign lasted so long and involved so much drama and intrigue."[15]

The few historians of the election who mention the Little Bighorn do so generally as an illustration of current events in 1876. For example, Evan Cornog and Richard Whelan's survey of presidential campaigns lists the Little Bighorn with the centennial celebrations, the publication of Mark Twain's *The Adventures of Tom Sawyer*, and the founding of baseball's National League as interesting things that happened that year. But they define the campaign issues as the economy, the corruption of both the Grant administration and Democratic political machines, and immigration.[16]

Roy Morris, Jr., briefly mentions the Little Bighorn in his book *Fraud of the Century*, but not as a campaign issue. Morris notes the irony that Custer's defeat had occurred amid the centennial festivities. He also knocks down the spurious assertion that Custer fought the Little Bighorn in hopes of securing the Democratic nomination himself through a dramatic victory. Such a scenario was virtually impossible given the length of time it would take to get news of the battle to the Democratic convention, which was scheduled to begin only two days after Custer launched his attack.[17]

The majority of Little Bighorn historians agree that Custer did not plan to use the battle to get to the White House, but they do tend to emphasize the importance of the battle as a campaign issue. Robert M. Utley, one of the most famous Custer historians and a retired National Park Service administrator, devotes an entire chapter of *Custer and the Great Controversy* to press coverage of the battle. In a passage often cited by others, Utley writes: "In the bitter election year of 1876, the Custer tragedy dropped as from heaven into the arms of Democrats struggling against Republican campaign orators seeking to clothe them in the bloody shirt of treason and disunion. The Little Bighorn disaster, laid on a backdrop of corruption in high places and scandalous frontier fraud, instantly became a pawn on the political chessboard." Utley concludes that within two weeks of the first report of the battle the press had spread the "first distorted" information about the battle, "and it had placed the 'massacre' in a political context that assured its rise to a national issue of the first magnitude."[18]

Brian W. Dippie, who analyzed the Southern response to the battle, agrees that it was viewed as a political issue: "The event itself was irrelevant; all that mattered was the various uses to which it could be put." The Democratic Party's reform platform tied in with blaming the Republican administration for mishandling the war. And the Democrats could counter the Republicans' "bloody shirt" rhetoric of southern disloyalty by defending Custer, a Union general during the Civil War, against charges of incompetence and by urging southerners to volunteer to fight the Indians.[19] Dippie notes in a book about the mythology of the Last Stand that Republicans responded in kind: "So virulent were the accusations which flew back and forth that it seemed for a while as though the election of 1876 might be fought over Custer's corpse."[20]

There is little doubt that, regardless of the location of newspapers, they were crucial in political campaigns. Most newspapers in 1876 devoted a lot of space to politics, covering the conventions in great detail. The amount and depth of the coverage indicated how important politics were to the public as well.[21] Certainly the politicians of the time were aware of the importance of the press, and the two presidential candidates were among the most press savvy of the era.

Tilden had been interested in politics since he was a boy. At eighteen he wrote a campaign paper in favor of Andrew Jackson's election in 1832. The piece, which was published anonymously in the Albany, New York, newspaper, was so well written that some observers thought vice presidential nominee Martin Van Buren had written it himself.[22] In his book on the press of the Reconstruction era, Mark Wahlgren Summers writes that "more than any presidential candidate before him, Tilden knew the uses of managed publicity." Tilden's home was a "political factory" where clerks tended to the press. His aides scoured newspapers for friendly articles and sent them to 1,200 local papers for republication, and they sent letters on boilerplate to weeklies throughout the country. The Republican *Hartford Daily Courant* noted with amusement that Tilden was trying to sell himself like patent medicine, an undignified tactic that was backfiring by angering the Democratic papers that did not get the letters.[23] Tilden also sent men to college campuses to find out what the students were interested in (which turned out to be reform), a foreshadowing of modern polling techniques.[24] Tilden biographer Alexander Flick emphasized the New York governor's knowledge of the press, describing him as poring over press clippings from around the country "with the eye of a trained prognosticator."[25]

The problem with Tilden's press relations was that he relied on pamphlets and statistics and lawyerly argument rather than "the raucous sort of propaganda that the party press did best." Tilden was even worse at responding to breaking news that attacked him. For example, he took a month to muster what he wanted to be the perfect response to *New York Times* charges against him of income tax evasion. Modern candidates have "war rooms" to respond immediately to such challenges, but even in 1876 most politicians would not let such negative stories linger. And Tilden's reliance on argument and manipulation of journalists was so well known that reporters were suspicious of him, and he gained the monikers "Shammy Tilden," "Slippery Sammy," and the "Spider of Gramercy Park."[26] But overall, at sixty-two Tilden was an outstanding politician and lawyer and the logical choice for the Democrats. He was a noted reformer of corrupt New York politics in a year when reform was one of the main issues. In the 1870s he had helped bring down the Tammany Hall ring led by William Marcy Tweed in New York City and the Canal Ring in upstate New York.[27]

According to Summers, Hayes was not considered as tricky as Tilden, but his understanding of the press may have been more "shrewd." He cultivated influential journalists in Ohio who advised him on his campaign. One of them, William Henry Smith of the Western Associated Press, distributed so many anti-Tilden stories that Democrats called the wire service the "Hayesociated Press." Murat Halstead of the *Cincinnati Commercial* gave valuable advice on publicity and served as a leading negotiator between southern Democrats and the Hayes camp over settling the disputed outcome of the election.[28]

Hayes, like Tilden, had a lifelong interest in politics and newspapers. His campaign biographer, in describing the Ohio governor's character and habits, noted his penchant for collecting newspaper articles on important topics, writing that "from these collections he has been able at any time to confront an opponent with the record of that opponent's political life from the outset." Indeed, in 1875 Hayes carefully listed in his diary all of the Ohio newspapers that supported him as a presidential candidate.[29]

Hayes and the Republicans would need all the support they could get, because of public dissatisfaction with their party. Still, Republicans believed they could win what they knew would be a close election because the bitterness of the Civil War was still fresh in the minds of many voters. Hayes told two leading Republicans that the "main issue" for their party must be convincing the voters that it was not safe to let former Rebels or Rebel sympathizers into power, and that the bloody shirt issue would take the voters' minds off hard economic times.[30]

Hayes, of course, also promised to reform the civil service. That reform would presumably include aspects of Grant's Indian policy, like the distribution of lucrative trading posts at frontier installations—a scandal that had implicated William Belknap, Grant's secretary of war. At the time of the two political conventions, voters were aware of the trading post scandals and that the frontier army was trying to subdue tribes declared hostile. It is logical to assume that news of the Little Bighorn disaster would make these issues more prominent in the presidential campaign. Certainly the battle was a dominant news story—something comparable to events like the sinking of the *Titanic*, the attack on Pearl Harbor, or the 9-11 terrorist attacks.

But the war itself was not a great news story and drew widespread attention only after Custer was killed. And that attention dissipated quickly after the news about Custer had been exhausted and the political campaign had heated up. Even though the army had devoted a large percentage of its combat units to the war, readers of most newspapers would have been hard pressed to know much about it. The news sections in most papers in June were devoted overwhelmingly to the political campaign and especially to the Republican convention in Cincinnati. Some papers closer to the fighting devoted more space to war news, but the political campaign was rarely connected to the military campaign, which seemed to be a nonissue. Even the *Bismarck Tribune,* Mark Kellogg's employer, attacked the Democrats as the party of rebellion as its main focus of an editorial explaining the issues of the upcoming campaign. The Sioux war was not mentioned at all, and the *Tribune* call for reform did not emphasize the Indian Bureau.[31]

In New York the major papers thought the election was much more important than the war. For example, on June 15 all seven columns of the *New York Times* front page featured convention material, much of which was carried onto the second page. The headline, "The Proceedings in Detail," was true to its word, reporting the texts of the speeches made at the convention. The speeches focused on preserving the outcome of the Civil War but did not discuss the ongoing Sioux war. Theodore M. Pomeroy, the temporary president of the convention, said emphatically, "The mission of the manhood of the Republican Party, our mission today, is to establish on sure foundations, and make secure for the coming ages, the fruits of the war, debt, and of taxation through which the present has been achieved."[32]

The following day the *Times* editorialized that the Republican platform adopted by the convention was "at once moderate in tone, and firm and explicit in its declarations concerning the prominent issues of the canvas." Among those prominent issues was reform, but the *Times* wrote that the "most notable" point in the platform urged a constitutional amendment against the funding of "sectarian schools." The *Times* claimed that the schools plank represented "a very large part of the American people."[33] Judging by the platform and the *Times* analysis of it, the American people were not interested in the Indian war, because it was not mentioned at all.

The first notable news story about the Indian campaign to appear in the *New York Times* during the convention was buried on page 7 on June 18. It was a one-paragraph dispatch from Gen. Alfred Terry, commander of the column that included Custer's regiment, reporting that on June 12 the column was looking for trails but had not yet found any signs of Indians. In the same edition, the *Times* editorialized that miners who invaded the Black Hills, which belonged to the Sioux, should obey government restrictions. "The Black Hills adventurers prefer their own lawless way, though it may lead to death and the scalping knife." Neither story referenced the election or the impact a change of administrations might have on the situation.[34]

Attendees to the Democratic convention in St. Louis seemed in more danger than travelers to the West. On the same day Custer and his men were being buried in shallow graves by their grieving, shell-shocked comrades, the *Times* carried a front-page story about the "unwashed" cursing and punching each other at the convention. The Republican *Times* reported with delight that a Missouri Tilden supporter was threatened by a drunken conventioneer who called him a "big-headed bloat" and that various western delegates were "made to feel the power of a New-York rough."[35]

The *New York Herald,* which was covering the Indian war more closely than the *Times,* also did not connect the war to its convention coverage. On June 16 it ran an editorial criticizing the Republican platform, especially its evasive stance on currency inflation, which the *Herald* argued was a "cowardly concession" to "western sentiment"; inflation would supposedly allow poor farmers to keep up payments on their property by paying with inflated currency. The Republicans previously had been in favor of curtailing inflation. An editorial adjacent to the convention piece castigated the country's Indian policy of "feeding these wild men of the woods in the vain hope that they could be civilized and Christianized, but during the whole history of the Republic the savage has gone upon the warpath whenever he grew tired of eating the bread he had not earned." The editorial made no mention that a Republican administration was responsible for the policy or that it should be an issue in the campaign, or that "western sentiment" would be interested in the prosecution of the Indian war. The *Herald* bemoaned the fact that the westerner Hayes was nominated over easterners James G. Blaine and Roscoe Conkling, claiming that this showed the West meant to rule the country by always demanding a westerner on the ticket, going back to Lincoln: "The President is not to come from the East for many years if the West can help it; and the West means to help it. While we are busy with commerce and manufactures, with the development of coal and iron, and heedless of partisan, and especially sectional politics, the West is making politics a business, and combining to have its own way in everything." But, again, the *Herald* was not worried about the West dictating Indian policy; rather, it was insisting to the East that "printed pieces of paper are dollars and that Western Presidents are to be chosen to show the power of the West through obnoxious and hurtful legislation."[36]

Hayes himself talked about the specie issue, the Centennial Exhibition, his nomination, and several other issues when a *Herald* correspondent tracked him down in Columbus, Ohio, "seated quietly in his room at the State Capitol," the day after he was nominated. Hayes, following the custom of the time, had not been at the convention but got the news of his nomination by telegraph. The reporter never asked Hayes about the Indian war, and the future president did not mention it on his own, instead voicing platitudes about other Republicans and the platform, which he admitted he had not read carefully—yet but "at a cursory glance I think it is an excellent one that cannot be improved upon." Hayes got most animated when he criticized the Democrats for talking about repealing the Resumption Act, which would put more paper money in circulation: "They do not make any proposition as to their next movement. I would like to know what the present democratic Congress has done to solve the financial question; absolutely nothing." The conversation was interrupted by a stream of well-wishers, including a group of black delegates and a Bavarian politician who had come to the United States to see the Centennial. One spectator told the reporter that the scene reminded him of the day Lincoln learned he had been nominated in 1860: Hayes "was extremely modest and courteous to all, and no ceremony whatever maintained in the admission of visitors, the doors of the Executive chamber being thrown open and all allowed to enter at pleasure."[37]

Hayes's personal qualities were what created widespread excitement among Republicans, according to the *Hartford Daily Courant,* which claimed it had not seen such enthusiasm for a nominee since Grant in 1868. Hayes "is a gentleman of dignified bearing, with none of the vulgar arts of the demagogue—one who has filled high office with ability, but has never sought to advance himself unless by a conscientious discharge of duty."[38]

In a speech at a reception for his nomination in his hometown of Fremont, Hayes indeed sounded modest and made a plea for a fair election in which both parties respected their opponents. He said he was touched by the warm reaction to his nomination, but especially by the comment of a friend who had said it was too bad Sardis Birchard, the uncle who had raised Hayes after his father died, had not lived to see the nomination. "But this is the order of Providence," Hayes told the crowd. "Events follow upon one another as wave follows wave upon the ocean. It is for each man to do what he can to make others happy. That is the prayer and that is the duty of life. Let us, my friends, in every position undertake to do this." Hayes said he was following the spirit of Lincoln, who said on his first nomination that he realized the tremendous responsibilities that faced him and that he prayed for "the Divine assistance without which I cannot succeed and with which I cannot fail." Lincoln, on his nomination, faced the threat of war, but Hayes was nominated when the country was actually at war on the frontier. Yet Hayes's speech indicates that he believed the main crisis facing the country was trying to heal the still-lingering wounds of Lincoln's Civil War. Whoever wins the election should be supported by the people, Hayes said. "My friends, there has been too much bitterness on such occasions in this country. Let us see to it that abuse or vituperation of the candidate that shall be named at St. Louis do not proceed from our lips. Let us on this Centennial occasion, this second century of our existence—set an example of what a free and intelligent nation can do."[39]

The war Hayes would inherit from Grant was not mentioned in the speech and did not seem to be of much concern to his supporters around the country other than as a crude joke. A group of Hayes enthusiasts in Chicago organized a club called the "Scalpers," named after Hayes's response to a call for him to campaign for Congress while he was in the army during the Civil War. Hayes wrote that any man who would do that should be scalped. The *Hartford Daily Courant,* on the day that many of Custer's men lay scalped on the Montana hills, noted approvingly that "Scalper" was a good name for the club.[40]

The *New York Herald,* too, had a short-lived feeling of national unity after the nomination of Tilden and called for a patriotic and intelligent campaign in the centennial year. "Every four years we have a revulsion and uprisal of all kinds of elements—defamation, hatred, misrepresentation. The press becomes a sewer. The fairest reputations are defamed. Honest differences of opinion grow into animosities." The *Herald* hoped for an election with "patriotisms and good feeling" but admitted that was not likely because the campaign already looked like it would be one of "strenuous, earnest controversy." The consolation, the *Herald* wrote, was that either Hayes or Tilden would make a good president.[41]

The *Herald* ran an editorial about the Sioux war on the same page, in which it worried that the Indian forces were stronger than the army and ended by asking, "Who is responsible for this war?" The editorial never made the obvious point that the Grant administration had started the war, nor did it raise the war as a possible issue in its campaign editorial, instead mentioning the school and money issue.[42]

The *Louisville Courier-Journal* mocked Hayes as "the Great Unknown" and, fittingly for horse country, wrote, "The dark horse from Ohio came in at an easy canter on the home-stretch, beating the favorite of the field by a full length and a half." Hayes's best quality was that he was inoffensive to the various factions of the Republican party, so he could unite them and in that sense would be a formidable candidate. The *Courier-Journal* devoted its entire front page to the election when reporting Hayes's nomination, but none of the lengthy analysis pieces on Hayes and the campaign mentioned the war or Indian policy, despite the fact that an editorial on the Republican platform claimed it was "spread out over every part of the political arena."[43]

The *Courier-Journal* immediately started touting Tilden as the best candidate to beat Hayes. It vigorously defended Tilden against charges that he had been a "peace democrat" hampering the Union effort during the war under the headline "A Scrap of a War Record." Another editorial on the same page discussed the issue of reforming the civil service but made no specific mention of reforming corruption in the Indian Bureau. For the *Courier-Journal,* as for so many newspapers around the country, "war" meant a war that had ended eleven years ago rather than the one that was being waged as they published their papers.[44]

In a subsequent editorial, the *Courier-Journal* argued that Democratic papers throughout the country, and especially the South, supported Tilden for the nomination because of his gubernatorial record, which "would inspire confidence and enthusiasm in his followers such as no man has done since the war. He is a true type of the old Jacksonian Democracy, and the people would rally to his support with entire confidence in his ability and determination to institute the most sweeping reforms in every department of the General Government." Again, the vantage point was the Civil War. The Indian war was not mentioned, even though an editorial directly below the Tilden piece urged Congress to transfer the Indian Bureau from the Interior Department to the War Department to stop corruption.[45]

The Republican *St. Louis Globe-Democrat* attacked Tilden's supporters over their Civil War records. The *Globe* mocked the various generals who had been listed by the *New York World* as endorsing Tilden, including George McClellan, Joseph Hooker, and William Rosecrans. It noted that the list was filled with malcontents and failures. "The *World* should add to its list the names of [John C.] Fremont and Fitz John Porter, and its roster of military frauds would be complete." But the *Globe* made no connection between Tilden's military supporters and the war he would inherit from Grant, or how he might prosecute it. An editorial published on the same page called for a winter campaign against the hostiles, but it made no connection to the presidential campaign.[46]

In San Francisco, the Republican *Alta California* also preferred using the Civil War to illustrate the political campaign. The paper claimed that Democrats metaphorically assassinated James G. Blaine by driving him to his dramatic collapse during the height of the Crédit Mobilier stock-influencing scandal. Blaine recovered physically after a few days, but the scandal likely cost him the presidential nomination. The *California* never mentioned the scandal's details but rather attacked "the traitors" who were continuing their work from the Civil War: "They have transferred the battle-fields of the Rebellion, from Vicksburg, and New Orleans from Gettysburg and the Wilderness to the Halls of Congress. Instead of the lives of Union officers and men, they now seek the reputations and the lives of our Union statesmen."[47]

The *California* was disappointed when Blaine lost the nomination but noted that it could rally around Hayes because he was honest and solid like Blaine on two issues: the support of the independence of schools from sectarian influence, and the support of hard money policy. The paper was also pleased with the Republican platform's support of the same issues, declaring it "one of the best, perhaps the best ever" presented to the American public. In none of the editorials did the *California* mention the Sioux war or Indian policy.[48]

One major paper that did link Indian policy to the election was the Democratic *New York World,* which in May used a term for reform that Franklin Roosevelt would popularize about sixty years later: "A wise, determined, far-sighted and sure-footed Indian policy, just to all parties concerned and clear of temptations to post-tradership roguery, is one of the many good things for which the country must look to a new deal in politics and Democratic Administration."[49] A subsequent editorial urged supporters to elect a Democratic Congress as well as president to achieve a host of important goals, including the reform of Indian policy: "The Democracy is not coming into power as an experiment, but coming with a duty to perform and coming to stay. The public debt must be funded, the tariff regulated, a humane and rational Indian policy established, the currency question taken out of politics, and the functions of the Federal Government brought within their proper limits."[50]

It is important to note that the *World* usually mentioned the Sioux war as an issue in passing, not as a main issue. In analyzing the two parties, the *World* like many other Democratic papers thought the Republicans could only campaign on the bloody shirt, which would not work because voters were "thoroughly sick of the civil war and of the long abuse of all its sufferings and all its victories for the low and selfish purposes of a single political party." The Democrats need only nominate honest candidates and denounce the "rascalities" of the Republicans to win. An editorial on the same page praised Custer and criticized Grant (although it was published on June 27, after Custer's death) but did not link the Sioux war to the campaign.[51]

For most papers, including the *World,* the election was the main story of the year because most editors believed their duties included informing the public about politics and promoting the party they favored. Henry Watterson of the *Louisville Courier-Journal*, for example, was such a strong supporter of Tilden that he acted like a campaign manager in some ways, advising him on strategy and introducing the provincial New Yorker, who knew hardly anyone outside his state, to movers and shakers in the South. Watterson's paper regularly ran a statement on the front page of its "hearty support" for the Democrats, noting that "no pains would be spared" to make it a useful tool for speakers and committee members to use in the campaign.[52]

Amid such coziness between politicians and journalists, it would seem natural that newspapers would interpret news like the Little Bighorn through partisan eyes. To some extent they did. But the papers by and large did not make the Little Bighorn or the Sioux war a major campaign issue; few ever linked the two directly. Disaster news typically becomes a major story for a brief time and then fades from view. Such was the case with the Little Bighorn. It dominated news coverage for a few weeks, but by the end of July it had been subordinated to the election, and war news was usually on the back news pages when it appeared at all.

As with Indian war coverage before the Little Bighorn, the war on the frontier remained a side issue. When the *World* got an advance copy of Reno's account of the battle in the *Army and Navy Journal,* it highlighted Reno's emotional description of Last Stand Hill and his pointed question to the American people of whether they should continue the current Indian policy. "This fierce question may cost Reno the favor of a dying administration," the *World* intoned, "but it was a manly thing to ask it, and the American people will answer it next November." Yet on the same page the *World* carried an editorial about three times as long as the Reno piece extolling Tilden's nomination and his reform record with no mention whatsoever of reforming Indian policy.[53] A few weeks later, when listing all of the accomplishments of the Democratic-controlled House in an editorial spanning a column and a half, the *World* devoted only one sentence to corruption in the Indian Bureau and one paragraph to post-tradership scandals in the War Department.[54]

Some editors accused their rivals of having opinions based solely on politics and using the battle to promote their favorite party in the upcoming election. The Republican *New York Tribune,* for example, implied that anyone who criticized Terry or Custer for the disaster was playing politics, although it never explained how this was the case. Presumably the reader understood Custer was a Democrat, so a newspaper's analysis of his actions was explained by its politics. "It is to be regretted that what are considered the exigencies of a political campaign should impel men to hasty judgments and unjust conclusion in matters of such seriousness. It ought not to be necessary to import into a Presidential canvas the brutalities of Indian warfare, and all good citizens will protest against any such use of the late disaster as that to which some partisan journals are endeavoring to put it."[55]

The *New York Times* was much more explicit in a July 8 editorial appropriately titled "Politics Run Mad," which chastised what it called a "besotted partisan press" for using the battle as an issue, particularly singling out its cross-town rival, the *New York World:* "As soon as the dreadful news is received in the *World* office that sheet goes into hysterical convulsions. The instant question with it is, how can this be made to help in the election? The frantic editor executes a war-dance, and shaking the gory scalps of the dead soldiers at the Republican Party, shrieks 'Vote for Tilden and Reform!' We venture to say that no such monstrous violation of public decency was ever before witnessed in American politics. The Sioux, bloody and vindictive though they are, have never yet touched the depth sounded by the *World,* which beats a tattoo on the coffins of the dead, and calling on all men to vote the Democratic ticket."[56]

The *World* editorial that set off the *Times* did attack Grant but was actually focused more on a defense of Custer. The editorial criticized Grant and Belknap for mismanaging Indian policy but did not, as the *Times* claimed, shriek at voters to choose Tilden. In fact, other election editorials on the same page excoriated Blaine's corruption and defended attacks by Republicans on Tilden's religious beliefs; neither mentioned the Little Bighorn or Indian policy as a campaign issue.[57] The *World* position was not as blatant as made out by the *Times* editors, who seemed to be using the battle to bolster their own side.

At any rate, the *Times* concluded its scolding with a call for reason that was actually a statement of its own political position: "Over his [Custer's] grave let the voices of criticism and partisan malice alike be hushed. Let the dead rest. The duty of the living is to strengthen those who remain. The problem of the government of wild and lawless tribes is not yet solved. A tragical experience has once more showed that the military arm cannot be weakened, nor the armed posts on the frontier be abandoned, while a single tribe remains nomadic and uncivilized. Least of all will the nation endure with patience the partisans who seize upon such a calamity as this to wrest this melancholy lesson to their own petty and selfish purposes!" On the same page, the Republican *Times* criticized Tilden in a pair of editorials but, true to its word, did not analyze how his positions would impact the Sioux war. One editorial argued that he was not as great a reformer as he pretended to be, the other accused him of manufacturing his alleged popularity through "systematic advertising and puffery."[58]

The pro-Hayes *Times* editors did not address their favorite's position on the war, either. When editorializing about Hayes's official letter accepting the nomination—an important part of campaigns in the 1870s—the *Times* emphasized his character while agreeing with his positions on the issues, none of which involved Indian policy. "It [the letter] is the manly, frank, and explicit declaration of a sincere and able man."[59] This was a theme the *Times* and many papers of both parties would follow throughout the campaign—character as one of the most important issues.

Character was important in the election because of the Grant administration scandals, one of which involved corruption in the Indian Bureau. But the *Times* denied any connection between that scandal and war. The Indians were fighting to keep their treaty lands. "The new [Indian] outbreak does not arise from the peace policy, or the misuse of Indian agencies. It is not chargeable on Gen. Grant or the Indian Board or the Republican party. It may be hard to confess, in the presence of the heroic dead, but they were killed because the nation, in its greed, had cheated these savage tribes." Editorials on the same page excoriated Tilden for the hypocrisy of accepting a running mate he did not agree with and for being an inadequate reformer in New York state. How Tilden might handle Indian policy was not mentioned.[60]

The *Times* editorials repeatedly argued that the whole country, not just the Republicans, was to blame for the problems with the Indians; therefore, the topic was not addressed as part of the campaign. When analyzing job training for Indians, the *Times* noted the difficulty of trying to get "the wildest and bravest savages who ever hunted over this continent" to do factory work. "There is little use in charging the President or his agents with the defects of our Indian policy. We are all sinners in the matter. We have sowed dishonesty and injustice, and are reaping disorder and bloodshed."[61]

After mid-July the *Times* no longer gave much importance to stories of Custer and the Sioux war, which fell off the front page for days at a time and got declining coverage for the rest of the election cycle. Out of seven columns, often three or more would be devoted to the election while the Sioux war, if it appeared on the front page at all, would get a partial column. By the end of August the war almost seemed to be a joke to the *Times* as it went back to its illusion that there was no war. One of the longer pieces about the war—and it was buried on page 5—was written in a lighthearted tone by a war correspondent who complained about short rations and "starving" for your country: "How great the thought of Delmonico's, the Café Brunswick, or the Hoffman, when, with a constitution which seems hollow clear down to one's boots, one sits down to a meal consisting of three small pieces of fried bacon, some fragments of 'hard-tack,' and half a pint of poor coffee, and this after a march of twenty-five or thirty miles!"[62]

By October, election news often took up most the front page, and during the last week of the campaign the entire front page of several editions consisted of nothing but election news. On October 29, only about a week before the election, the *Times* finally carried a story explicitly linking the election to the war. It reported that a meeting of Democrats had endorsed Tilden and listed several demands from the government, including government payment for "Indian depredations" and the transfer of the Indian Bureau to the War Department. The Democrats in question were meeting at the Wyoming Territory convention, and their story was buried on page 10.[63] For the *Times* and its eastern readers, the war was simply not much of an issue.

The war was a more important issue for readers in the West, where newspapers were close to the front if not actually in areas that still saw Indian raids. Major western papers like the *Alta California* in San Francisco put war news and election news on the front page almost daily in July, August, and September. But even the *California* reduced its war coverage during the final months of the election campaign, running war stories only about every other day while publishing several election stories on the front page every day.

When writing about the war, the *California*, unlike the *Times*, often referred possessively to "our little Army" and "Our Indian Campaign," as in an editorial of that name that blamed the army's defeat on a cheapskate Democratic House of Representatives that had not appropriated enough money for the military: "The Democrats have been determined to destroy the efficiency of our little army by cutting down its numbers, diminishing the numbers of its officers, and so making it as little formidable as possible. As the Secesh [secessionist] element has the supremacy in the House, they naturally hate the Army which stood true to the Government when they were false to it."[64]

The San Francisco paper hardly ever made such an explicit connection between the Sioux war and the election. One of the rare examples argued that Democrats were trying to cut military funding in order to appear as reformers: "The Democratic House has resolved itself into a reform organization, and with them the suppression of this Indian outbreak, and the protection of our frontiers, and the lives of our skeleton regiments are as nothing when in the balance against a little cheap political capital, made for the Democratic party and the Presidential nominee, under the grand sound of economy."[65]

But for the most part, western papers chose not to use the war to make political points. The *Missoulian* in Montana praised the speech of its territorial delegate to Congress for letting the government know about the danger of Indian raids, particularly after the Little Bighorn. An adjacent editorial about Tilden praised him as a better reformer than Hayes but made no mention of his Indian policies or the war. The *California* frequently criticized the government's Indian policy of providing supplies—including weapons—to tribes that used them to kill whites. But the Indian policy was being implemented by the Republican Grant administration, and the Republican *California* did not tie the issue to the election. For example, on July 13, only a few days after it first reported the Little Bighorn, the *California* raged against a report that the hostiles were returning to their agencies to rearm: "When his ammunition has been exhausted in this, to him, enjoyable work, he returns to the Reservation with his scalps and his Indian glory, to once more grow fat upon Government bounty. . . . This is [a] specimen of our Indian policy." On the same page the *California* published an editorial about Tilden's problem in uniting the various factions of the Democratic Party, but it did not mention the war or what his Indian policy might be.[66]

The *California* repeated its criticism of the government's Indian policy throughout the fall:

We are somewhat weary with hammering away at this, one of the greatest and most unjust follies of our American system. It is cruel and unjust even to the Indians themselves, for they are cheated; allowed to own their own ponies and to acquire the best arms, and to supply themselves with ammunition, and go out upon their real or pretended hunts, thus tempted into making war, or else only murdering the few unprotected whites they may chance to meet on the plains or in the hills, and whenever wearied with such hunting and perhaps short of provisions, allowed to return as before and be rationed. This is extra and unreasonable benevolence which leads the Indian to think himself master, and eventually to lead him to destruction.[67]

The article went on to rail against the Indian agents and government, concluding that, "if the world abroad had a fair idea of our system of Indian humbug, and all its lungs could be united in one guffaw of ridicule, it would blow up the Indian Ring and Sitting Bull with it."

But the *California* never advocated blowing up the Grant administration or the Republican Party. In one of its last critiques of Indian policy before the election it emphasized that it did not mean to impugn the character of all government employees: "In all our references heretofore to the Indians and the troubles they have given us, no purpose or intention was entertained of reflecting upon the Administration of President Grant. The system has grown up through the years of doubts and changes, not only of the system, but frequent changes in the agents and the Government."[68]

The *California* did not generally comment on what changes a Hayes or Tilden administration might make in Indian policy. One of the best examples of this was its August 5 editorial page, which declared that the reservation system was a "convenience for the hostile redskins," who could reequip after fighting U.S. troops. "It is enough to make an honest, earnest man pull out his hair—provided he is not bald—to read and think of the rascalities of the Indian Ring, and its ramifications all through Indian territory, wherever the Government has undertaken to feed the Savage." The paper argued in another editorial in favor of civil service reform but did not mention anything about reforming the Indian Bureau or changing Indian policy. Similarly, it criticized Thomas Hendricks, Tilden's running mate, on monetary policy but was silent on Indian policy.[69]

The candidates and their representatives did not bring up the issue, and that was all right for the *California*. Hayes's letter of acceptance of the Republican nomination did not touch on the war but instead emphasized reform, education, and Reconstruction. The *California* noted approvingly, "Hayes has said everything that we wished for, and nothing that we dislike." When a *California* reporter got a chance to interview Hayes in September, a rarity in that presidential candidates at that time usually let their surrogates do the campaigning, the reporter apparently never asked Hayes about the Sioux war or Indian policy. The reporter, who interviewed Hayes in Columbus, Ohio, wrote that the governor was in "an affable and entertaining mood." They watched a small parade of Civil War veterans and talked about the Republicans' prospects, the economy and reform, but not reforming the Indian Bureau.[70] Although the *California* served a readership that arguably was in the theater of war—parts of the state had recently experienced Indian warfare—the editors simply did not seem to think the Little Bighorn or the Sioux war were major election issues.

The *St. Louis Dispatch,* an independent newspaper in the center of the country, had a similar attitude toward the war: the editors covered it extensively but rarely if ever linked it to the election, which they argued was boring: "The political canvass thus far for the Presidency does not enlist any special enthusiasm. 'General apathy' appears to be in command of the forces on both sides, and the general public are not caring which whips, so much as they used to. The campaign, aside from its stupidity, has no marked features. There are no log cabin and hard cider meetings, no Wide-Awake or Little Giant processions—nothing, in fact, to indicate that two great parties are engaged in a struggle for the enormous patronage and tempting pickings of the National Government for the next four years."[71] An editorial published adjacent to the analysis of the lack of electoral excitement noted, "The Indian question is beginning to assume a more interesting phase than for some time past" because of increasing trouble on the reservations.[72] But the *Dispatch* did not make the connection between this "interesting" story and the election, which might have become less boring with some debate about patronage as it affected Indian policy.

The *Dispatch* argued later that month that the voters were tired of the reform issue because they did not believe either party was sincere about it: "It is dawning upon the public mind more and more clearly every day that the whole thing is a sham and a humbug." Furthermore, the people were more interested in the economy: "The people are evidently becoming tired of barren issues. They feel the pinch of hard times resulting mainly from the depressed condition of business. Their great desire is the Government shall provide a stable and uniform currency, properly regulated and governed in value and volume, and adjusted to the requirements of business." By the end of the month, the *Dispatch* noted that business was improving, in part because hard times had forced people to concentrate on work instead of the "costly nonsense" of election campaigns: "The people's interests generally suffer just in the proportion that the interests of the professional politician are enhanced. Hard times have awakened the people to this fact, and they are now placing the business interests of the country in the forefront, and with a success that is gratifying."[73]

Although the *Dispatch* found the election boring, it found violence—crime and war—interesting and usually had a healthy dose of one or both on its pages. Its front page featured a regular column titled "Crimes and Casualties." On July 22, the crimes column featured a gory murder story with the sensational headline, "An Italian Cut to Pieces with a Razor, for Money." Two of the other six columns on that typical *Dispatch* front page featured news about the Sioux war, and the other main headline covered international news. But the *Dispatch* avoided connecting the war to an endorsement of either Tilden or Hayes. For example, when it editorialized about the "great issues" of the campaign, it mentioned reform, schools, monetary policy, and the war—the Civil War—which it said some Republicans were still fighting. On September 22 it carried a piece about the Republican nominee for Indiana governor, Benjamin Harrison, that defended the party's "bloody shirt" campaign. The Harrison piece was sandwiched between editorials castigating the country's Indian policy, but the articles made no mention of the effect a new administration might have on that policy.[74] In other words, politicians waved the bloody shirt of the Civil War, but the editors of the *Dispatch* left the bloody buckskins from the Sioux war furled.

Some southern newspapers, representing a readership that felt victimized by the bloody shirt rhetoric, did wave the bloody buckskins at the Republicans, albeit briefly. The most passionate example was Watterson's

Louisville Courier-Journal, which argued that the best solution for the country's Indian problem was to elect Tilden: "Next year, with Tilden at the White House, every gross irregularity like this Indian business will be corrected. Indian wars under the old Democratic regime were rare, and when the party of peace comes once more into power a proper Indian policy will be adopted, which will be satisfactory to the Indians themselves." Although Hayes was clearly for reform and had tried to distance himself from the Grant administration scandals, the *Courier-Journal* would have none of it. Hayes, the paper argued in another editorial, would "continue the wretched, mismanaged [Indian] department, for he indorses Grant's administration."[75]

Other prominent southern newspapers also took shots at the Republicans. The *New Orleans Picayune* blamed the Little Bighorn on the Grant administration for not providing enough troops for the frontier: "A gallant officer, with his two brothers and their entire force, fell in an unequal contest with the savages, while a large portion of the military of the country were living in pampered idleness in the South and elsewhere. At the very time of its occurrence we are told that the President, with the Secretary of War and the Attorney General, were in consultation respecting the disposition they would make of the army in the South during the approaching elections. This was a more important subject to them than a massing of the Indian tribes in the West and the slaughter of immigrants and the burning of whole villages."[76]

The Kentucky *Woodford Weekly* claimed that the Grant administration was thoroughly incompetent and that only corrupt Indian agents and traders would benefit from an expensive Indian war, which it claimed cost the government about $1 million for every Indian killed. "Will the people see that nothing short of the absolute overthrow of the Republican party can save this country from all manner of entanglements both in home and foreign relations, from utter disgrace and degredation, from individual and national bankruptcy?" the *Weekly* asked, and then made a prediction about the election: "We believe they will."[77]

The *Fort Worth Democrat* in Texas reacted similarly, describing Custer's defeat by "a few thousand untutored savages" as in insult to the national honor that should "mantle the cheek of every proud American." How long would this happen? "As long as Grant and his kind control the government."[78]

But as summer turned to fall, the southern press, too, largely forgot the Little Bighorn as a campaign issue. A September editorial in the *Courier-Journal* headlined "The Latest News from the Front" meant the political campaign as the front, and the campaign had nothing to do with Indians. An editorial published immediately below it urged the transfer of the Indian Bureau to the War Department, but it made no connection to the election, and the editor did not even bother to distinguish it with a headline.[79]

The *Picayune* noted that both political parties campaigned for reform, "but what is to be reformed?" For southern newspapers like the *Picayune,* state issues were more important than national issues. The *Picayune* made its position clear in an appropriately named editorial, "Louisiana First," which argued, "We have, of course, much to gain by the success of a Conservative ticket in the national election; but by far the greater number of our ills have resulted from the maladministration of the State authorities." In a foreshadowing of the tacit agreement made after the disputed election that southerners would accept Hayes in return for control of their states, the *Picayune* editorialized, "Let us see Louisiana free, give us an honest State administration, and we might endure even another term of Radical Federal administration."[80]

With such an attitude, it is easy to see why the *Picayune* carried far fewer stories about the Sioux war than did its northern counterparts. The *Picayune* usually carried only a few stories a week about the war but several stories a day on local, state, or national politics. For the *Picayune,* the main campaign issue was clear, and it was not the Sioux war: "The one great, overshadowing issue of the pending political canvas in this State is the adjustment of the relations between the black and white races. Other and minor issues are presented; but nearly all of them would be at once determined by the reconciliation of the black man to the white man, and of the white man to the black man." The newspaper argued that blacks had learned that "radical misrule" was hurting everyone in the state, and it urged whites to be conciliatory toward blacks and persuade them "that an alliance of the two races is necessary to the preservation of their common safety."[81]

The election was important to the *Picayune,* certainly more so than for the *St. Louis Dispatch,* which had noted that the campaign was boring and bad for business. The *Picayune,* on the other hand, argued that the reverse was true: politics had suffered because businessmen had withdrawn from it. "It will be admitted by any one who will devote a moment's reflection to the subject, that this republican government of ours requires, more than any other, the intelligent co-operation of all its citizens. The policy, the laws, the destiny of a state depend upon the collective will of the individual citizens who compose it. When, from this aggregate, a large proportion of the better element is voluntarily withdrawn, the loss is felt by the whole body politic. The privilege of self-government carries with it a heavy responsibility." For the *Picayune,* however, the main responsibility was toward Louisiana issues, not national issues like the Sioux war or reforming the Indian Bureau.[82]

Some editors thought the national election would have little impact on the Sioux war or Indian policy in any case. The *Emporia News* on July 14 noted that, "if ever a people were entirely disgusted with Indian policy, the people of the United States are now, and yet there is little chance of any administration making an improvement of the various policies tried up to this time." The *New York Herald* only a month before the election published a story about possible dereliction of duty by some Little Bighorn survivors that might have lost the battle, but it pointedly argued that this should not be part of the election campaign: "At the present moment the country is too much occupied with the work of selecting a new king to undertake an inquiry into the causes which led to the Custer massacre; but as soon as the elections are over an investigation must be had." Both Hayes and Tilden were for reform of Indian policy, but the *Herald* was skeptical either one would make significant changes and end the cycle of treaties and war: "So far as Tilden or Hayes is concerned the Indian question will go on as usual, and continue to be settled until it has been finally put an end to by the disappearance of the Indians. But the politicians may console themselves with the reflection that the Indian question will not have much weight in the coming election, the only danger to the republican success arising from the German vote."[83]

The Little Bighorn was an interesting conversation topic rather than an issue of direct concern to the average person. As one Washington reporter wrote about two weeks after the battle was first reported: "People must have something to talk about, and just now we are happy in the possession of two most prolific themes—politics and the Indian war. As regards the first, every section, nay, almost every petty locality, has its peculiar views in reference thereto. But the other presents the same phase throughout the country. It is much to be deplored, but we have certainly entered upon a long and terrible war."[84]

Nevertheless, for most of the country it was a long and terrible war for someone else: the settlers on the frontier, the volunteer soldiers in the country's tiny regular army, the Indians who were swindled but nevertheless now had to be taught to stay out of the way of progress and out of the news pages.

≫→

The Little Bighorn was a huge news story in 1876 because it had many of the main "news values" that journalists use to define the importance of a story: conflict, human interest, prominence, novelty, and impact. Those first four values were evident because the battle involved the tragic death of a famous officer and half his command in a devastating, unexpected, and yet heroic defeat. When covering a disaster like the Little Bighorn journalists always ask why, and the question has never been answered satisfactorily precisely because of the complex circumstances of the battle. Reasonable people disagreed then and disagree now on who owns the lion's share of the blame. Editors in 1876, usually working for newspapers that took a clear political stance, viewed the battle through a partisan lens, but that did not necessarily make their opinions on the subject illegitimate or encourage them to use the battle as a campaign issue.

The Little Bighorn's significance to the election was never as great as that of Reconstruction, government corruption, or the economy. Furthermore, its relevance to the campaign dissipated rather quickly as the initial shock of the disaster faded and people returned to the more pressing concerns of their own lives. It is true that Custer's defeat was a costly embarrassment for the national government and that it affected Americans in the tangential way that any government failure affects them. But for most newspaper readers the Little Bighorn and the Sioux war had little direct impact on their lives. There was no draft, and the regular army was a minuscule percentage of the population. Serving in that army had little glory compared to serving in the Civil War. A *New York Herald* story on a recruiting office—located in the former mansion of a "low comedian" named William Burton—described "hundreds of unemployed and hungry men" trying to get one of the two thousand enlistments authorized by Congress: "There is little of the old romance of the war of the rebellion about this recruiting office. All is stern business and quiet and orderly silences and work; no big bounties or stories of charging or captured batteries or rescued flags to enchant the tired and hungry recruit. For these men, if they fall in battle, there will be only a lonely grave in the prairie grass or hurried pile of stones in some far-off rocky canyon bed, where there will be naught but the howl of the coyote for a requiem."[85]

The Indian campaign area was so isolated from the populated part of the country—what frontier soldiers sometimes referred to as "the States"—that the Sioux war had about as much direct connection to readers as the wars going on in Europe and others parts of the world. People in the North were more concerned about the economy. People in the South were more concerned about the federal troops patrolling their war-ravaged states than about the troops struggling against hostile tribes halfway across the country. People in the West were more concerned about the Sioux war than their fellow citizens were, but even there the main issues were the economy and reform. That the Sioux war was not taken completely seriously in much of the country is illustrated by the *Globe-Democrat* headline over a column of war stories, including Rain-in-the-Face's purported removal of Tom Custer's heart: "Subjects for Dime Novels."[86]

In truth, the Little Bighorn was not a great campaign issue because the country was in broad terms united on what to do about it: punish the hostile tribes so that they could not make war again. "This is in no respect a party question," the *New York Herald* argued in an editorial urging a prompt and firm effort to end the war. "Democrats and republicans are united as to our duty with the Indians. For this reason the leaders of the two parties should enter into the work with conscientious energy."[87]

Both parties agreed that the government needed to be reformed but realized that it was needed throughout the government—the corruption in the Indian Bureau and the post tradership scandals were just part of a systemic problem. Even the controversy over Custer's actions did not keep the country from reaching consensus that he was a hero. The Republican *California* wrote as much when it urged the government to retrieve Custer's remains from the battlefield and suitably entomb them before the wolf or the "surly and malignant Sitting Bull" could defile them. "This is not a question of party, but of honor; not of law, but of gratitude. . . . it is one of patriotic love, and of military policy, which would show to our little Army something of the sentiments of an appreciative people toward their gallant defenders, who are ready to throw away their lives in their defence."[88]

Both Hayes and Tilden were shrewd politicians and could have made the Little Bighorn and the war a campaign issue if they had wanted to, but both realized that voters were interested in other topics. Certainly their surrogates did not make it an issue. It was common for papers to run political speeches verbatim, and in an era without tweeting or instant messaging speeches were *long* and expected to be so. The *Globe,* for example, published the speech of Illinois senator and former Union general John A. Logan that took an entire column of the front page on September 16 as well as the majority of page 3. In all of his praise of Hayes and castigation of Tilden, he mentioned corruption in the Indian Bureau in two paragraphs, arguing that it had been worse under the administration of James Buchanan than under "Republican rule." Logan was careful not to name the disgraced Grant in reference to the Indian Bureau, for this was not a winning issue for Republicans.[89]

But Democratic speakers did not make the Little Bighorn or Indian policy a campaign issue either. The *Courier-Journal* on September 4 published a speech by Joseph Pulitzer that spanned half of the paper's oversize eight-column front page. Pulitzer, who spoke in German to appeal to the German voters of Indianapolis, concluded like a twenty-first-century politician with a ringing call for change: "We demand a change that reform and purity shall prevail in our government. We demand a change that the American people, solemnly condemning corruption and commending honesty, may rise above prejudices and partisanship to real patriotism. We demand a change to preserve the Republic!" The *Courier-Journal* published the speech in English, but in any language it was clear that the main issue was reform, and since Pulitzer never mentioned the Indian Bureau reform of Indian policy was a side issue.[90]

The *California* warned its San Francisco readers right before the election that a vote cast for Tilden was a vote for "another war, and another scene of horror and hatred."[91] But the *California* was referring to another Civil War, which was the constant looming presence in readers' minds, not the Sioux war. Concern over a resurgence of the Civil War was the reason many newspapers, particularly those east of the Mississippi River, covered the Hamburg race riot with as much intensity as the Sioux war. Only a handful of people died in that small South Carolina town compared to the 250 or so soldiers killed at the Little Bighorn. But the so-called Hamburg Massacre brought back memories of a war in which casualities in some battles approached 25,000 or more. It is easy to see why the Little Bighorn did not become a major campaign issue when there were so many other things for voters to worry about.

The election would be decided on issues closer to home than the Little Bighorn.

HARPER'S WEEKLY.

A JOURNAL OF CIVILIZATION

Vol. VIII.—No. 577.]   NEW YORK, SATURDAY, MARCH 19, 1864.   [$4.00 FOR FOUR MONTHS.
$3.00 PER YEAR IN ADVANCE.

Entered according to Act of Congress, in the Year 1864, by Harper & Brothers, in the Clerk's Office of the District Court for the Southern District of New York.

BRIGADIER-GENERAL GEORGE A. CUSTER.—Photographed by Brady.—[See Page 187.]

Harper's Weekly helped make Custer a media star during the Civil War with this 1864 cover of an unnamed battle. Americans expected their cavalrymen to be dashing figures, and Custer literally fit the image.

This 1865 photograph shows the charismatic look Custer had developed by the end of the Civil War, wearing oversized boots, long hair, and a uniform of his own design. Custer said the red necktie was intended to let his men know where he was on the battlefield. His Civil War soldiers began wearing the necktie, too.

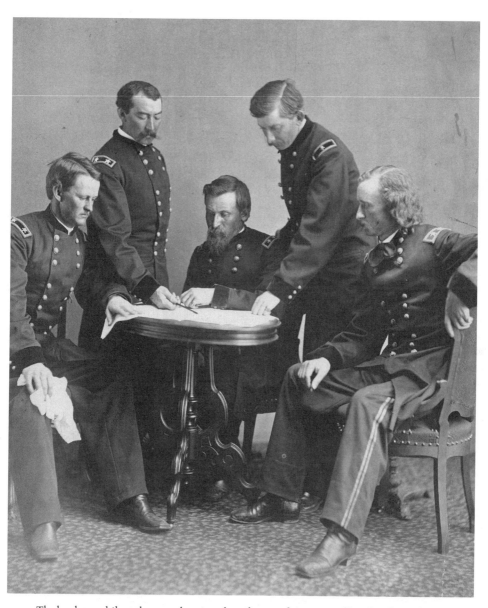

The hard war philosophy waged against the tribes was first practiced by Sheridan and Custer during the Civil War. From left, Wesley Merritt, Philip Sheridan, George Crook, James William Forsyth, and Custer, photographed by Alexander Gardener in 1865, when they were closing in on victory in the Civil War. Crook would lead a column into the Battle of the Rosebud during the Great Sioux War.

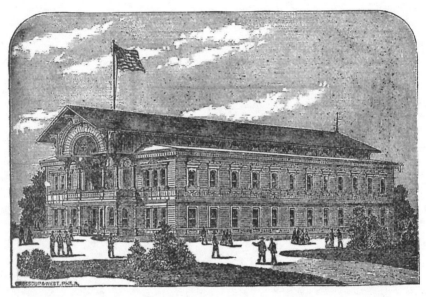

The Newspaper Pavilion at the Centennial Exhibition in Philadelphia provided fairgoers with copies of most newspapers in the United States. The newspaper industry was growing in 1876 and was an entertainment as well as a news medium. Still, pavilion organizer George P. Rowell complained that fairgoers seemed more interested in displays like a giant silver nugget from Nevada. From *Centennial Newspaper Exhibition.*

INDIAN TENT IN THE GOVERNMENT BUILDING AT THE CENTENNIAL EXHIBITION.
[FROM A SKETCH BY OUR SPECIAL ARTIST.]

This sketch from the *Daily Graphic* shows tourists examining a tipi at the Centennial in Philadelphia. While fairgoers were gawking at replicas, Custer and his men were being killed while attacking a real village. From the *New York Daily Graphic*

"BLEST BE THE TIE THAT BINDS."

Wendell Phillips.— This, my friends, is the gallant Scout whom Du Guesclin, Chevalier Bayard, and Sir Philip Sidney would receive as a brother. We are bound together by a common humanity, and oh! let us assist each other to the best of our powers. Let us honor the brave, and this dear brother shall scalp them.

This sarcastic *Daily Graphic* portrayal of Indian rights activist Wendell Phillips joined at the rib with a warrior carrying a bloody knife captured the emotions of many readers after the Little Bighorn. An editorial cartoon conveys only one side of the argument, and this cartoon missed the fact the many editors wrote sympathetically about the Indian viewpoint, including the opinion that whites had started the war. From the *New York Daily Graphic*

Newspapers often portrayed the great Sioux leader Sitting Bull as a villain, but they also gave him credit—sometimes too much—for his military genius. Americans in 1876 enjoyed puns, and Sitting Bull's name lent itself to countless jokes aimed at both Indians and the U.S. Army.

CUSTER MONUMENT BALL AT WHITE SULPHUR SPRINGS HOTEL, VA., LAST FRIDAY.

Former Yankee and Rebel journalists united in mourning the death of Custer. Northern newspapers covered a charity ball organized by southerners to raise money for a monument to their former enemy. The *Daily Graphic* made one mistake in this illustration: the ball was held in West Virginia, not Virginia. From the *New York Daily Graphic*

Columbia, in mourning over the Little Bighorn dead in the background, shames
Democratic House Speaker Samuel J. Randall for his party's efforts to cut the size of the
army. Debate over the size of the army erupted in the wake of Custer's death, but such
issues as reforming government overshadowed it during the fall political campaign.
From the *New York Daily Graphic*

DECLARATION OF EQUALITY.—*Justice* "Five more Wanted."

The Hamburg Massacre pushed the Little Bighorn off the front pages of most newspapers. *Harper's Weekly* illustrated the outrage of many journalists, who argued that the whites involved in the riot were more savage than the Indians who fought Custer. The fear of a renewal of the Civil War overshadowed the active war being waged in the West. Photograph courtesy of HarpWeek.

118

Rutherford B. Hayes was a savvy politician who knew how to use the media, cultivating journalists who could help his campaigns. Although he had known Custer from the Civil War, he did not make the death of his fellow Ohio veteran or the Great Sioux War an issue in the 1876 election.

New York governor Samuel J. Tilden made his national reputation by taking on corruption in his home state. Like Hayes, he was a media-savvy politician and did not make the Little Bighorn or the Great Sioux War an important part of his campaign. This campaign song emphasized his honesty. Republican newspapers would instead call him "Slippery" Sam, an adjective they would also apply to the Sioux.

CHAPTER 5

"The Old Rebel Spirit"

The Hamburg Massacre Bumps Custer off the Front Page

At least five times as many men were killed at the Little Bighorn than in the Hamburg Massacre, but the news of the South Carolina race fight sent chills through many people around the United States. Custer's death and the almost unbelievable defeat of the Seventh Cavalry, coupled with the sensational details of savage mutilation of the bodies, made for thrilling news copy. Nevertheless, the Little Bighorn was warfare, and the dead were soldiers who fell on the battlefield. That the Indians took no prisoners and mutilated the corpses was horrifying but something generally expected in that type of war. The Hamburg fight, on the other hand, was between two supposedly civilized forces yet involved the murdering of unarmed black prisoners by white southerners. To many Americans, even some northern Democrats who usually sided with their southern brethren, the Hamburg Massacre represented an attack on democratic government and humanity.

"All of the other issues involved in the next election are insignificant with the great issue which this massacre has so strongly brought forth," the *Chicago Tribune* declared in an editorial that excoriated Tilden for not addressing the massacre in his acceptance letter of the Democratic nomination. The paper made its dramatic claim only a little more than a month after the battle of the Little Bighorn was reported.[1]

Papers like the *Tribune* thought the Hamburg battle was more important than the Little Bighorn because it symbolized the problems with Reconstruction, problems that meant a return to Civil War could be imminent. A contemporary history of the administration of South

Carolina governor D. H. Chamberlain asserted that "undoubtedly this event [Hamburg] was the turning point in the course of the political affairs in South Carolina." The Hamburg Massacre was the first indication that the violence of the Ku Klux Klan, which had been inactive because of Chamberlain's strict policies, was reviving in South Carolina.[2]

Chamberlain himself compared the Hamburg Massacre to the Little Bighorn in letters and speeches soon after the riot. In a letter dated July 13 to Senator T. J. Robertson, Chamberlain wrote, "If you can find words to characterize its atrocity and barbarism, the triviality of the causes, and the murderous and inhuman spirit which marked it in all its stages, your power of language exceeds mine. It presents a darker picture of human cruelty than the slaughter of Custer and his soldiers, as they were shot in open battle. The victims at Hamburg were murdered in cold blood after they had surrendered, and were utterly defenseless." The letter was published in several newspapers on August 18. In a campaign speech in Beaufort on July 16, Chamberlain did not mention the Little Bighorn specifically but did say that the Hamburg victims were "shot down with more than Indian barbarity and cruelty."[3]

The news of both events hit the country at about the same time. Most newspapers reported the Little Bighorn on July 6, and most reported the Hamburg fight about three days later. Hamburg, which is just across the border from Augusta, Georgia, had a majority black population, and most of the prominent people in town and in public office were black. It was in fact considered a center of "black power," and local whites complained of various abuses such as not being able to drink from the public fountain and forced to make way for drills by the town's black militia unit. One such episode precipitated the Hamburg Massacre, when two white men demanded that the militia, which was gathered for a Fourth of July celebration, get out of the way of their carriage. The black militia and the white men argued, with the militia ultimately opening its ranks to let the carriage through. But the father of one of the men returned later to demand the militia captain be arrested for blocking the road. The militia captain argued with the judge, Prince Rivers, who then charged him with contempt of court and set trial for July 8.

The militia and a group of armed white men gathered in town on the trial day. A prominent white man, M. C. Butler (a former confederate general), demanded that the black militia disarm, and they refused. The militia retreated to the town armory. Butler left Hamburg but returned that day with reinforcements, including a cannon. A black man and a white man were killed in an exchange of gunfire, but the militia soon tried to flee the armory after a brief siege punctuated by cannon fire.

One white and at least two blacks were killed in the battle, and twenty-nine blacks were captured by the whites. Four of the most prominent blacks were taken from the group of prisoners and shot in cold blood while they were being taken to the Aiken County jail. In the aftermath of the fight, the white mob sacked the town.[4]

Press reaction generally split along partisan lines. Republican newspapers claimed the event epitomized problems throughout the South and called for a strong federal response to guarantee the peace and protect the rights of black citizens. Democratic newspapers in the South tended to defend the action of the whites, and Democratic northern papers sometimes defended the whites but at other times criticized them, especially for giving the Republicans a campaign issue. Regardless of the editorial position of the paper, the Hamburg incident was a huge news story that quickly overshadowed the Little Bighorn for a time in many parts of the country. But because of the close timing of the two fights, newspapers, like politicians, often connected them, and the two became intertwined in decisions about the size of the army and the number of troops to be stationed in the South.

The press reaction to the Hamburg Massacre cannot be understood without placing it in the context of the Civil War. Donald A. Sutherland argues in *A Savage Conflict* that guerrilla warfare was decisive in the Civil War and certainly left a horrific impression on the participants, including Hayes, who was "appalled" by the frequent murder of his soldiers by bushwhackers when he served in West Virginia. Even in parts of northern states such as Iowa, Ohio, Illinois, and Indiana, civilians lived in fear of raids by partisan groups—often bands of deserters and desperadoes who raped, murdered, and stole with little regard to the politics of their victims. Indiana senator Oliver P. Morton, famous for waiving the bloody shirt in every election, especially in 1876, had been governor of the state during the war. He sent a message to Lincoln's War Department declaring that Indianans lived "in a state of intense alarm."[5]

Little wonder then that, when the prominent Republican *Hartford Daily Courant* first reported the Hamburg fight, it used the headline "War in South Carolina," mirroring the headline "War in the West" over a series of wire reports about the Sioux war. According to the *Courant* coverage, war was occurring in both the West and the South and was equally brutal in both places: "Of the character of the negro massacre at Hamburg there can be no question. . . . The barbarities even extended to the mutilation of the dead. The whole proceeding was one which in this country could only have occurred in the south or among the hostile Indians."[6] But the better comparison for the *Courant* was the Bleeding Kansas violence of slaveholding Missouri "border ruffians" abusing the free-staters in Kansas in the 1850s. In both cases, Democrats excused the violence, the *Courant* editorialized. "They have learned nothing by the war. They treat the Hamburg massacre exactly as they treated the 'Kansas outrages.' Now, as then, they are on the side of disorder and brutality, taking always the part of the 'dominant race,' without any sense of justice or fair play."[7]

When the *Courant* criticized Tilden—and as a Republican paper it did so often—it castigated him for not speaking out about the massacre: "The whole white sentiment is in favor of the murderers, no prominent lawyer volunteers on the side of justice, humanity and law, and it is almost certain that criminals will escape without punishment, and will only be held in greater esteem for their cowardly deeds. And Governor Tilden did not dare say one word in condemnation of the outrage for fear of discouraging his southern workers." Tilden's opinion on the Sioux war was of no interest to the *Courant*.[8]

The Washington *Courant* correspondent reported that several Democratic congressmen were trying to kill a bill to increase the size of the army to provide reinforcements to fight the Sioux. The story, headlined "The Latest Rebel Exhibition," described "rebel objectors" threatening to filibuster the bill: "The leading democrats saw plainly the great political blunder of this opposition, but none of them could control those hotheaded men who swaggered around saying if the President wanted help to get his troops in the Sioux country out of trouble, let him take them out of the south." The next day the *Courant* warned its readers in an editorial to expect southerners to start complaining about "bayonet" rule in the South by federal troops: "Where no fraud or violence is intended there will be no fear of federal bayonets; but where it is designed or carried out there ought to be such fear, and all good citizens will hope that punishment will speedily follow crime."[9]

The *Courant* published stories about Hamburg and other violence in the South as much as updates on the Sioux war and frequently emphasized the former. On September 26 a one-paragraph story about Democrats murdering four black Republicans in Mississippi was announced with three screaming headlines, the first of which blared "Another Southern Outrage." A longer story on Sitting Bull reportedly marching on Fort Sully got the generic headline "The Indian War."[10]

When the *Courant* did publish stories about the Sioux war, such as an account of treaty negotiations, it connected them to the Civil War. A Sioux chief named American Horse told the U.S. peace commissioners to get the soldiers out of Indian land because they did not belong there. To the *Courant,* he sounded like a slaveholder of the old South:

> The Sioux Indians appear to understand the thing as perfectly as if they had been studying the states rights theory of the democrats all their lives. . . . And the savage naturally thinks his rights are interfered with when he is disturbed in his favorite summer pastime of war. He regards the Union or the government, for his purposes of war, exactly as the slaveholder formerly regarded it for his purpose of slavery. The latter all the time desired the government to support and defend his "system" to extend it, to catch the runaways and pay the damages of his loss of slave property; and yet it denied the power of the government to in any way interfere with slavery in the states, for it was a "local institution."[11]

As election day approached, the *Courant* became ever more strident, headlining a campaign editorial "The Election War." But this headline was no mere campaign rhetoric. The *Courant* journalists called the violence in Hamburg and other places a Democratic "war policy" that was leading to a collapse in social order. What could Connecticut voters do? Be sure their state went Republican to offset the success of Democrats in South Carolina: Connecticut's "responsibility is vastly increased by the condition of affairs in South Carolina. For it is not now merely whether she shall vote for the election of Tilden, but whether her vote shall sanction the old rebel spirit that carries elections by violence."[12]

Waiting for election day was nerve-wracking: "Not since the days when we waited in painful uncertainty the news from Gettysburg, the news of the repulse of Lee's march in the north, has there been a deeper anxiety. We expected to hear of a victory then, and we expect a victory now, but the cases have their differences; then our good news depended upon the valor of the soldiers, now it depends upon our own vigilance." The final *Courant* editorial before the election laid out the reasons to vote for Hayes, which concluded that, "with Hayes elected, we may expect that the old rebellion spirit will be so subdued that even in Texas the flying of the Union flag will not be considered an impropriety."[13]

The "old rebel spirit" was something that today we would call "code words" for partisans to use to advance their cause. It was used often and throughout the country in connection with Hamburg and southern violence. Even the *New York Times,* which was generally considered moderate in tone, picked up the phrase fairly quickly as it shifted from Little Bighorn to Hamburg coverage. The Little Bighorn was still on the front page on July 9, with the first report of what the *Times* called "Trouble in Hamburg" on page 7. But the next day, four days after the Little Bighorn was first reported, the *Times* thought the Hamburg incident was the bigger story. A one-paragraph story on troops being sent west was the only mention of the Indian war on the front page; it appeared immediately below a lengthy story about the violent end of the Hamburg riot.[14] On July 14 the paper devoted more than two full front-page columns to a detailed account of the riot under the headline "The Old Rebel Spirit." The story described white men shooting their black prisoners in cold blood and noted that two bodies were mutilated. An editorial in the same issue argued that "the conduct of the white ruffians in the matter was wholly without legal excuse, and was cruel and savage in the last degree." The editorial asserted that the *Times* did not want to take "partisan advantage" of the riot, but it immediately proceeded to do so: "But we venture to ask all candid men whether the ruffians like Butler and his gang would have more or less license than now in South Carolina if Tilden and Hendricks were elected next Fall!"[15]

The *Times* continued this theme of connecting Hamburg to the election by using the headline "Democratic Campaigning," with the subhead "The Hamburg Massacre," over a story about congressional debate over keeping federal troops in South Carolina to deal with the race violence. In continuing coverage, the paper referred to the incident as a "massacre" instead of "trouble" or "disturbance," and on the editorial page it regularly flayed Democrats over Hamburg. The Democratic newspaper stories about the massacre were neither truthful nor believable, the *Times* wrote, and it was obvious that incidents like Hamburg would be used to keep blacks and Republicans from voting. The *Times* asserted its positions occasionally in a collection of one-paragraph comments in a column called "Notes of the Campaign." One such paragraph noted, "The negroes in Hamburg, S.C., are now very quiet—especially the dead ones."[16]

In the West, Kansas Republican papers were even more sensational in their demonization of southerners and Democrats in connection with Hamburg, which replaced the Little Bighorn as the top news story for a time. The *Lawrence Republican Journal* on July 28 reprinted the *Times* "The Old Rebel Spirit" piece but added a series of evocative subheads including "Honeycombed with Bullets," "Four Men Weltering in Their Own Gore," and "Some of the Bodies Mutilated."[17]

The mutilations conjured images of Custer's troopers, and newspapers like the *Chanute Times* in Kansas drew the comparison for the readers who could not make the connection on their own: "The two subjects which have most occupied the public mind for the last week, are the misnamed Custer massacre in Montana and the real Butler massacre in South Carolina," wrote a Washington correspondent under the byline "Life." The reporter argued that the Little Bighorn was brought about by a "rash and impetuous officer" who died in legitimate warfare, whereas Hamburg was perpetrated by "a cold-blooded devil incarnate" who encouraged the murder of defenseless men. "The Butler massacre, at Hamburg, has become significantly suggestive, by reason of its standing out so prominently in all its particulars. The usual cry of 'bloody shirt' is of no avail in covering up the enormity of the transaction. People stand aghast at such a display of horrid cruelty, and the question is asked, are we living in a Christian country, or in a land of fiends."[18]

"Fiend" was a word used frequently by Republicans to describe the Hamburg aggressors. For example, the *Atchison Daily Champion* in Kansas headlined Hamburg as a "Fiendish Massacre" with the subheadline that "The Rebel 'Chivalry' Surpass the Sioux." The story first appeared in the *Chicago Tribune* under the less dramatic headline "The South Carolina

Massacre," but the message was the same in all papers that carried it: the massacre was at least as bad as the Little Bighorn, and the federal government needed to step in. The story noted that some of the dead militiamen had been "mutilated with hatchets and bayonets, Sitting Bull fashion." Democratic newspapers that call for revenge against Sitting Bull should look to this story of white men massacring blacks, and the guilty should be punished. "If the state is powerless to arrest them, then the United States must do it."[19] The *Chicago Inter-Ocean* agreed, arguing that the Hamburg incident justified action by the federal government, else South Carolina would become "the theater of outrages matching in cruelty and horror the terrible Indian massacres on our Western frontier."[20]

The *Burlington Weekly Patriot* in Kansas also compared the southerners to the hostiles, noting that "the infuriated mob fell upon their fancied tormentors, the Negroes, disarming them and afterwards butchering them up in a manner that would shame even the bloodthirsty Indian." The *Patriot* claimed it would not blame all Democrats for the actions of a few, but it urged citizens to vote Republican—the party against violence— because "all Democrats are not disloyal, but all disloyal men are Democrats, therefore the party which contains this disloyal element should be mistrusted."[21]

The *Illinois Daily State Journal* claimed the racial fights in the South were worse than the Indian wars: "Talk as we may about the . . . atrocity of the massacre of soldiers by the Modocs or the Sioux, all the Indian massacres of the past few years have been paralleled by the assassination of unarmed colored men and others in the South within the same time." A news story on the same page of the *Journal* was headlined "Southern Tildenism," linking the atrocity to the election.[22]

Unlike the way they covered the Little Bighorn, most papers made an explicit connection between Hamburg and the election. The *Washington Republican* in Kansas, for example, sarcastically wrote in its own story, again headlined "Fiendish Massacre," that "another blow for Tilden was struck by the Democrats of a South Carolina town, named Hamburg," and that "the Southern Democracy can discount the Sioux."[23]

The *St. Louis Globe-Democrat* also used sarcastic humor when addressing Hamburg. A subhead of its main news story about the event mocked the southerners: "The Young Men of Augusta, Ga., Amuse Themselves with Slaughtering a Dozen or so of South Carolina Negroes." An editorial argued that the murders were obviously done to affect the election in that state just as violence had been used by Democrats in Mississippi the year before: "'To kill off the niggers,' is the shortest road to Democratic victory in the South."[24] The word "slaughter" was a favorite of *Globe-Democrat* headline writers and was used over both Indian fights and racial confrontations in the South, as in "Official Report of the Hamburg Slaughter" and "The Sioux Slaughter." The paper mocked Democrats for wanting to remove troops from the South to be sent to the West, arguing that most of the troops in the South were patrolling the Mexican border. The argument about troops was one the *Globe-Democrat* and many other Republican papers voiced repeatedly, denigrating the "silly story" that troops in the South were needed in the West: "There are 5,000 soldiers in the North; why not send those?" It was a simple argument made so often that it, too, resembled modern "talking points." For example, the *Chicago Inter-Ocean* mocked southerners "howling" about military oppression, noting that the number of soldiers per state was much higher in the North than in the South. "On behalf of the North, we howl," concluded the *Inter-Ocean*.[25] The *Illinois Daily State Journal* argued that troops were needed in the South in part to control local violence "to the eternal disgrace" of the instigators but were also needed for national defense: "The anxiety to get the troops, absolutely needed for the maintenance of our coast defenses, out of the way, and even to leave the Rio Grande border unguarded, is an indication of a deep and wicked purpose, to carry the Southern States for Tilden and Hendricks at the coming election at any cost, not even excepting assassination and the virtual inauguration of civil war."[26]

The *Globe-Democrat* also mercilessly mocked the claim of Mississippi congressman Lucious Q. C. Lamar, a former Confederate officer who said that southerners were prostrate and had no real power over their own states. "The people of the South may be prostrate as a general rule, but the experience of Hamburg shows that on a very trifling provocation they are capable of suddenly erecting themselves and depriving a great many of their oppressors not only of the rights of citizenship, but of life," the paper editorialized, using the terms of the Civil War. "Never since the rebels were restored to their forfeited rights by the clemency of the Republican party has there been a single instance in which an ex-rebel has been restricted in his political freedom. . . . The bloody shirt is an unwelcome exhibition at all times, but worn by Mr. Lamar its hypocrisy is as brutal as it is transparent, and before he flaunts it in Congress he should let the echoes of the Hamburg revolvers die away."[27]

When Democrats complained that black Democrats were intimidated by black Republicans from voting in the South, the *Globe-Democrat* doubted the claim. The simple solution, the *Globe-Democrat* argued, was to send more troops to the South to police the election since both parties now believed voter intimidation was a problem.[28]

One *Globe* rival, the *St. Louis Dispatch*, argued that southern Democrats had made a mistake by giving the Republican administration an excuse to send troops to the region: "In the name of all that is reasonable, what do they mean down in South Carolina and Georgia, to commence the work of slaughtering negroes now?" asked the *Dispatch* on July 14. "Have the Southern Democrats become the slaves of fate? Are they incarnations of folly? Of all things which they have it in their power to do, policy would dictate that this one thing ought not to be done. Count the Democracy 50,000 votes less in the North, and charge the number to the account of Hamburgh, South Carolina." The next day the *Dispatch* suggested that the violence would allow Governor Chamberlain to succeed in his request for federal troops: "The consummate folly of the unreasoning and vicious authors of that butchery is something past the comprehension of ordinary minds. The worst enemy of the Democratic party could not have desired for it a greater misfortune than the course pursued by some of its Southern adherents. . . . With a few more Hamburg affairs, to bear through the campaign, the last lingering hope which the Democracy may entertain of carrying the election will die."[29]

In Custer's hometown of Monroe, Michigan, feelings also ran high about Hamburg and the bloody shirt, although the incident did not push coverage of the Little Bighorn aside. The paper gave almost three full columns to coverage of local political speeches, one by Charles Rynd, a University of Michigan regent who abandoned any attempt at academic dispassion in addressing the election. "If the democrats were tired of hearing about the bloody shirt, they should stop making shirts bloody," the *Commercial* quoted Rynd as saying. "He believed that every man of whatever nationality, white or black, should receive the full protection of the law, but the democrat party did not believe in any such thing. They were in sympathy with oppression and wrong. They were preaching honesty, but they have been the most notorious thieves the world ever saw. For years and years they stole the earnings of human beings." The paper itself was one of the most strident in its condemnation of Hamburg, which it claimed Tilden would ignore if he were elected: "The fact is this was a political massacre pure and simple—a massacre of southern republicans by southern democrats—a political massacre in the interest of Tilden and 'reform.' It is the kind of bloody work that will be frequently perpetrated in the south, not only upon negroes but upon whites as well, if the democrats succeed to power, and if either blacks or whites dare to express a sentiment or to take any action in opposition to the democratic party."[30]

In the West, the *York Republican* in Nebraska agreed that more violence would occur if Tilden were elected. "The barbarities of this South Carolina [chivalry] are about on a par with the Black Hills Sioux," the paper editorialized, using terms sure to chill its readers. "And yet the whole of . . . Aiken have volunteered to defend these Hamburg murderers."[31]

On the West Coast, the *Alta California* of San Francisco also thought that the Hamburg incident was an atrocity, but its main complaint against Democrats was that they wanted to reduce the size of the army. The *California*, like many western papers, maintained heavy news coverage of the Little Bighorn and the Sioux war even when the story broke about Hamburg. On July 11 it published its first news of Hamburg—a paragraph in a column of briefs that noted dispassionately that "some of the prisoners" were shot. In contrast, the front page contained three stories on the Sioux war, including an interview with an Indian fighter in Salt Lake City who claimed he could raise five thousand volunteers. The paper did not put Hamburg on the front page until July 16, and then as the fifth subhead under a story about Congress. The fourth subhead reported the debate over reducing the size of the army. The fifth subhead noted, "Republicans Say No, and Point to the Late Massacre of Negroes in South Carolina." On page 2 the *California* editorialized against what it called "unreconstructed rebels," but it was most outraged at an incident in Plattsburg, Missouri, where some residents marched in the Fourth of July parade with a Confederate flag, "flaunting it in the faces of the people; bearing it through the streets and daring any one to attempt to cut it down. Even the Sheriff was not able to suppress this open and impudent act of treason."[32] No mention was made of the unreconstructed rebels in South Carolina who actually killed people.

On July 20 the *California* mentioned Hamburg in an editorial, but with more outrage about the effect the proposed reduction in the army would have on the Sioux war than about the South Carolina murders: "Had this Sioux uprising occurred in the South, as did the Chickasaw, Cherokee, Creek and Seminole wars, there would have come from every cotton and cane plantation, rice swamp, city, town and newspaper office a howl and yell, united call for vengeance, as ever run in the ears of the country during the war of the rebellion," the paper noted. "But the South is fortunately free from Indian troubles, and a President is to be elected, and the consequence is that the destruction of our little army, whether by Congressional action or the rifle of the Sioux, is a matter of almost indifference with the Democratic members."[33]

The next day the *California* again criticized Democrats over Hamburg, this time for using violence to win elections, and suggested that troops were needed in the South to keep order. "But can we call ours a Republican Government, although our Constitutions and Bills of Rights declare all men equal before the law, if one race are allowed year after year to carry elections by force, by reducing the majority of one race to a minority through violence, murder and assassination; or, through terror, deterring the more timid negro from going to the polls to vote? No wonder members of Congress who endorse this system of creating majorities, desire the United States troops withdrawn from the South."[34]

Some Democratic newspapers condemned the Hamburg Massacre, but Republican editors were usually suspicious of their motives. The *Atchison Daily Champion* in Kansas, for example, wrote that "the southern Democratic newspapers are sorry for it, but they are sorry because it has happened on the eve of a Presidential election, and their sorrow is not of that genuine kind which demands that compensation shall be made for this murder. They demand no punishment."[35]

For southern Democratic newspapers like the *New Orleans Picayune,* the Little Bighorn meant that troops stationed in the South should be sent west. The *Picayune*, which billed itself as the largest newspaper of the "Southwest," immediately called for troops to be taken out of the South and sent to the Indian war. In an editorial on July 7, the first day it reported the Little Bighorn, the *Picayune* lionized the Democrat Custer and criticized the Republican Grant administration: "General Custer was one of the most efficient and gallant officers in the service. . . . As a successful Indian fighter no man in the army had a better record." The U.S. Army was second to none in courage and discipline but was too small for the Sioux war. The war should be vigorously waged, but the *Picayune* doubted Grant would send the necessary troops: "The general election is near at hand, and a large number of troops will be needed to overcome the Conservative majorities in the Southern States. Gen. Custer has been already sacrificed, and the Republican party would prefer to see the whole army murdered in detachments to risking the results of a fair election."[36]

The *Picayune* followed with a lengthier editorial the next day, admitting that "even the Indians should not wholly be denied justice" in the sense that the corrupt Grant administration had "robbed" them, so they were not completely to blame for fighting. But the Little Bighorn debacle has now forced the government to use its army to protect "every immigrant, white, red or black," who wants to move west.[37]

But on July 10, Hamburg, which got two front-page stories, pushed the Little Bighorn off the *Picayune* front page. The first story contained a paragraph of boldface headlines telling the story from the white point of view: "Serious Trouble in Hamburg, S.C.—A Negro Military Company Defies the Law—They Provoke a Conflict and Intrench Themselves in a Building—Citizens lay Siege to the Intrenched Rioters." The second story reported the end of the incident, writing about the black militia as if it were a foreign army: "Further Particulars of the Riot—A Disastrous Termination—Several Negroes Killed—They are Dislodged from the Building—Prisoners Taken and Reported Shot—Many Escape to the Country."[38]

About a week later the *Picayune* devoted almost three full columns to a page 12 story reprinted from the *Charleston News and Courier*. The story was headlined "The Hamburg Butchery" and purported to be an unbiased "history" of the "shocking affair." The story did not cover up the killing of the prisoners, which a subhead called "Murdering the Prisoners," and it suggested that the whites used the buggy incident as a pretext to disarm the black militia. But the story justified the disarming, describing Hamburg as a haven for criminals: "That they [these negroes] were not fit characters to be entrusted with firearms is sufficiently well known and is granted on every hand. The town had become a rendezvous for the worst characters in the country, and nothing of property was safe within a radius of ten miles from the place, which was a city of refuge for the thieves and cut-throats of Augusta and elsewhere, all of whom [thought] themselves assuredly safe when . . . within the purlieus of their fortress and under the protection of its military and civil defenders." When the *Picayune* reported on July 19 that Chamberlain's request for federal troops was denied, its headlines revealed its glee at the news: "An Administration Snub for his Excellency" and "The Soldiers Needed to Fight Indians."[39]

Judging by its lack of coverage of the Sioux war compared to Hamburg, the *Picayune* did not care all that much about where the soldiers were needed as long as they were out of the South. Furthermore, the paper's main concern about what it called the "Hamburg Riot" was that it was being used as a way to "enfeeble the vigor" of the Democratic campaign by making Democrats "explain or defend" the episode. The *Picayune* defense was that such incidents were not widespread, and that the local residents brought the perpetrators to justice. Similar riots happened in the North and West, the newspaper asserted: "What would elsewhere be regarded as a circumstance for which neither the community nor the Government was responsible—one of those occurrences which may happen in the best regulated governments as well as families—would here be magnified into an evidence of rooted and active disloyalty. This violent discrimination of conclusions from similar events is the effect of the energetic handling of Southern affairs by a class of politicians whom the accident of war cast to the surface."[40]

The *Picayune* asserted that federal troops were not needed in South Carolina because local citizens could handle riots: "Gov. Chamberlain possessed all the requisite ability at home to preserve the peace of the State. The people had no sympathy with the affair at Hamburg, and he would have experienced no difficulty in raising any *posse* of citizens to restore quiet and arrest criminals." The paper accused Chamberlain of exaggerating the situation when he went to Washington to plead for troops: "Gov. Chamberlain has been to Washington and told his dismal tale, doubtless with all the embellishments an excited imagination could lend. South Carolina was in a state of revolt, and the carpet-bag Governor, true to the traditions of his party in the South, wanted troops to coerce them into docility. The troops were refused and South Carolina's

Executive was returned to his home with the salutary intimation that the constitutional method must be employed." The *Picayune*, however, was skeptical that the Grant administration would "consistently" uphold the constitutional rights of the states in an election year.[41]

The *Daily Constitution* of Atlanta, another large Democratic newspaper in the South, had coverage similar to that of the *Picayune*. The *Constitution* also first reported the Little Bighorn on July 7, but two days later it was giving the Hamburg fight equal billing on the front page. The Hamburg headline, "The Siege of Hamburg," was more dramatic than the Little Bighorn headline. A subhead shouted "The Negroes in Arms Across from Augusta." The Little Bighorn story's headline was a mere label—"Rosebud Valley"—followed by the subhead "The Excitement Incident to the Massacre of Custer's Legion."[42]

In a front-page editorial about Hamburg, the *Constitution* called the episode a "civil war" between the militia and the posse. "The facts are fully enough stated to show the lawlessness of the colored troopers and we are glad to know that there can be no lies plausibly told about it being a political persecution." But as more facts became available, the *Constitution* backed off on some of its sensational claims: "The unfortunate affair is deplored by all good citizens of both races, and there is deep regret that better counsels did not prevail. . . . The whites and blacks intermingled freely, there were deep regrets but no threats that blood had been shed and that lives were lost. There is no further trouble anticipated." The *Constitution* editorial admitted that from the first reports the riot appeared to be the type of incident that occasionally happens in the area—where the civil power has to use force to maintain order: "We hoped to receive confirmation of this intelligence so strong as to make it impossible for misrepresentation to feed its hungry and bloody maw upon the details of the unfortunate conflict. We print what has been received, but we are not ready to say that we feel satisfied with the information. That there will be greater conflict of opinion and statement concerning the matter than actually occurred in the riot, is already too well assured." But the *Constitution* asserted that it appeared the blacks did not start the fight, and it deplored the "gross outrageousness of the coercive warfare, as it was conducted by the outsiders." Unless the whites could prove there was a good reason for their conduct, "the public will hold them guilty of a great outrage."[43]

The *Constitution* occasionally ran front-page stories on the Sioux war through July, but much of its editorial page was spent arguing with northern papers about Hamburg. The paper chastised the *Washington Chronicle* for a headline about the riot that indicated Hamburg had started "The Campaign of Blood in the South." The *Chronicle* writer was "an able-bodied liar" who had written the story without waiting for all the facts to be determined, the *Constitution* asserted. "We know wrong was perpetrated in some things done at Hamburg, but we are inclined to believe if they had been done to the . . . liar of the above named paper they would have been supreme acts of justice." On the front page of the July 13 issue, the *Constitution* quoted two stories from the *Chronicle*, one that stated that Hamburg was "the usual killing of negroes previous to a presidential election" and one that mocked the "two scions of the first families" for starting the fight when they could not break the militia ranks with their buggy. The *Constitution* asserted that a man who would write the first piece was the sort who would swear "a damning shame upon his mother for a dollar," and the author of the second piece, "had he lived in Pilate's day, would have perjured himself for a dime by swearing a lie against the Lord." The "hired liar" who wrote the story did so before he knew the facts. "So ready a cur deserves having the city 'dog tax' on his worthless life paid a year in advance." The *Constitution* also quoted a *New York Herald* story that described Hamburg as being opposite Atlanta, a mistake that prompted the *Constitution* writer to urge the *Herald* to "cram in geography before it grinds out vituperations upon an innocent people."[44]

In a lengthy editorial on page 2 of the same issue, the *Constitution* argued in more detail with the *Herald* claim that violence like that in Hamburg would allow Republicans to raise the bloody shirt and win the election. The *Constitution* editorial acknowledged that it respected the opinion of the Democratic *Herald*, but that the riot in Hamburg was not related to the election and was no different from riots among miners in Pennsylvania. "Let the Hamburg riot be fully investigated. The state government of South Carolina is a republican one, and can surely be relied upon to make no partisan report favorable to 'rebels' and 'kuklux.' Until they have used all endeavors to do justice and punish crime, and have failed, stop this premature warfare upon the entire people of our section."[45]

Hamburg, by the middle of July, dominated the front page of the *Constitution* as well as the editorial pages. In fact, the paper sent its own reporter to Hamburg to cover the inquest into the affair. The first-person narrative of the inquest and a wire story about congressional debate about the riot took up almost a third of the front page on July 19 while news of the Sioux war was relegated to a brief on page 2. The narrative news story about the inquest contained detailed descriptions of the town, the judge, and the jury. The story was highly skeptical of the blacks and respectful of the whites. For example, the reporter described Rivers, the trial justice, as a political appointee without any ability: "His forehead recedes back considerably, and as his hair is cut very close, I noticed that the back of his head is rather pointed. A flat nose and dark skin show that he is an unadulterated specimen of his race, and lacking in the shrewdness and ability which so often characterized the mixed representatives of the two races. . . . Prince Rivers fails to impress the observer as being a negro of great intelligence or ability." The reporter was also unimpressed with the all-black jury, noting that "some are shiftless, ignorant-looking fellows," but admitted that they listened to the testimony closely and conducted themselves "with due propriety." In contrast, Butler's denial that he was at the scene when the prisoners were shot was reported without editorial comment.[46]

The *Constitution* rarely commented on the Sioux war other than to take brief one-paragraph shots at Grant or his son Fred. On July 18 it urged the president in a front-page paragraph to replace the 3,334 federal troops stationed in the South with volunteers so the regulars could go fight the Sioux. "Of course it would not be safe to leave the eleven turbulent states, filled as they are with warlike and savage races of barbarians, without bayonets of some kind," the Constitution wrote sarcastically. "Never mind the coming elections. You can't carry them anyway, Mr. Grant, without upsetting the republican cart this year in the northern states. The people of those states are finding out your tricks."[47]

The *Louisville Courier-Journal* editorialized that Hamburg "has furnished the Republican party with its favorite campaign material, and they began on Saturday to swing the bloody shirt in the halls of Congress." The paper admitted that the shooting of the black militiamen was "inexcusable" but argued that the militia companies were used to intimidate white voters and should be disarmed. Governor Chamberlain could use the state militia to put down any violence between the races but wanted federal troops to protect the Republican voters and preserve his radical government.[48]

The *Courier-Journal,* like the *Constitution,* frequently castigated northern newspapers for criticizing the South over Hamburg, and especially what it saw as the hypocrisy of their reaction to a riot in Newark, New Jersey. "The Newark affair, however, which resulted in the butchery of seven men, was only 'a dangerous exercise of authority,'" the paper wrote in sarcastic response to a *Pittsburgh Gazette* editorial. "If lynch law needs the attention of the secretary of war in one State, it needs his attention in all. There is no talk of sending troops to New Jersey, however." And according to the *Courier-Journal,* the *Boston Journal* was advocating the mob law it supposedly was against when it asked in an editorial why southerners did not just "string up the ringleaders" of the Hamburg riot. "The answer to this query is a very simple one. The southern Democrats are not running the government of the State of South Carolina, or they would see that the laws against mobs and lynching are promptly executed. The Radicals have possession of the State, but they have never been known to do anything to suppress mob law when a negro gets killed. On the contrary, in South Carolina and other Southern States where Radicalism prevails, bloody riots have been encouraged on the principle that the blood of a few negroes will greatly help the Republican party."[49] The *Courier-Journal* even taunted the Democratic *New York Herald,* which had criticized the Hamburg massacre. The Kentucky paper quoted the *Herald* coverage of a burglary/murder in New York and asserted, "When thieves and burglars in New York have got so strong that they 'can take the upper hand of society,' it is about time for the Herald to devote itself to the salvation of its immediate vicinity, instead of backing the Republican party in its bloody shirt crusade against the South."[50]

Through most of July the *Courier-Journal* regularly covered the Sioux war and in fact usually devoted more stories to the war than to Hamburg or related incidents. But toward late August, as the presidential campaign heated up and the Grant administration debated sending troops to South Carolina to stop the violence, the paper's columns became more excitable. They mocked the administration's order to send troops to the South instead of to the West because the order quoted a House resolution calling for the rights of all citizens to be respected as a reason for issuing it: "When the president and secretary of war have sufficiently enjoyed themselves over the grim joke they have perpetrated on the Democracy by punctuating their resolution with the point of a bayonet, it is to be hoped that they will discontinue their warlike designs on the citizens of our country, and permit General Sherman to send re-enforcements to the distressed handful of our worthy soldiers who vainly, against overwhelming numbers, are endeavoring to subdue 'the savages of the Western frontier.'"[51]

When the House passed a bill enlarging the army, the *Courier-Journal* argued that the troops were not necessary but that the Democratic congressmen had to vote for the bill or else be blamed for any defeat in the Sioux war:

> General Grant, as the chief of the Hayes conspiracy, is conducting his campaign on those rules of warfare which governed him during the war. It matters little to him how many black men in the South or white men in the West are sacrificed, so that the end is attained. If the Democrats had refused the additional troopers asked by the War Department we should have had another Custer slaughter planned and arranged by the president. Now that the lower house of Congress has, by furnishing the useless accession to the military establishment, cut the Central Republican managers off from their strategic opportunity to make capital for Hayes off the blood of the private soldier, Messrs. Morton, Chandler and Boutwell are driven back upon their old expedient of organizing a system of disturbance in the Southern States, having in view the use of the army as an intimidator and looking finally to a pretext for forcibly retaining possession of the Government in the event of Tilden's election.[52]

When it reported that the trial for the Hamburg cases was delayed until January, the *Courier-Journal* concluded that it could only mean "that the Republicans have squeezed out of the lemon all the campaign juice they can get. It is apparent that the trial, if [held] before the November election, would develop the fraudulent nature of the charges printed in the Republican newspapers. The great men who run the Republican party are unwilling to have a campaign lie spoiled. They are satisfied with the little capital they made out of the dead negroes at Hamburg."[53]

The *New York World* took the *Courier-Journal* arguments one step further. The *World,* like the Kentucky paper, called the troop order a "grim joke" but was even more emotional in its appeal to readers, arguing that sending the new troops to the South would expose the frontier army to another Little Bighorn. "This must, indeed, be sad consolation to the friends at home whose prayers go up night and morning for the welfare of those devoted men, of whose sacrifice they fear they may hear by every pulsation of the telegraph. Especially since they are now assured by the highest authority that no more relief or support shall be sent them, must their solicitude and apprehensions be immeasurably increased." The paper called the order "wicked" and claimed the American people had not "sunk so low in moral and political integrity" that they would tolerate such threat to self-government. "If this military order is sanctioned at the election in November next, then we set a precedent and authorize any ambitious ruler hereafter to use the army of the United States to perpetuate his power or to uphold his party."[54]

Although the *World* occasionally blamed the administration for "sending Custer's little band to death, while the bulk of the army was kept for dragooning the South,"[55] it reserved its most inflammatory copy and headlines for Hamburg and assorted racial troubles as the presidential campaign proceeded. "It seems pretty clear that parts of South Carolina are in a state of anarchy," the *World* wrote in a typical editorial. "The negroes under control of white politicians, who are anxious for bloodshed, in the belief that bloodshed at the South means Republican success at the North, are armed, aggressive and insolent. The whites, outnumbered but determined, are ready for resistance. . . . That ancient commonwealth, once a community proud, intelligent and law-abiding, is lapsing slowly but surely into riotous ruin. Something must be done to rescue it. How long will the Northern people continue to intrust the management of the nation to a party which breeds such calamities and threatens us with such catastrophe."[56]

Shrieking headlines also painted a portrait of chaos and approaching Armageddon. "Deeds of Negro Fiends," "A Black Reign of Terror," and "Negro Lawlessness" were typical headlines the *World* used to describe violence in the Hamburg area. The latter story included the subhead "Colored Ruffians Assault a Farmer's Wife and Wreck a Train." It told of various skirmishes and riots over the two incidents, in which one white man was wounded and six blacks killed, although it admitted "the city is full of rumors." The story was published on the front page next to a series of reports from the Indian war including a fight between Crook and the Sioux that resulted in about fifty casualties for both sides and the destruction of thirty-five Indian lodges. But this story was labeled simply "The Indian War," with one subhead explaining that it was from official reports of the fighting.[57]

For the *World,* the violence in the South was "The War of Races," as it titled a story about blacks arming themselves in Monroe, Louisiana. The Indian war, in contrast, was sometimes treated as insignificant. For example, on August 23 the *World* devoted one paragraph to an editorial about Sitting Bull possibly attacking Canadian Indians but spent more than a full column bloviating about Chamberlain's actions in South Carolina.[58]

The *World,* like many papers, had a schizophrenic attitude toward the southern violence that manifested itself in sometimes conflicting editorial positions. On the news pages it trumped up violence, but on the editorial pages it claimed there was no need for federal troops to keep the peace. The Indian war was sometimes used to support arguments about the use of troops but more often than not got lost in the debate over the southern violence. The *World* claimed the troop order should be parsed carefully by all Americans. "It is an order to hold all the troops not ready for Indian service in readiness to move," the *World* began its analysis. "As everybody knows, there is no war nor rumor of war, foreign or domestic, in the country. There is no legitimate use of troops anywhere in the country. What this order means, and all it can mean, is that the Administration means to use troops to prevent free elections in the Southern states."[59] But a reader analyzing this editorial as carefully as the paper analyzed the order would note that the *World* referred to "Indian service," not an Indian war, and that the paper believed there was no war in the country, which had to mean that the paper did not consider the western U.S. territories part of the country. Obviously the *World* coverage of the Sioux war indicated that its editorial writer knew there was fighting on the frontier, but the language used suggested that this was really small potatoes compared to the potential reopening of the Civil War in the South.

Although a Democratic newspaper, the *New York Herald* chastised what it variously called "white madmen," "scoundrels," "bullies," "brutes," and "roughs" who perpetrated the Hamburg Massacre. "Is it any wonder that peaceful men in the North mourn over this bloodshed and ask if there can be law and order where public opinion justifies these outbreaks?" the *Herald* asked when the riot was first reported. "We await with deep interest the full details of this new contest. So far as the report now goes it looks as if these Southern white madmen had resolved to elect Hayes and Wheeler. They are doing yeoman's service in Augusta. One or two Hamburg riots will settle the business."[60]

The *Herald* made no bones that the main significance of the Hamburg riot was its effect on the election. The subhead for an early story about the reaction in Washington said the story would explain the "Effect of the Outrage in a Political Point of View." The story noted that Democrats were split on how to react to Hamburg and that prominent Republicans would use it to push their agenda. "It appears here that the whites were the aggressors in every stage of the event. As the details become more certainly known it is apparent here that this affair is likely to have an important influence upon men of republican antecedents, who were moved to vote the democratic ticket. Such people ask what would happen in such a case if Governor Tilden were in the White House?"[61]

Unlike other Democratic papers, throughout its coverage of Hamburg, which was extensive and frequent, the *Herald* was usually sympathetic to southern blacks, who it argued were wrongly being accused of having a vicious nature. During the Civil War, blacks committed few outrages against their masters. "They are really a docile, affectionate race, as is shown by the patience with which they bore centuries of slavery and wrong."[62]

The *Herald*, despite its intense coverage of the Little Bighorn and the Sioux war, saw the racial and sectional strife that Hamburg represented as more important to the election than the issue of sending troops to the frontier. It argued that state militia should ideally handle problems like Hamburg but that the army might be needed in some cases: "Affairs like that at Hamburg, if they are to be repeated, make troops as necessary as the rebellious ideas of Sitting Bull; and if such massacres are encouraged the white men who promote them can only expect the treatment that is accorded to other savages." Like several other papers, the *Herald* called the administration's troop order a joke, but it argued that troops would not be sent South: "We regard this recent order as mere *brutum fulmen*— a harmless thunderbolt launched in too ready compliance with astute politicians, who did not wish their party to risk so tempting a chance to lash the democrats with a withe of their own cutting. We appreciate the joke, but are sorry that the President was complaisant enough to take part in it."[63]

Nevertheless, as the election drew near and troops were ordered South, like most papers the *Herald* became more strident, with stories comparing the arrest of South Carolina citizens by federal troops to despotic governments: "This is not Mexico; but these acts of Governor Chamberlain, this misuse of federal troops and federal power, would if continued four years longer, set us a long way toward Mexico. If it is granted that the political party which happens to possess the federal government may march its soldiers in the States for political purposes, then we have paved the way broadly for general civil disorder." Headlines about South Carolina shrieked "The Bayonet," "The Palmetto State: Democratic Leaders to Be Arrested on the Eve of the Election," and "The Enslaved State."[64]

From the time Hamburg was first reported until the election, the *Herald* never let up on its coverage of the riot, because it saw it as emblematic of the key issues facing the country. "We do not mean to let this matter drop," the *Herald* asserted in a July editorial nagging Chamberlain to push an investigation of the riot. "It is a crucial event. Here can be brought to light the truth about such outrages, and we can learn whether they happened because the republican State government fails to do its duty in punishing crime, or whether the white people are to blame. Riot and murder were done in open daylight by men who were neither masked nor unknown."[65]

≫→

Not all newspapers thought Hamburg was as crucial an event as the *Herald* portrayed it, and certainly over the course of the year more ink was spilled over the Little Bighorn than over Hamburg. The standards of news judgment applied; in general, the further from Hamburg, the less frequent or passionate the editorials about it. Nevertheless, Hamburg was more important than the Little Bighorn in election coverage because it involved the key issues.

Even in the Far West, in what could be considered the war zone, newspapers that were intimately familiar with the ferocity of the Indian campaigns were horrified by news of Hamburg. "If there is one person, whatever his political proclivities may be, who can read the accounts of these cold-blooded murders in the south without having his blood boil in his veins, he must be the possessor of more *sang froid* than usually falls to the lot of mankind," thundered the *Laramie Daily Sentinel*. "For the sake of humanity and credit of our common country, we should be glad to believe that the stories of these atrocities were false, or at least greatly exaggerated, but on the contrary the half is not told." The *Sentinel* then asked all Democrats, and particularly the editor of the local Democratic newspaper, if they would oppose federal troops being used to stop these "atrocities." Using the inflammatory language of the guerrilla operations of the Civil War, the *Sentinel* attacked its rival editor: "The Missouri bushwhacker who runs the Democratic organ and aspires to run the Democratic party of this Territory, probably sympathizes with, and may for ought we know, claim to belong to this southern chivalry, but we doubt if the Democrats generally will endorse or even attempt to apologize for the damnable outrages."[66]

Comparing coverage of Hamburg and the Little Bighorn shows that the latter was big news more because it was an interesting story rather than an impact story. Hamburg as a news story had less drama, but its meaning spoke deeply to the frightening, painful memories of the Civil War. The *Hartford Daily Courant* commented that it was always difficult to "exactly understand the work of the period" in which a person lives. But the paper suggested that history would ultimately judge the postwar years by one standard: "By and by, it may be in fifty years, it may be in a century, will appear in all its simple and grand proportions, the great struggle for the equal rights of man, regardless of color, which characterizes the third quarter of the nineteenth century in America. The work of this epoch will then be clearly seen, stripped of all its incidents of half-heartedness, of betrayal, of demagogism, of public and private corruption. What will history have to say of it?" The answer, the *Courant* suggested, would depend on whether the Republican party fought and won the election to stand up for the rights of blacks secured during the Civil War.[67]

Left unmentioned in the argument for equal rights for all men, regardless of color, were the rights of the so-called red man. The black men killed at Hamburg were seen as victims. The red men at the Little Bighorn were seen as enemy combatants. That fact created an obvious difference in the coverage of the two groups, but the native peoples were not without their supporters as journalists struggled with the dramatic questions of their epoch.

CHAPTER 6

"Asses Who Are Braying for Extermination"

The Indians in Little Bighorn Coverage

In the emotional reaction to the Little Bighorn, particularly the mutilation of the bodies of Custer's men, some journalists called the Indians monsters—literally. The Indians "have, of their own accord, thrown down the gauntlet, and seem willing to take the consequences," thundered the *St. Louis Dispatch*. "Their treatment of the dead whites after Custer's last battle proves that the Sioux have learned nothing from civilization. The same instincts, that found a home in the hearts of those savages when found on this continent, are alive today. . . . In a word, the 'noble red man of the forest' is a sarcasm on that sentiment, and since our efforts to domesticate him have proved futile, it would seem that the only recourse left is to declare the hostile element of this race dangerous to the lives and property of good citizens, and they should therefore be exterminated, as we would exterminate other vampires of the woods."[1]

The *Chicago Tribune,* although a loyal Republican paper, derided the administration's peace policy. Instead, it repeated a version of the famous quote—usually attributed to Phil Sheridan—to define a "good" Indian. "The best use to make of an Indian who will not stay upon a reservation is to kill him," the *Tribune* wrote chillingly. "It is time that the dawdling, maudlin peace-policy was abandoned."[2]

But the emotional sentiment was not universal. As Marc H. Abrams notes in *Sioux War Dispatches*, an alternate view at the time was that the Little Bighorn was a battle in a war, not a "massacre."[3] Even in the home city of Sheridan's military headquarters, the press disagreed with the general's quote. The *Chicago Times* took issue with its rival *Tribune* and other papers around the country in a detailed analysis that presented what its headline called "Facts for the Serious Consideration of the Asses Who Are Braying for Extermination." The article, which took up most of the front page of the July 22 issue, traced the history of Indian warfare from colonial times to the present campaign and concluded that "the aggressive policy of the Anglo-Saxon has resulted in almost innumerable wars." Sitting Bull's "nomadic bandits" have been a source of trouble, the *Times* admitted, yet the whites had cheated the Indians and still owed the Sioux money from a previous treaty. The *Times* reported lengthy statistics on the achievements of the tribes in the Indian Territory and concluded that "enough has been given to demonstrate that TO KILL AN INDIAN is the poorest use he can be put to, and that his civilization is something which can be accomplished."[4]

The irascible publisher of the *Times,* Wilbur F. Storey, had been a supporter of the rights of American Indians dating back to the 1850s, when he owned the *Detroit Free Press.* Storey, however, was consistently hostile to the rights of blacks, who he believed were "not ready for freedom." He often used racial slurs in his headlines about blacks, and his stories about the Little Bighorn sometimes called the Indians "fiends" because he believed nonreservation Indians like Sitting Bull were "bandits."[5] His attitude was much more sympathetic toward peaceful Indians. Storey could not be neatly classified in his attitudes toward human rights in general and Indians in particular. In that sense, his coverage was emblematic of Little Bighorn coverage in the American press as a whole, which included a wide range of opinion on what almost everyone called "the Indian problem."

Historian John Coward notes in his book on Indian war reporting that there were four main attitudes toward Indians in the nineteenth-century press—extermination, war short of genocide, removal to reservations, and assimilation—ideas so common that they were found in newspapers of all regions of the country and were not mutually exclusive.[6] In other words, editors like Storey could recommend defeating Sitting Bull's band but at the same time recognize Indians' rights and recommend that they be taught to adapt to modern civilization in order to survive.

Editors also expressed a variety of opinions on who was to blame for the Sioux war, although they were almost universally united in their opinion that the government had no choice but to win the war. In that sense, the press reaction to the Little Bighorn was similar to its reaction to other attacks on the nation, like Pearl Harbor or 9-11, both of which inspired an outpouring of support for the military, retribution against the enemy, and complete victory in the war. Winning the Great Sioux War by the definition of nineteenth-century editors almost always entailed confining the tribes to reservations until they were assimilated into society. Editors, however, disagreed frequently on how to assimilate Indians and indeed whether they were capable of assimilation at all or would simply die out as a race.

Calls for extermination in newspapers were not always racially based but rather can be better understood as a continuation of the hard war attitudes formed during the Civil War, when widespread guerrilla fighting contributed to calls for extermination from both North and South. Guerrilla fighting occurred throughout much of the country, and not just in border states like Missouri, where the ferocity of the fighting included at times scalping and mutilating corpses as in the Indian wars. Indeed, guerrilla raids, like the sacking of Lawrence, Kansas, were sometimes referred to in the press as massacres. Union forces retaliated with brutal raids of their own wherever guerrillas were a problem, leading one resident of Greensboro, North Carolina, to say that the Yankees "would exterminate our race if they could." The rebel civilian was not wrong about the sentiments of some federal officers. Gen. Edward R. Wild, who burned homes, executed prisoners, and took women as hostages, told his superior officer that his tactics would "exterminate" the guerrillas. And one Illinois soldier serving in Mississippi wrote that "confiscation and extermination is our motto."[7] When Lincoln was shot at the end of the war, some southern papers rejoiced, and the *Texas Republican* wrote that the president was a "tyrant" who had waged a war of "subjugation and extermination."[8]

It is important to note that the main developers of the hard war tactics of taking the fight to civilians were Grant and Sherman. Sheridan and Custer were the tip of the spear in implementing these tactics in the Shenandoah Valley, where they hung some captured guerrillas and destroyed farms throughout the region. Since these tactics, including Sherman's infamous march to "make Georgia howl," had helped win the war, it would be ridiculous to expect journalists, many of whom covered the war or fought in it, to condemn harsh tactics used against the Indians or express sympathy for the groups they considered the enemy. Furthermore, Indian fighting was often considered a war of "exterminate or be exterminated." For example, the *New-York Daily Times* described Sioux motivation for attacks on settlers in Iowa and Minnesota in 1857 as "a war of extermination on our North-Western frontiers."[9]

The same type of thinking was prevalent in 1876, including in two of the main St. Louis dailies. In an editorial discussing the history of the peace policy, the *Dispatch* argued that continuation of the policy would lead to the killing of all white settlers: "The Quakers have been particularly officious as the advocates of peace. Their policy has been experimented upon, but like all other theories has failed. People who live far from the scenes of Indian vengeance, the bloody work of his tomahawk and scalping knife, are not the safest or most intelligent counselors. If their line of policy were observed, settlers upon the borders of western civilization would become the indiscriminate subjects of savage cruelty—if not total extermination." The *Globe-Democrat* likewise opined that "it is very hard to think of the extermination of a tribe of Indians, but it is still harder to think of white men being exposed to extermination by a tribe of Indians whose intervals of murder are passed under the security of the Government, and feeding and fattening at the expense of the white men. Of the two alternatives, we decidedly prefer the extermination of the Indians."[10]

The word "extermination" was a popular description for any type of fierce fighting long before Custer's Last Stand. Nevertheless, editors called out the old war horse and whipped it vigorously immediately after the news of the Little Bighorn. Others used similar terms like "annihilate" or "wipe out." Such editorials could be found in newspapers throughout the country and reflected the views of many. A *New York Herald* correspondent wrote that the Little Bighorn had generated more anger at Indians than the murder of Gen. Edward Canby during peace negotiations with the Modocs in 1873: "As the details of the fight come to hand they arouse the most intense and indignant feelings of resentment against the Indians and the so-called peace policy of dealing with them. Even prominent officers of the War Department have not hesitated to pass severe strictures upon the President and his advisors for the encouragement which they have given to the farce and hypocrisy of the peace movement. . . . It is not too much to say that the prevailing feeling favors the policy of extermination."[11]

In Illinois, the *Peoria Daily Transcript* explained in an editorial appropriately headlined "How to Avenge Custer" that the government should recruit frontiersmen to deal with the hostiles. "So far as this tribe is concerned, the policy of the government ought to be complete extermination. . . . To adopt this course would doubtless be to sacrifice some substantially innocent persons, but this is not a case where it is possible to deal with individuals. These wild Indians will not be civilized. That experiment has been fully tried with them. Let the word be no more Indian massacres, and no more Indian wars, because there will be no more Indians." The *Ottawa Republican* noted that Custer's command "was exterminated" and then suggested that the country wanted the same thing for the Indians: "The feeling of the country in regard to this unlooked for disaster is one of intense bitterness towards the savages. The belief being general that nothing short of the partial or total extermination of the roving bands will affect a cure."[12]

Texans, who were still engaged in active Indian warfare, took the Little Bighorn news personally. The *Galveston News* boasted that Texans could avenge Custer: "Following the humiliating lesson just taught the government by the Sioux, should a call be made for troops equal to the emergency, Texas could furnish a regiment of men inured to the sort of service required, and nothing would suit the frontiersmen better than an opportunity to pay back, with interest, the heavy obligations laid on them by the murderous Indians. . . . Give Texas a fair show at the exultant Sioux, and there will be consternation and mourning in their wigwams before many moons have passed. The red devils must be wiped out or reduced to complete impotency, and Texans are the men to do it. Only give them a call."[13]

Another southern newspaper did not offer volunteers but did suggest the same solution, albeit in reluctant tones. The *New Orleans Picayune* expressed some sympathy for the Indians, writing that the war was not the fault of the tribes alone: "The Indian has been cajoled, and robbed, and starved, while the satellites of the Government under the Delano administration fattened on the plunder on his misery, and his final resentment was but the logical result of continued ill usage and broken faith." Nevertheless, the *Picayune* argued that the day of making treaties was over and that the government should do whatever necessary to make the frontier safe: "If the hostility of the Indian to the white settler is such as cannot be appeased, there is nothing left apparently but a war of extermination, should such an extreme course be forced upon the consideration of the Government by the savagery of the Indian foe."[14]

In Topeka, *The Commonwealth* story "Our Trouble with the Sioux" called for destroying the hostile tribes: "The war which has gone on for fourteen years ought to be brought to a swift conclusion, and the policy this time should be no treaty, no yielding of a foot of land, nothing but war, till the Sioux nation is nothing but a recollection." Farther west in the Dakota Territory, the *Black Hills Pioneer* in Deadwood City called for local volunteers to fight the Sioux, asserting that such outfits do better against the Indians than the regular army: "There is but one sentiment on the Indian question here—the hostile Sioux should be exterminated, and white men engaged in trading ammunition to them should be hung wherever found. Let the Government call out a Black Hills Brigade and put it in the field, and the efficacy of carrying out this policy would soon be made apparent."[15]

It is important to note, however, that the policy recommended by the *Pioneer* advocated extermination of the *hostile* Sioux, not all Sioux, and certainly not all Indians. Most of the hyperbolic language published after the Little Bighorn included some type of caveat like that used by the *Pioneer* and emphasized winning the war as the ultimate goal. Innocents would be hurt, but as in the Civil War that was acknowledged as the price of victory. It did not mean killing every Indian or taking no prisoners. Even the *Bismarck Tribune,* published by Custerphile Lounsberry, who was himself a wounded Civil War veteran, tempered its bloodthirsty call for all-out war. Lounsberry's headlines over a Little Bighorn news story succinctly described his reaction: "Now It's Business," "No More Foolishness," and "Troops and Supplies Enroute." Lounsberry advocated waging a "vigorous" war in an accompanying editorial whose headline challenged "What Will Be Done about It?" "Wipe out all treaties, rub out all agencies and reservations, and treat the Indians as they are, criminals and paupers. Feed those that justice to distressed humanity requires should be fed; hang or shoot the murderers, whose crimes are clearly proven; confine those who deserve punishment of a less degree; give the remainder the chance that white men have to gain land, property or a living, and hold them accountable to the same laws that white men and negroes are required to respect, or cause them to suffer the consequences of a violation of those laws." Lounsberry claimed that he was not an "Indian hater" but believed those who commit crimes should be punished.[16]

Editors who claimed to be friends of the Indians argued that this "tough love" of defeating them militarily and forcing them onto reservations was ultimately the best thing for them. The *Omaha Herald* wrote that the scope of the Little Bighorn battle meant neither side would stop fighting until there was total defeat: "As a friend and defender of this perishing race, we see no other way to solve this part of the Indian problem except through cruel rigorous war." The *Herald* argued that the Sioux would have to be moved out of the Black Hills because the gold rush meant they would never live in peace there. "The Sioux Indian cherry is a large one, but the country has reached a point where it would be folly to make two bites of it," the *Herald* wrote, explaining that wise Indian leaders must acknowledge the inevitable and seek the best terms they could get. "This done, and the best welfare of the red man will be gained, the future civilization of the continent assured, and the Indian, hunted down no longer by the merciless spirit of the superior race, will be allowed the poor privilege of perishing in peace."[17]

Many editors around the country urged the United States to show mercy. The *Missoulian,* a newspaper so close to the seat of war one would think it would urge extermination, in fact warned against it: "A radical change in government policy seems to be now demanded in dealing with the savages." The paper then called for terms that would have been familiar to any reader who knew what made Unconditional Surrender Grant famous when he won his first major Civil War victory at Fort Donelson: "They extend no quarter and take no prisoners; but they are wily enough and have sufficient knowledge of our magnanimity to surrender when their annuities are spent and they are overpowered in numbers. It is not necessary for us to become savages by pursuing a war of extermination; but the government should demand an unconditional surrender with all that is implied by that act. The Indians should be thoroughly and forever disarmed and put to agricultural pursuits. The attempt to civilize Indians and repress disorders, while allowing them to pursue a life of vagabondage, is one of folly."[18]

The attitude of some western papers defied stereotype, including their condemnation of false reports about Indian raids. Elmo Scott Watson, one of the earliest Indian war press historians, claimed that much news about Indian fighting in western papers was "propaganda" to get more troops for "threatened" areas to boost the economy.[19] But a reading of area newspapers after the Little Bighorn showed the opposite: editors feared panic over Indian fighting would ruin their fledgling communities. For example, the *Laramie Sentinel* wrote that newspapers that reported rumors about Indian raids "would keep money and business out of a locality, or deter visitors from coming there," and were untrustworthy. A follow-up editorial mocked anyone taken in by the rumors:

> We are having our periodical Indian scare, which comes around as regularly as the ague on the Maumee. "Tenderfeet" and nervous, hysterical women are the only ones afflicted with it to any serious extent. We are really sorry for them. For the weak-brained sensation loving local who helps it along for the sake of a little temporary, cheap notoriety, we have no feeling but that of contempt. To the timid ones we beg leave to say that there is not, and has not been, a hostile Indian on the whole Laramie plains this year, and wont be one. All the reports gotten up about them are either pure fabrication, or have no better foundation than a band of elk, two or three hunters or herdsmen, a gang of tramps, or a party of children out hunting strawberries.[20]

In fact, John Wallace (Captain Jack) Crawford, a miner, army scout, and correspondent for the *Omaha Daily Bee,* wrote in a story published before the Little Bighorn that a businessman in the Dakota Territory urged him to "not say anything about these Indian scares; it will injure the country." But Crawford assured his readers that he would tell the truth about the dangers in the territory, "and when I hear of any scalping or horse-stealing, I will let you know, for I want no man, woman or child to ever say that I kept back information that would have saved a single life."[21]

Eastern newspapers like the *New York World* did not worry about panicking their readers over local raids, but the editors did fret that the shocking news of the Little Bighorn would stoke the fires of vengeance. The *World* blamed Grant and the Republicans for mismanaging Indian policy and predicted dire consequences: "To those who have looked with hope to the establishment of a true peace policy, the results of the counterfeit will be a matter of especial grief; for in the face of the present disaster there will be less inclination among the people to consider what may be done for the future welfare of the Indians, than what may be done for immediate revenge. We fear the nation will now rush from the policy of civilization to the policy of extermination." The public anger was misplaced, the *World* argued in an editorial a week later, after reports were published that the Indians were well armed with rifles and ammunition they received from their agents, who made a lot of money from the government. "The 'peace policy' is, happily, abandoned forever," the *World* concluded. "The Custer massacre has effectually estopped that absurdity. But before we exterminate the Indians, let's begin with the agents. After they are eliminated we can more readily dispose of their customers." The *World* did not mean all Indians, but rather the hostile tribes embodied by Sitting Bull's band. A subsequent editorial noted that one government official said the choice was to either feed the Indians or fight them. "He advises the former method as the cheaper of the two, and we suppose it will be adopted so far as the friendly Indians are concerned. As for Sitting Bull, he repudiates all compromise. Therefore, as we cannot give him bread, we are forced to give him bullets."[22]

All the ink and talk about using bullets on the Indians prompted Wendell Phillips, a human rights activist with a long record of fighting for civil rights for minorities, to write a widely published open letter to Sherman accusing him and the press of encouraging public support for extermination. According to Phillips it was widely believed that the Indians had been cheated and abused by the white man, and he quoted some of Sherman's own statements that agreed with that position. He demanded that Sherman publicly address whether or not he supported extermination as official military policy. "If, indeed, this is the counsel you give from your high place then, for the sake of the Christianity which we profess and that civilization we claim, I wish it understood that one, at least, of your fellow citizens believes that you misrepresent the army, whose best officers have often protested against our heinous injustice to these wards of the nation, and that you . . . disgrace the post Washington once filled and the uniform that Thomas, Greene and Hamilton have worn."[23]

The *New York Herald,* which prominently published Phillips's letter under four headlines, agreed with him that the white man had wronged the Indians but stated that Phillips did Sherman "an injustice" by accusing him of favoring extermination. "There are a few people on the frontier who hold this most extreme notion and think the only good Indian is a dead one," the *Herald* admitted, but it argued that this feeling had to be understood in the context of the atrocities committed by Indians against frontier communities. Still, the *Herald* declared that the United States was a Christian nation and should treat the Indians with mercy and according to the rules of war: "But our duty now is to end this Indian business. We do not mean to kill the Indians or to impose any privation upon them. Even if we were to capture Sitting Bull, Rain-in-the-Face or any of the chiefs who warred upon Custer, we should advise no policy of vengeance or retaliation." The best way to end the business, the *Herald* concluded, was to field an army large enough to force the hostiles onto a reservation where they could "pursue the avocations of civilized life" and where the military could watch over them. "This is the only way to settle the Indian question. It will prevent those perfidies on the part of traders and irresponsible agents of which Mr. Phillips complains. It will prevent those atrocities toward settlers which every year shock the country. It will give peace to the red man and the white and enable us to go on in the work of developing and extending our civilizations."[24]

The *Herald* compared the war to British efforts in India to stop practices like "widow burning and child killing" and argued that American Indians must be taught civilized practices. "That is our duty, and the government cannot discharge it with too much loyalty. The whole question has become one of barbarism against civilization. Our first duty is to defend ourselves by an aggressive and vigorous war. Our next duty is to bring every Indian under the beneficent influence of the laws. Let us prosecute the war so that we may have a lasting peace."[25]

In fact, the *Herald* opinion—in favor of a tough, quick prosecution of the war, forcing the hostiles onto reservations where they could be assimilated—was the majority opinion in U.S. newspapers. The foremost advocate of this idea and the most optimistic of its success was the Indian-friendly *Chicago Times.* A July 23 editorial asked plaintively "What is an Indian?" The *Times* answered that Indians were no more ferocious that whites: "Our late civil war, in the matter of atrocities, long continuance, and the number of slain, eclipses any war ever waged by Indians on this continent." In fact, Indians were the equal of or superior to whites in terms of agriculture, hunting, fishing, craftsmanship, leadership, warfare, and diplomacy. The *Times* editorial described the Indian talent in detail in each of these fields: "As natural orators, the Indians have no superiors among the white races. They are eloquent, poetical, fervid, and persuasive. In the arts of diplomacy, the Indian is gifted by nature and education. This has repeatedly been shown in the alliances formed between tribes long unfriendly, and well illustrated last fall by the visit of the Sioux chiefs to Washington." The *Times* claimed that the problem throughout the nation's history was that whites never accorded the Indian consistent, equal status:

> He is not a citizen, nor a foreigner, not an alien, not an ally; at least he is none of these continuously. When we want to get his lands, then we call him a foreigner, and his tribe a nation, and proceed to make a treaty, as we do with Russia or Spain. If another country wishes to regard the tribe, as a nation, and the land it occupies as its territory, we at once object. When it is our selfish policy to regard an Indian tribe as a nation, we so regard it till we get what we want. Having obtained what we want, we call the Indians "red devils," whom we have the right to treat as we choose, and claim the right to prevent other people from interfering with them. Our system of jurisprudence has established the legal status of everything that is animate or inanimate except an Indian. The nation mourns the loss of the brave Custer and his band, but few stop to inquire on whose hands the stain of their blood rests. Who stops to calmly inquire into the causes of the war with the Sioux while the people demand that the "red devils" be exterminated? What is an Indian? No one can answer the question.[26]

Times rival *Chicago Inter-Ocean* argued that the answer to the Indian question was gun control. In an editorial headlined "Disarm the Indians" the *Inter-Ocean* asked, "Why are the Indians allowed to bear firearms?" The rationale for the government to give Indians guns is that it allows the Indians to hunt, but Indians had subsisted just fine before they had modern weapons, the paper argued. "In a civilized society the carrying of deadly weapons is frequently prohibited, and good citizens bow cheerfully to a regulation which they see is for the common good.

It is certainly no worse to deprive savages of the power to kill than it is to deprive civilized men of a like power; and especially is this so if the former are furnished with the necessaries of life by the latter, and enabled to subsist without personal effort. We owe a certain duty to the Indians, but we also owe a duty to ourselves and to our defenders, and the solution of this problem of Indian massacres seems so simple that the wonder grows why it has not been adopted."[27]

The *New Orleans Picayune* wrote that the simple solution was training the Indians to be farmers. The paper's earlier call for extermination proved to be rhetorical hyperbole apparently written in the emotion of first hearing the news of the battle. A few weeks after the Little Bighorn was first reported, the *Picayune* argued for transferring the supervision of Indians from the Interior Department to the War Department for their own protection. There were only two ways to deal with the Indians, the *Picayune* argued, "inspire them with proper fear of the strength of the white man, and . . . engender respect by a manly fulfillment of pledges." Since the Indians had been constantly cheated under the Interior Department, the best idea was to place them under the control of the War Department. "This presents the double advantage of a full exercise of the troops in keeping the Indians within the reservation and in the presumable honesty and principle of soldiers in the distribution of supplies. There is little danger that they will rob the Indians and compromise the nation for their own enrichment, as in the Department of the Interior, as it exists, and the protection of the Indian would be incalculably less expensive and less burdensome on the Government."[28]

When the government sent peace negotiators to meet with the tribes, the *Picayune* hoped they would be successful: "Certainly there is little glory to be gained for the United States in warring upon the Indians, even if the war resulted in their final extermination. Especially is this the case when the aggressions of the savages have been provoked by bad faith on the part of the Government." The *Picayune* argued that it would be better for the Sioux if they gave up the Black Hills and moved to the Indian Territory, because the latter had superior farmland: "The territory itself is secured to the Indian people. Association with the Indian tribes already settled in that country, who have more or less adapted themselves to a civilized mode of life, will also be likely to have a beneficial effect in reclaiming the savage Sioux. The friends of civilization everywhere would doubtless hail with satisfaction an arrangement of this nature, which will be calculated to put a peaceful termination to this embarrassing and vexatious question."[29]

The *New York Times* agreed that Indians could be taught to adapt to white civilization. One editorial noted the success of a program to teach Indians to work in factories and to have their own home gardens. The story described a modern village including a steam-powered sawmill completely operated by Indians. "When it was considered what these savages had been a short time before, the whole village was a remarkable scene of industry, good order and budding civilization." The editorial admitted that Sitting Bull's tribe would be "difficult subjects" but thought that they could also benefit from this system.[30]

On the Kansas frontier, the *Burlington Weekly Patriot* noted that what to do with the Indians was "a most vexed question." The paper criticized easterners for having a romantic view of Indians that they imagined after reading novels and poems like Longfellow's *Hiawatha*. "Their ideas, therefore, are of the highly classic mould, and would vanish directly at sight of a greasy, dirty Osage or Soux brave." But, despite the tough talk, the *Patriot* advocated a radical solution:

> We believe the true policy to pursue with the Indian is to make him ame-
> nable to the same laws as the whites are. Make him by proclamation or
> statute a citizen of the Republic, at once to enjoy the same privileges and
> subject to the same restrictions that surround other citizens, and do away
> with this farcical wardship that has been practiced so long and at such
> frightful cost. Give him the same right to enter or homestead his hundred
> and sixty acres of land that the white man or the negro has, and then if
> he does not choose to avail himself of it, make him submit to the occu-
> pancy of the soil by those who do choose. If numbers of them attempt to
> assemble for riotous or unlawful purposes, disperse them or arrest and
> punish them the same you would a party of white or black rowdies.

The *Patriot* did suggest that those who did not follow such a policy should be dispatched to the "happy hunting grounds of their forefathers" or to prison, but it noted that those were the same punishments for white and black criminals. In advocating citizenship for Indians, this dramatically written story was about fifty years ahead of its time.[31]

Most newspapers, regardless of the region of the country they served, expressed this sort of conflicted opinion. They would advocate a vigorous war but include a tinge of reluctance that it was necessary. In New England, the *Hartford Daily Courant* captured this feeling well in an editorial that admitted the Indians "had been provoked by a most wanton and inexcusable breach of faith," and that Custer himself was to blame for the gold rush into their lands that had now created a long war. "Nothing remains now but to make an energetic campaign against the Sioux, and to chastise them into obedience and peace. The subject of their grievances must now be postponed until they have been taught that they can have no grievances which will justify them in resorting to the war-path."[32]

Regardless of their position on the war, most newspapers, like the *Courant*, acknowledged the Indian side of the story. The *New York Times* blamed whites for the war: "It may be hard to confess, in the presence of the heroic dead, but they were killed because the nation, in its greed, had cheated these savage tribes." The *Times* argued that Sitting Bull and his followers had never agreed to the treaty confining them to areas west of the Missouri River, and that railroads, miners, and military survey expeditions had frightened away the game they depended on. "We disregarded these wrongs, though the other side had not assented to the treaty. We notified the chiefs that they would be treated as enemies unless they removed to the new reservations. The wild leaders, embittered by a sense of their wrongs, burst into war, or more correctly resisted invasion—and on the late occasion only too successfully." In a subsequent editorial, the *Times* blamed all branches of the government and the population as a whole for the war. "We are all sinners in the matter. We have sowed dishonesty and injustice, and are reaping disorder and bloodshed."[33]

The concept of sin and the question of how a Christian nation should treat the Indians was a common theme in the secular press and, of course, in the religious press. A Presbyterian newspaper in Kentucky argued that the Little Bighorn was God's punishment for white men's sins against the Indians. "Our sympathies are with the Indians. They can [be] civilized—some of them have been. They have souls and can be saved—many of them have been saved, and the Gospel is the power of God. Keep whiskey and white scoundrels away from them, and use the Army, not to butcher them, but as a police force to govern and protect them."[34]

Another Kentucky newspaper, the *Owensboro Examiner,* wrote that the Indians at the Little Bighorn were defending their land and doing their duty, just like the white soldiers. "In the past but little respect has been paid to treaties made with our red neighbors, whenever the cupidity or rapacity of the white man required their violation. This is not right, and if the Indian is ever to be civilized and Christianized, he should be dealt honestly with by the white man."[35]

Although the *Louisville Courier-Journal* mocked the *Inter-Ocean* editor for suggesting gun control, noting that "it evidently has not occurred to this pundit that the disarming of ten thousand Sioux warriors, who have had a taste of blood, involves, no little difficulty," the paper blamed the whites for the war. In an editorial headlined "The True Issue," the *Courier-Journal* argued that the Indians left the agencies because they were starving from inadequate rations provided by the Indian Bureau. "Had the Indians been properly fed it is certain that they could have been kept quiet until some honorable arrangement could have been made for the transfer of the reservation to the Government." The paper admitted that the 1868 treaty giving the Sioux the Black Hills was a mistake, but, nevertheless, the government must act in good faith: "It involves the expenditure of a great deal of money to feed these red wards, but we have got their land and are duty bound to give them a quid pro quo as long as they continue to live, and as long as treaties are ratified with them."[36] According to the *Courier-Journal,* the case of who was right was clear: "The Indians observed their part of the treaty by withdrawing their opposition to the railroads and remaining on their reservations, which fact is stated in the Indian Commissioner's report for 1874. The United States, however, did permit and encourage white men not only to pass through the reservation set apart by the treaty of 1868, but sent an army to punish the Indians for resisting the open violation of the treaty on the part of the Government."[37]

Like other papers, the *Courier-Journal* asserted that Indians should be treated fairly, which was the crux of its argument for transferring Indian agencies from the Interior Department to the War Department, where "there will then be some possibility that both Indian and whites will have equal and exact justice administered to them." The *Courier-Journal* argued with the *Detroit Free Press*, which had stated that because of the status of the Indian tribes there was technically "no law to punish an

Indian for murdering a white man." The *Courier-Journal* pointed out that such a law would not be necessary "if, at the start, there had been a law to punish a white man for murdering an Indian."[38]

The *Baltimore American* noted that Indians were not the only ones who committed savage crimes, using the famous Missouri James gang of bank robbers and the Hamburg fight as examples: "The Missouri robbers and the South Carolina murderers in some respects have not the excuses that might be made for Sitting Bull. He, at least, was fighting, as the long-established customs of his race taught him, for his own rights and on his own land, against those who had come to dispossess him of both, whilst in the other cases the robbery and murders were committed by those who at least profess to be subject to the laws of civilization."[39]

The *Hartford Daily Courant* blamed lawless miners for the Little Big-horn: "There are many persons who believed that the Indians are as much sinned against as sinning in their present act of hostility to the white man. Promises made to them have been constantly broken. They have been driven from their lands as often as the demands of 'civilization' could be made to require. New reservations have been allotted to them with solemn promises that here they could remain undisturbed, but the restive and lawless frontiersman has been on their path before the ink of the treaty was dry." Still, the *Courant* believed the hostiles should be punished severely and reported in a subsequent editorial that many people in Custer's hometown were "in favor of the utter annihilation of every red devil on the face of the globe who is not civilized" and then added that the last four words were not needed.[40]

A few weeks later, however, the *Courant* softened its stance and again blamed greedy miners for provoking the tribes: "Behind the problem of the government management of the Indians is always the fact that the crowding whites want every desirable bit of land that the Indians claim. And a century of experience with the savages has taught us no better method than alternately crowding them and fighting them. Treaties are only truces."[41]

In August the *Courant* expanded on that theme in a much lengthier editorial that claimed the treaty system was a "mistake" and would ultimately lead to the extermination of the Indians. The supplies provided to the Indians under the treaty system encouraged idleness and gave them the wherewithal to wage war against the whites.

No one, it seems to us, can uphold our present policy on the score of humanity. Its fruits are alternate massacres on either side; and under it the Indian is actually disappearing as fast as if we waged such a war of extermination as the Michigan settlers waged on the wolves. It would be better for the Indians and for us if we said to them:—"We do not recognize either your independence nor any paramount right in the soil. You may stay where you are and live as you please, provided you are peaceful and make no war on civilization. If you can't get a living by hunting and fighting your neighbors, then go to work; come within the lines of protection, and occupy and cultivate land, every family of you can have a quarter section. We will do no more to feed or clothe you than any other settlers, but we will aid you by all the encouragements of our civilization to earn your own living. If you will be idle, you shall have no help. If you won't behave, you shall be punished."[42]

The *Courant,* like most newspapers, distinguished between the hostile, or "wild," tribes, often represented in stories by Sitting Bull's band, and peaceful tribes. John Coward notes in his book on press coverage of Indians in the nineteenth century that "the evolving national myth of white dominance and manifest destiny" required both villains and heroes, and that the press used Custer and Sitting Bull to fit those respective roles in its coverage of the Little Bighorn. An example of the *Courant* using Sitting Bull for the villain role occurred when it reported that the public was confused about the character of Sitting Bull because there were two chiefs with the same name. The paper cleared things up by noting that the chief at the Little Bighorn was "a notorious scoundrel, chief of the Unkspapa tribe of Sioux, who has for the past 15 years made his home in the valley of the Yellowstone and the Montana tributaries. He has presently refused to go upon a reservation or to take part in any conference, and by repeated acts of hostility has proved himself an outlaw who merits extermination."[43]

Part of the press obsession with Sitting Bull was the need to have one person represent the Indian side of the story, but government officials contributed to his fame by emphasizing him in their debates about Indian policy. A widely published story about Sitting Bull quoted a Montana territorial delegate to Congress who blamed the war on "Sitting Bull and the outlaw Sioux." The delegate contrasted Sitting Bull with Red

Cloud and Spotted Tail, Lakota chiefs who had signed treaties with the federal government and were living peacefully on agencies. The delegate said the government had no choice but to subdue Sitting Bull. "Any other course would be a cowardly and wicked surrender of our frontier settlers and our friendly Indian allies and subject them to a barbarous and determined enemy of our country." Another widely published story featured a letter from the secretary of war, James Cameron, to Grant that claimed Sitting Bull's band had acted with contempt toward the Sioux peace treaty the majority of the Sioux were honoring.[44]

The *Baltimore American,* which gave dramatic play to both of those stories, editorialized that it was pleased the government would fight the war "sharply and vigorously" and punish Sitting Bull's tribe, which it called "the outlaws and land pirates of the West." But the editorial noted the wide range of public opinion on what to do with the Indians and cautioned against treating them all as outlaws:

> There is no disturbance in the Indian country which will not be used as an argument against the peace policy, and the recent massacre affords the advocates of harsh dealing a text upon which they can elaborate with a force that is all the more keenly felt now because the public mind is excited and indignant. But while it is entirely true that the hostile savages can scarcely be too severely punished, it must be remembered that the nucleus of Sitting Bull's force consists of Sioux Indians, who have always been outside of the treaty pale, and who not even the great chiefs of the Sioux nation have been able to hold in subjection. Undoubtedly there has been a failure to furnish supplies at the Sioux reservations, and the scarcity of food has caused many young warriors to join Sitting Bull.[45]

Although Sitting Bull was seen as the instigator of the Sioux war, most papers gave a grudging admiration to his military leadership and his fighting skills and those of Indians in general. Even the virulently anti-Indian *Rocky Mountain News* compared the hostiles' success to "Napoleon's genius" in defeating two of the three prongs of the army's offensive: "In the fatal fight in which Custer lost his life, the two divisions were attacked when separated, and both in general and particulars, the Sioux have pursued the course of Bonaparte in the first Italian campaign, when, at the head of hardly a quarter of that number, he successfully vanquished an Austrian army of 80,000 men moving in three divisions."[46]

The *St. Louis Dispatch* used the same comparison when it analyzed the Little Bighorn and the Rosebud, attributing the two battles to Sitting Bull's martial prowess, although in reality Sitting Bull was not present at the Rosebud and in both battles the Indians were reacting to immediate threats rather than planning a grand strategy to deal with the army's assorted columns: "As soon as Sitting Bull saw Crook fall back, he withdrew and concentrated his forces for an attack upon the other two columns, and Gibbon's command suffered next. Thus has the Sioux warrior exhibited thorough skill as a military leader, never before known among Indian nations. It was this Napoleonic talent of the red captain that has enabled him to defeat the troops, and led to the annihilation of Custer and his command." The *Dispatch* even defended Sitting Bull from critics when it was learned that he did not direct the Little Bighorn from the front but stayed in the village. The critics "forget that the Indians are adopting some of the strategies of civilized generalship, and do not risk their leader in a conflict where they know that his loss would, in all probability, in an even fight turn the battle against them."[47]

Some newspapers published rumors that Sitting Bull had gone to West Point, or was fluent in French, or had a white advisor named Milburn. The *St. Louis Globe-Democrat,* which printed several such stories, including one that Milburn had died with Sitting Bull at the Little Bighorn, admitted its error when a reporter ran into the aforesaid Milburn "stalking along Fourth street." According to the *Globe,* Milburn's full name was Charles Emmett, but he went by "Dashing Charlie" as well as the alias Milburn. The reporter was startled by seeing Emmett, who indignantly denied that he was a renegade who had joined the Sioux. "He had not been on the plains during the present Indian war, and therefore, had not been much killed on either side of the slaughter." Emmett, who had lived with the Sioux for seventeen years, said whites, including Custer, greatly underestimated them, and the current expedition was not strong enough to defeat them. "They are the best marksmen in the world. They ride horses that can travel over any kind of ground. He lives on nothing but meat and drinks alkali water. Two hours sleep will do them, and they can go three days without food."[48]

Of course, no newspaper had correspondents with the hostiles, so they relied on secondhand reports like those from Emmett to explain the Indian character. But most published some version of the Indian side of the story by interviewing Indians on the reservations who supposedly had talked to the hostiles. One widely published story quoted Sitting Bull through Bear-Stands-Up, an Indian from the Spotted Tail Agency who said he had been in Sitting Bull's camp. Bear-Stands-Up said that Sitting Bull would not attack anyone south of the Black Hills but would fight any whites who entered the Black Hills. "He does not want to fight the whites, but only to steal from them, as they have done. The whites kill themselves, and make the Black Hills stink, there are so many dead men." Sitting Bull told Bear-Stands-Up that, if no troops were sent after him, he would visit the agency and counsel his people to make peace.[49]

Medicine Cloud, an Indian from the Fort Peck agency, carried a message from Sitting Bull to Indian agent Thomas J. Mitchell that was also widely published. Sitting Bull's quote, as published in the *New York Herald,* portrayed a leader who wanted to negotiate peace: "Tell him I am coming before long to his post to trade. Tell him I did not commence the war; that I am getting old; that I do not want to fight the whites, but that the whites rush on me and I am compelled to defend myself; that but for the soldiers stationed on the Rosebud, I, with my people, would have been there before; that if I was assured of the protection of the Great Father I would go to Fort Peck for the purposed of making peace. I and the other chiefs want the Black Hills abandoned and we will make peace."[50]

Stories about negotiations over the sale of the Black Hills between the Indian Commission and the peaceful Sioux under Spotted Tail included lengthy quotes from the Indians. The *Courant* devoted almost a half column to what it headlined "Great Speech by Spotted Tail," in which the chief described the broken promises made to his tribe leading to the current war. "Half of our country is at war, and we have come upon very difficult times," Spotted Tail said. "This war did not spring up here in our land. It was brought upon us by children of the great father, who came to take our land from us without price, and who do a great many evil things." The storehouses on the reservation were empty, but the country was instead filled with soldiers who kept the Indians from hunting to feed themselves, he said. "It seems to me there is a better way than this when people come to trouble. . . . "It is better for both parties to come together without arms, talk it over, and find some peaceful way to settle."[51]

Not all editors were impressed. The *Globe-Democrat,* which also published Spotted Tail's comments, mocked his speech, claiming his interpreters must have studied at the "American School of Speakers. If there is anything which can rival the neatness and completeness of the aboriginal manipulation of the scalping-knife, it is the injured innocence of the rhetorical humility of the red devils when they begin to talk to their 'Great Father.'"[52]

The *New York Herald* published drawings from Sitting Bull's pictographic autobiography, which the paper claimed showed his lack of humility in chronicling exploits like killing a soldier and capturing horses from the Crows. The paper printed twenty-one drawings in two editions, a huge number of illustrations in a era when it was impossible for newspapers to publish photographs and most drawings were published in illustrated newspapers such as *Harper's Weekly*. An army surgeon named James C. Kimball had acquired the drawings in some unexplained way in 1870 while stationed at Fort Buford in the Dakota Territory. The *Herald* called the drawings "commonplace" in its accompanying news story but wrote that everything about the "the Napoleon of the Sioux" was interesting because of his role at the Little Bighorn. The news story described the drawings as the "daring deeds of the Chief," but the *Herald* commented on the editorial page that the autobiography, especially the drawing of Sitting Bulling killing a soldier, showed the savagery of "the Irreconcilables of the frontier" who had rejected civilization. "The book from which this is taken contains fifty-five similar drawings, each recounting some deed of bloodshed, cruelty, theft or inhumanity. These make up the life of the model savage whom our philanthropists love to feed, the child of nature whom the Indian Ring is never weary of praising and swindling. It adds a pang to the bitterness of the death of the gallant Custer and his heroic command that they fell at the hands of such a savage, in whom everything that is cruel and vicious is a matter of ostentation and pride."[53]

Despite its criticism of Sitting Bull, the fact remains that the *Herald* let readers see the chief's own portrayal of his life, and it is likely that some readers were sympathetic. For although the *Herald* criticized the government peace policy and activists like Wendell Phillips, it also admitted that whites had wronged the Indians, and it urged treating those who surrendered with mercy. It was an opinion that most editors held to varying degrees. The *Baltimore American,* for example, called for a modified peace policy. It urged distinguishing among peaceful Indians, the hostiles, and Indians on the reservations who pretended to want peace but gave aid to Sitting Bull's band: "Still, all this is no reason for ceasing efforts to tame and civilize the Indian. It merely amounts to a demonstration that there are occasions for severity and distrust as well as for kindness . . . in dealing with the savages; that the policy ought to be modified according to circumstances, and that different Indians require different treatment. . . . Let us have the most merciful application of the peace policy wherever possible, but let it be administered with discretion and not with that unreasoning heedlessness which permit the 'bad Indian' to take advantage of it."[54]

The *American* took Sherman's side in his spat with Wendell Phillips. It is interesting that Sherman felt compelled to deny he wanted to exterminate the Indians and said he favored "protecting and caring for" Indians on the reservation. The *American* said that it was "needless" for Sherman to have to defend his record, but that his comments provided the public with good information from a respected authority.[55]

There was also organized support for the peace policy. The *American* published a news brief about a group called the Universal Peace Union, which met in Philadelphia and adopted a resolution "counseling adherence to the peace policy in dealing with the Indians, and calling on President Grant to veto any bill for the transfer of the Indian Bureau to the War Department."[56]

≫→

Although most newspapers expressed some sympathy with the Indians, if only to show that they had considered all the facts before urging total war, some stories showed that journalists, their sources, and their readers had a limited understanding of Indian culture. One story in the *American* purported to explain the origin of Indian names. Its "expert" source was Gen. Fitzhugh Lee, who had fought Comanches before the Civil War. The story sounded like pure conjecture, such as claiming that

Sitting Bull was named when a buffalo bull was driven into camp, was wounded, and then sat down at the time of Sitting Bull's birth. Crazy Horse supposedly received his name because a wild horse ran through camp when he was born. In reality, both men had different names as children and, as was the standard practice, were given new names as adults. Sitting Bull was originally called "Slow," but his father gave the boy his own name after Slow had performed a heroic act in battle. Crazy Horse was called "Curly Hair" as a boy. Crazy Horse's father, like Sitting Bull's father, gave his son his own name after he had won honors in battle.[57]

The confusion about Indian naming practices was emblematic of the general confusion and conflicting thoughts about the "Indian question" in the minds of many Americans, including journalists. They saw their country as a Christian nation, but they wanted revenge for Custer and total defeat of the enemy. They wanted to expand the United States and promote their civilization, but they admired the courage and nobility of the native peoples.

One response to such confusion is laughter. Americans have always maintained a sense of humor through their darkest times. Newspapers reprinted a Mark Twain piece satirizing the way the whites treated Indians. The answer, Twain wrote, instead of massacring the Indians, was "soap and education," which would be equally deadly and "strike at the foundation of his being."[58] It was by no means the only joke newspapers printed about Indians and the Sioux War as Americans struggled to understand a national tragedy.

CHAPTER 7

"Custer's Death Was Sioux-icide"
Humor and the Little Bighorn

The day after reporting Custer's death, the editor of the *Laramie Sentinel* joked that he was glad he was not at the Little Bighorn because he did not want the embarrassment of being tomahawked while wearing dirty socks and having an unpaid laundry bill in his pocket.

> The more we think it over, the more we congratulate ourselves that we didn't go as a reporter with the Indian Expedition, for although it is very pleasant to write up a long Indian fight, it rather knocks the romance out of it to write up the item in Paradise, or in case that no passes are granted to editors and reporters, to be obliged to get up an account of the engagement on fire-proof parchment, and run the risk of securing a reliable medium by which to convey it to our paper, all these things taken into consideration we are glad we didn't go. Of course what the country needs is good patriotic volunteers, to go forward and sustain the flag, and all that sort of thing but the reason we don't hanker for such active life is that we object to being promoted so precipitately. We have never been noted for our precipitation, and to be promoted from an ordinary newspaper reporter to a shining angel without any scalp is an honor to which we do not aspire.[1]

The writer continued for two more paragraphs in the piece, which was headlined "Thanksgiving," cracking wise about things like wanting to live long enough to see how many votes Hayes got in the election. "Of course there isn't much fun in being a local editor, and getting licked every day for giving some ill-tempered man a pleasant little puff, but we'd rather do it, and see the circus once in a while, than to spend the summer with the Hebrew children and Lazarus, while the bloody Sioux perform the difficult figures of the 'can can' around a lock of our sorrel back hair."

The editor of the *Rocky Mountain News* saw the piece and commented drily, "The editor of the *Laramie Sentinel* is indulging in much thanksgiving because he didn't go out with Custer's party on a reporting expedition, but the people of Laramie have yet to be heard from."[2]

Such joking about death and scalping was widespread in newspapers in the immediate aftermath of the Little Bighorn. Even the *Louisville Courier-Journal,* edited by Custer friend Henry Watterson, could not resist making tasteless jokes. After reporting the amount of various life insurance policies held by officers of Custer's command, the paper commented, "If Sitting Bull doesn't mind, he'll 'bust up' somebody's insurance company the first thing he knows."[3]

Americans in 1876 believed that they were a people who enjoyed humor and were better at it than people from other countries. The *St. Louis Globe-Democrat* ran a series on American humorists in August and September 1876, extolling the superiority of the American funny bone: "There is no doubt that the Americans are decidedly a humorous people, and that their humor is not only original but unique. Even the English, very slow to admit our intellectual capacities of any kind, are forced to acknowledge our possession of a distinct humor. Indeed, they relish it more than we do, and show an undue appreciation of it by pirating the books of our funny writers, just as we pirate the books of their serious writers. It took the English a long while to understand our humor; but now they have the key, they enjoy it immensely, and are inclined to believe all comicality in print as emanating from Yankee sources." The writer claimed his London friends often would mistakenly think humorists such as Francis Burnand were Americans and would be shocked when he told them they were British. "I forebore to say that . . . in our opinion, Burnand is extraordinarily stupid."[4]

James R. Aswell wrote that although Americans tend to think such humorists as Mark Twain were mavericks in the nineteenth century, the period was actually filled with robust humor, much of it printed in newspapers by anonymous contributors, including soldiers and others from all walks of life who "rubbed elbows, daily with the vigorous life of their times and reported it with shrewdly humorous insights. In laughing at the hurly-burly of America, *they knowingly laughed at themselves as part and parcel of it.* That is the core of our native sense of humor."[5]

These jokes were often shared among newspapers around the country through the "exchange" system, which quite literally meant editors exchanged editions of their papers and were free to copy from them. Editors in 1876 needed filler, and journalists wrote brief jokes, especially puns, to meet the need.[6] The *Globe-Democrat* humor analyst praised writers like Mark Twain and Bret Harte but wrote that American newspapers tried too hard to be funny: "The consciousness that we are a nation of humorists causes us to overwork the humorous vein, especially in the newspapers. Nearly every journal of any prominence, nowadays, is afflicted with a funny man, who, in continuous grinding of mental wheat, must grind a good deal of an inferior sort. That funny man may have a fair fund of natural humor, but he soon exhausts himself, and yet he innocently keeps on until you hear the pump in everything he does." The humor in the exchanges was "depressing in the extreme" because it was repeated over and over and diluted. Yet any editor who was told that he was not funny was apt to reply that the critic had no sense of humor. The writer compared it to a man who was given an emetic as a joke: "While he was retching and suffering, the administrator said: 'I see, my dear boy, that you can't take a joke.'"[7]

Many of the newspaper jokes in 1876 were tinged with cruelty or violence. The Republican *Hartford Daily Courant,* for example, wrote about a four-year-old boy who accidentally drank a pint of lye. The *Courant* noted that the boy would recover, "though the doctor says he will never be good for anything but to edit a democratic newspaper."[8] Jokes in poor taste were so common that Samuel Cox argued in his 1876 analysis of American humor that it needed to be more refined and moderate. Cox, who was Speaker of the House of Representatives, no doubt had first-hand knowledge of being the butt of jokes, particularly in American newspapers. He explained that journalistic humor typically "consists in giving a comic account of a catastrophe, and then, by a sudden and serious turn, leaving a suggestive hiatus, making a conclusion which connects the premises." Cox cited many violent examples, such as these: "A woman put her tongue to a flat-iron to see if it was hot. That household has been remarkably quiet since." "A young man in Louisville thought a circular buzz-saw was standing still; he felt it. Several fingers are pre-served in the best of spirits." Or, the most tasteless example cited by Cox: "A youth showed his father's pistol to little Dickey. 'Eight years of age,' was the inscription on the little casket.'"[9]

Such jokes may seem harsh in the politically correct mood of the early twenty-first century until one considers jokes about current tragedies. Barry Blake's analysis of humor points out that many current jokes are about death, disease, and disaster. He gives as an example that within a day or so of Hurricane Katrina, which devastated the Gulf Coast in 2005, some people were repeating the line that the "first bar to re-open on Bourbon and Water Street found it didn't take long for the regular customers to drift in." Yet Blake admits that some disasters, like the 9/11 terror attacks, are too emotional for any comedians to joke about with-out a substantial amount of time passing.[10] Jimmy Carr, a professional comedian, and his coauthor Lucy Greeves, express an opinion similar to Blake's in their book on humor: "There's an old saying that comedy is tragedy plus time. And Charlie Chaplin is credited with the observation that 'life is a tragedy when seen in close-up, but a comedy in long-shot.' Some tragedies seem so cataclysmic that in the immediate aftermath it seems wrong to laugh at *anything,* let alone at jokes about the tragedy itself. In New York, following the attacks on the Twin Towers in 2001, the comedy clubs were strange, furtive places for months. People wanted to laugh, but they needed to be given permission." They wrote that a few weeks after the attack comedian Gilbert Gottfried told an audience that he wanted to get a direct flight to California but couldn't because they wanted him to stop at the Empire State Building first. No one laughed, and someone shouted, "Too soon!" Gottfried got the crowd back on his side only after telling an extraordinarily dirty joke known to most comedians as "the Aristocrats"—a joke that had nothing to do with cur-rent events.[11]

But the days immediately following the first reports of the Little Bighorn disaster were not too soon for Americans to laugh at the vari-ous aspects of the Sioux war. Jokes abounded on the incompetence of the military and the savagery of the hostiles, especially the custom of scalping. Although fairly rare, even jokes about Custer were made little more than a week after his reported death. The title for this chapter, as an example, was published as a one-liner in the July 14 edition of Ken-tucky's *Owensboro Examiner.*

Why were such jokes common so soon after a battle in which several hundred people were killed? It is difficult to find the answer, because humor itself is hard to explain. As communication scholar John C. Meyer writes on the functions of humor, "If one has to explain a joke, it is probably no longer funny."[12] Nevertheless, that difficulty has not stopped scholars from doing so and developing different ways of analyzing humor. These ideas are useful in understanding the reasons newspaper editors mocked various aspects of the Great Sioux War and why the public presumably found them amusing.

One of the more common ways of analyzing the creation of humor divides it into three types: relief, incongruity, and superiority. Relief theory suggests that some jokes are created to relieve tension over uncomfortable or fearful situations that could include fear of injury. Superiority theory explains that some jokes make the audience feel superior or triumphant over the butt of the joke. Incongruity theory suggests that people laugh at things that are surprising or absurd. Meyer suggests that humor can also be analyzed by looking at its functions, which could be to unite or to divide the audience. He writes that speakers, especially politicians, use humor to identify with their audience and explain their positions on issues with funny and memorable short jokes. On the other hand, people can use humor to separate themselves from "the other." For example, a politician can use a joke to show how his views differ from his opponents, or he can mock his opponent for violating some social custom. Meyer points out that humor can be difficult to analyze because some jokes fall into more than one category. A joke could serve to help the speaker relate to his audience while serving to separate him from his political opponent.[13]

Some jokes about the Little Bighorn could fit into more than one category, but the various humor theories illustrate that jokes helped journalists and their readers make sense of a horrific event, reduce tension, and distinguish civilized from savage behavior. In addition, the jokes could quickly and effectively make points about a newspaper's position on the war, the election, or Indian policy. In fact, Indians, and Sitting Bull in particular, were the object of the majority of jokes published in the aftermath of the Little Bighorn. The names of Indians and the words "Sioux" and "Little Bighorn" lend themselves to word play, making such brief jokes a natural for the column of fillers most newspapers carried. Such columns were often published on the editorial page, which was appropriate because they usually fit under the superiority theory of humor; they assured typical readers that their culture, including naming customs, was superior to that of the hostile tribes. The jokes, by reducing the stature of Indians and leaders like Sitting Bull, also served to relieve tension for readers by making the enemy seem less threatening.

Historian John Coward argues that newspapers made Sitting Bull the "near-perfect Indian villain" in their coverage of the Little Bighorn, sometimes erroneously crediting him with killing Custer.[14] Editors certainly made Sitting Bull a comic villain through countless puns on his name and jokes about his character and life. One popular joke suggested the army would catch Sitting Bull: "Uncle Sam's—Taking Sitting Bull by the Little Horn."[15] The *Louisville Sunday Review* even poked fun at another newspaper's version of the joke: "The New York Com. Adv. wants someone to take S. Bull by the horn. Now, we don't wish to be profane, but the man who does that is liable to be gored." The *New York Herald* published a slightly different version: "Terry says he will yet catch Sitting Bull. In a Big Horn."[16]

The most popular puns about Sitting Bull mocked his name, emphasizing the fact that he came from a culture considered inferior to white society. A few of the myriad examples follow:

"The position of Sitting Bull is a standing shame."[17]

"The Indian question: How can Sitting Bull be cowed?"[18]

The Army will make things so hard for Sitting Bull "that he will have little time for sitting."[19]

"That rascally Sitting Bull fights as well as most Indians do standing up. It begins to look as if they will have to get him to lie down if they want to whip him."[20]

The *Bozeman Avant Courier* thought Sitting Bull was just another in a line of enemies the United States had defeated: "Deacon Smith being asked the other day what he was thinking about, shook off his revery, and replied, '1776, John Bull; in 1876, Sitting Bull.'" The *New York Herald* compared him to an insect: "There is poetry even in that Sitting Bull of winged torments the uneasy mosquito. Think, young man, as you listen to his grace before meat, that the bill that feeds upon your marble forehead may only a little while since have caressed the damask cheek of her whom you love."[21]

Another time the *Herald* imagined the chief fighting the whites using an effeminate technique: "Sitting Bull says that if he ever gets hold of Terry he'll snatch him bald-headed." The *Herald* also imagined the chief's interest in white culture: "Sitting Bull says the government's hostility to him has prejudiced the people against him so that he cannot consistently visit the Centennial."[22]

Some newspapers treated their readers to fictional profiles of Sitting Bull. The Republican *Bismarck Tribune*, which identified Sitting Bull's politics as Democratic, claimed that he got his name from "*setting* down on lonesome subjects of the American Republic whenever an Indian Agent 'kicked' and would not divide even." The story mocked his limp, claiming one of his legs was shorter than the other: "This deformity sorter bothers the military, as it gives him an uncertain warbling gait, and they can't tell whether he is bound for the Big Horn mountains or the British Possessions." Although his formal education was limited, Sitting Bull "can cipher a government contract down as close as a Q.M. [quartermaster] clerk.[23]

The *Hartford Daily Courant* had fun with the reports that Sitting Bull was a graduate of West Point. Some newspapers reported the stories as true, but the *Courant* ran it on a page of fantastic pieces like a "fish story" about a huge pickerel in a Wisconsin lake that attacked boats with the force of a sperm whale and was "as cunning as a Sioux warrior."[24] The story about Sitting Bull claimed he was actually "a strapping Western youth" who was kicked out of the military academy for getting in a drunken brawl in the village of Buttermilk Falls. He roamed around the West like an early Forest Gump, fighting desperadoes and future Civil War heroes in Texas, Arizona, and California before landing in the Black Hills, where he put his military training to use against Custer. But the conclusion of the story, which was originally published in the *Baltimore Gazette,* was an anecdote about Sitting Bull being teased at the academy. Sitting Bull was supposedly nicknamed "Bison" at the academy and had first entered the school with long, shaggy hair and a patchy beard. Some mischievous cadets told Bison he needed a regulation haircut and shave and directed him to a dorm room where some other cadets pretended to be barbers. They shaved only half of Bison's face and closely cut only one side of his head, telling him they had to stop work abruptly at eight o'clock. When the officer of the guard saw the half-shaven Bison walking around, he asked him what happened.

> "'The barber told me he couldn't shave after eight o'clock.'
> 'What barber?'
> 'In that room there,' pointing to the abode of the wicked cadets.
> 'Oh, it was there, was it? Come with me.' (The officer of the guard enters and finds the amateur barbers still in costume.) 'Mr. Burnside did you half shave this cadet?'
> 'Yes, Sir.'
> 'Well, finish your work, Sir,' whereupon Sitting Bull sat down and General Ambrose Burnside shaved him."[25]

The image of the great Sioux leader, feared for his scalping knife, being shaved by a Civil War hero known for his wild facial hair must have been hilarious for nineteenth-century readers. They no doubt also enjoyed a story of Sitting Bull's white childhood written by "A Schoolmate" that originally appeared in the *Minneapolis Tribune:* "I well remember the infantile days of Sitting Bull, the guileless innocence of his childhood, and how we used to give him a truthful little hatchet and butcher knife and the old yellow cat all for to play with," the writer recalled. "I should judge that he must have scalped that old cat as much as sixteen or seventeen hundred times before he was three years old. It was [beautiful] to observe what an interest that child took in dumb animals—particularly that cat."[26]

Journalists found scalping humorous, at least judging by the number of jokes referring to the practice. According to humor theory, such jokes would help ease tension over a fearful situation and also divide the reader from the Indian, emphasizing the idea that the hostiles were savages with practices outside the norms of civilized society. Many of the jokes mocked soldiers, frontiersman, and war correspondents for being afraid of losing their scalps or teasing them that they might lose them. Actual incidents of mutilations were generally not topics of jokes unless it was the scalping of hostiles by whites or Indian allies. The *Bismarck Tribune,* for example, interviewed a black man who was on the *Far West*—the ship that brought Custer's wounded back from the battle—to ask him if whites had scalped an Indian who killed a scout. "Tom answered with abhorrence, in exclamation, 'Scalp him! Why yes, cut his har close, and fotch him in on de boat in quarters! Eugh! Eugh! Golly! Fat Injun, I tell you!'"[27]

On the other hand, two Denver newspapers made light of erroneous reports that a young war correspondent had been killed and scalped. The *Rocky Mountain Herald* wrote: "Mr. Richardson, the young newspaper correspondent who *wasn't* scalped by the Sioux, after all, is revisiting Denver. He disclaims any connection with that 'canard;' in fact denounces it as an outrage—on both himself and the Sioux." The *Rocky Mountain News* joked that it would try to reduce such false reports: "Hereafter all persons who may be reported killed and scalped by the Indians will be required to furnish proper and sufficient proof of the fact in order to secure an obituary notice in the News. It will not be necessary for them to bring in the news and accompanying vouchers in person, but when such matter is sent in for publication the party presenting it must be vouched for by some responsible citizen—a property owner preferred."[28]

Other reporters were mocked for their baldness, which would be a protection against scalping. The *Chicago Tribune* joked that its correspondent, Phocion Howard, "had his few straggling hairs clipped close to his scalp" before he left to cover the Sioux war. The Chicago newspapers had a strong rivalry in 1876, and the *Chicago Times* consistently mocked the rival *Inter-Ocean* for covering the war with wire reports but writing in such a way as to give the reader the impression it had a correspondent at the front. The *Times* wrote that the *Inter-Ocean* special correspondent supposedly with Gen. George Crook must have lost his scalp, because "to an astonished congregation . . . he walked into . . . [a] church on yesterday with his hat on."[29]

The *New York Times* wrote that hiring Indian women as maids would end the fighting on the frontier while helping their new city employers deal with the gas man or other bill collectors:

[The] new maid from the West would need her favorite recreation to keep her happy. She must have an occasional plumber given to her for purposes of torture, and must be allowed to scalp the man who comes to inspect the gas meter. These innocent and harmless sports would not only bring happiness to her unsophisticated bosom, but would doubtless have an excellent affect upon the plumbers and gas inspectors. Even the most hardened plumber, who had been for years in the habit of charging a full day's pay for sitting one hour on the edge of a bath-tub, and making up his mind that he had forgotten to bring his tools, could not help being benefitted by being tied to a post in the back-yard while the Sioux cook could take a frequent hack at him with the hatchet while waiting for the potatoes to boil or the beef to roast.[30]

The *Times* joke was included in a lengthy satirical piece about the war, but many newspapers printed one-liners about scalping. For example, the *Louisville Sunday Review* wrote, "The young gentleman who asks if we know of an effective depilitory, is respectfully referred to Sitting Bull." The *St. Louis Dispatch* quipped, "The first scalping operation— taking time by the forelock." The *Louisville Courier-Journal* noted that "A Sioux Indian on the war-path is the most ha(i)rra(i)sing of wild beasts." When the paper wrote that Young-Man-Afraid-of-His-Horses had told peace commissioners, "I have never made any man's heart feel bad," it could not resist adding, "Oh, no; you never made any man's heart feel bad, but what about his *hair?*"[31]

As much as newspapers joked about scalping in order to relieve tension over the ferocity of the Indian enemy, they also sought to reduce fear over the threat by mocking Indian customs, intelligence, and bravery. This type of humor allows the jokester and audience to feel superior to the butt of the joke. Some of these jokes indicated confidence in the army. The *St. Louis Globe-Democrat,* for example, repeated a joke that predicted an easy victory: "If Terry kills half the Sioux and routs the other half, the burying-ground might Sioux-tably be called a semi-Terry." The *Bozeman Avant Courier* mentioned the motivation of the army's Crow scouts: "The Crows have caws to per-Sioux their old enemies."[32]

The *Courier-Journal,* like many newspapers, frequently mocked Indians names: "Such names as the Ogallalla Indians do have! For instance, there are Man-Afraid-of-the-Bear and Young-Man-Afraid-of-His-Horses. To be afraid of a bear is not so bad, but for a full-grown young warrior to be afraid of his horses is simply ridiculous." The *New York Herald* mocked Indian women: "Sioux squaws do not wear striped stockings. Three streaks of green paint are cooler and cheaper." The *Williamstown*

Sentinel ridiculed Indian men in an article headlined "Loathe the Poor Indian," a play on the then common expression "Lo! The Poor Indian." It described a local Indian who begged for whiskey by presenting a certificate to white men. The certificate assured that "the bearer . . . never lifted a scalp nor robbed a hen-roost by daylight. He is the father of some of his children, and uses no cologne. He has that noble attribute of his race, an untutored mind."[33]

Indian courage was mocked in a *Clark County Democrat* story about some soldiers who fired a mountain howitzer without first unpacking it from the back of a mule. The recoil knocked the mule toward the Indians, starting a panic. "One of the Indians being captured and asked why he ran so, replied—'Me big Ingun not afraid of little guns, but when white men load up and fire a whole jackass at Injun, me don't know what to do.'" The *Louisville Courier-Journal* reported that peaceful Indians were panicked by news of the Last Stand because they thought they would be blamed: "When news of the Little Horn first reached St. Paul, all the Indians in the city not on duty at the cigar stands quickly disappeared, fearing a pale-face mob."[34]

A *New York Herald* war correspondent made fun the of the army's Crow allies, describing a scene in which an officer fed them lavishly as a way to try to persuade them to fight the Sioux. "The scene, however, was far from giving a high idea of the Indian race. As the groups lay around patiently waiting their share of sugar, bacon, hardtack and coffee, men, boys and women amused themselves hunting in each other's raven locks and evidently relishing the captured game. There is a strange mixture of cleanliness and squalidity in the Indian's diet. But as he never seems to change his underclothing he has at all times an odor repugnant to our olfactories."[35]

There was also newspaper humor aimed at the military and the government. The motivation for this humor was complex. It could function as a relief from an intense situation, but it could also make the jokester and the audience feel superior to soldiers who had made mistakes or to government officials who had developed a failed Indian policy. The *Republican Daily Journal* mocked local militiamen who gloried in their uniforms until they faced the prospect of being sent to face the hostiles. The paper wrote that the typical nightmare of a militiaman involved a fight with the Sioux and running "barefooted forty miles through goosberry bushes with a saddler's girth around their heads to keep down their scalps, or having passed a pleasant half-hour on some 'big Injun's' toasting fork while the squaws and little ones stuck straws into them to see if they were 'done.'" The story included anecdotes about a recruit who crossed the street covering his face with his hat whenever he ran across a local Indian who apparently was a town drunk. "And there is another young recruit who sat at dinner yesterday and was asked if he would be helped to some custard. 'Help nobody' said he excitedly, 'I shan't go now, there.'"[36]

According the *New York Times,* regulars in the field were also jumpy. The *Times* correspondent joked that soldiers were so nervous after the Little Bighorn that they almost shot him when he returned to camp after a brief ride. The *Chicago Tribune* mocked nervous troops who "captured" a camp of Rees, an allied tribe that provided scouts for the army. The camp was filled with old men, women, and children because all the warriors were on a hunting party. "I[n] true military style they flanked and closed in on the village, and captured every soul without shedding a drop of blood! When the squaws and decrepit old 'bucks' were paraded before the Colonel, the l[a]ugh was loud and long."[37]

But most of the newspapers' mockery was reserved for the generals, not the privates. One popular joke compared the Little Bighorn to the disastrous defeat of Edward Braddock at the Battle of the Monongahela in the French and Indian War: "It was Gen. Braddock who first discovered that one white man could not whip a dozen Indians. Braddock is dead, but the war office still lives."[38]

Phil Sheridan was a frequent target of jokes—usually in the form of one-liners or briefs—because he was at the military department's headquarters in Chicago instead of in the field. Southern newspapers like the *New Orleans Picayune* were angry at Sheridan for his military duties in Reconstruction, and that might have been partly the reason behind jokes like this one: "According to a contemporary, gallant Phil. Sheridan still flits about the telegraph office in Chicago, and makes the savage Sioux tremble." Another southern newspaper, the *Vicksburg Herald,* reflected the region's bitterness by asking, "Why didn't Sheridan lead that charge? He would have made a better dead man than Custer." The *Austin Daily Democratic Statesman* also ridiculed Sheridan for visiting the Centennial during the campaign: "While Sitting Bull was slaughtering Custer's braves, Sheridan was the sitting ass presiding over a body of jolly junketers in a carousel at Philadelphia."[39]

A Democratic Kansas newspaper, the *Leavenworth Daily Appeal*, also mocked Sheridan's courage: "The nation rejoiced that the massacre of the gallant Custer was to be speedily avenged, and the gallant Phil was to be the man to do it. The hats they threw up in the air had hardly come down, when it was again flashed over the wires that he was stationed on the west portico of the Sherman House, in Chicago, where he had planted his (telegraph) battery, and with clenched fists was daring them to 'come on.'" The *Missoulian* noted that "General Sheridan doesn't scare much, but then a man seldom does when his hair is safe." The *Bismarck Tribune* believed Sheridan should command a punitive expedition but nevertheless quoted an unnamed southern newspaper that "wants Sitting Bull and his men declared banditti, and suggests Sheridan would be the proper man to subdue them. Correct, though intended for a joke." In 1875, Sheridan had asked the secretary of war to set up military tribunals to try white supremacists in Louisiana as "banditti."[40]

Crook, who unlike Sheridan was in the field against the Sioux, was also the butt of a few jabs because of his botched campaign and the indecisive Rosebud battle. The *Rocky Mountain Herald* mocked him: "[We] congratulate you on preserving your scalp." This sentiment was echoed by the *Bismarck Tribune,* which noted that Crook had captured some "defenceless" Indians near the Red Cloud agency. "He makes a great parade over this feat, and says this is the first gleam of daylight we have had in this Indian business. A different course on the part of Crook during the summer would have given the country many gleams of daylight and saved much hard fighting for the future." The *Missoulian* wrote simply that "the news about Crook looks a trifle Sioux-picious."[41]

The *Louisville Courier-Journal* implied that Crook and Terry were incompetent in a piece that claimed Sitting Bull's real name was Hooking-the-Ground-Bull—a more accurate name because he was too active for the army to catch him: "His chief of staff, Long Dog, may occasionally seek repose, but he himself was born to make the dirt fly, as we have already seen," the paper wrote in late August, when it became evident the army would not avenge Custer that summer. "Crook and Terry always clamber over the fence when Hooking-the-Ground-Bull stiffens his tail and undulates his horns. They at least do not get him mixed up in their minds with that less-enterprising Indian commander, Get-Up-and-Run-a-Little-Way-and-Then-Sit-Down-Again. The thunder of his hoofs is too recent in their ears. Until after the election, at least, Hooking-the-Ground-Bull will have his own way, and it behooves the press to see that his name gets into the papers right.[42]

In a subsequent issue, the *Courier-Journal* noted that some newspapers were accusing Hooking-the-Ground-Bull of being a dirty drunkard. "His recent Napoleonic achievements have set going the tongues of Envy and Malice. . . . But a discriminating public is already too familiar with the denunciation of heroes to pay much attention to such charges. No doubt Bull is deeply pained when he sees them in print, and wishes he had never seen either the Big Horn or the Little Horn, but time will vindicate him, and bring more scalps to his belt."[43]

A few weeks later the *Courier-Journal* imagined Sitting Bull bragging about his victory in the boastful language of a frontiersman like Davey Crockett or Mike Fink: "The campaign against the Sioux is over, and the Sitting Bull, proud of the result, walks off, pawing up the ground, to the admiration of the smiling squaws, and boastfully bellowing, '*I'm* your howling hyena of the hills and your patent old he-hair-raiser of the per-raries—*I'm* your rip-roaring Sitting Bully-boy with the glass eye, and your gaul-darned and double-fisted son of a steam-injine—*I'm* the high-pressure, iron-jawed sassage machine to chaw up your Crooks and Terrys—you heerd *my* horn!' And poor Crook and Terry, *they* must feel sorry they ever learned the business. And they don't seem to have learned it much either."[44]

The *St. Louis Globe-Democrat* wrote that the campaign was similar to an old joke about a North Carolinian hunting a bear: "He followed the trail until it began to get a little too warm, when he turned back. Crook and Terry hunted quite vigorously until they 'struck the largest trail ever seen on the plains,' when they discovered their provisions were out, and 'returned to refit.' There is no better sport in the world than hunting Indians—the trouble begins when they have been found."[45]

Other jokes ridiculed Terry and Crook for being too slow in their pursuit of the hostiles. The *New York Herald* wrote, "Many of the Sioux warriors are called 'Sitting' this or 'Sitting' that; but the trouble is that they don't sit still long enough to give Terry a chance." The *Courier-Journal* went into more detail, writing that "one of the Ogallalla Indians is named Good Bull and another Slow Bull. The first named is perhaps too pious to do much fighting, but if Slow Bull would take command of the Sioux in place of Sitting of that ilk, there would perhaps be some little hope that Crook and Terry would overtake them." The *Courier-Journal* also imagined Crook's response to Sherman's statement that he did not want to exterminate the tribes: "This, then, accounts for Gen. Crook's apparent disinclination to overtake the Indians—he's afraid of exterminating them."[46]

According to some jokes, the Indians did not fear the army. The *Cheyenne Leader* emphasized the Indians' confidence after the Little Bighorn, reporting that well-armed Indians were leaving reservations to join the hostiles: "A band of them being stopped by white men, were asked where they were going, and the chief replied: 'None damn business. Go where we please." The *Bismarck Tribune* noted that Blackfoot chief John Grass teased army officers at a negotiation. Grass, whose band was at peace with the government, had helped the army capture Kill Eagle's hostile band. Grass argued for leniency for Kill Eagle's band because they had left the reservation only to hunt and not to fight. The *Tribune* admitted that Grass made a good joke when he smiled and gave the soldiers an old, worn-out flintlock musket to take to the "Great Father" for hunting.[47]

The *Louisville Courier-Journal* noted that Spotted Tail had criticized Grant in some of the negotiations and compared it to attacks on the president from fellow Republicans upset about his scandal-plagued administration: "Spotted Tail in his speech to the commissioners made some very ugly charges against the Great Father. He may possibly have been reading Carl Schurz's speeches."[48]

Several newspapers found amusement in the fact that at peace negotiations in September Chief American Horse joked that the "Great Father" should send soldiers to the North in the United States because there were plenty of bad men to arrest there. If American Horse had read Republican newspapers, the Democratic *New Orleans Picayune* noted tongue in cheek, he would know the soldiers were needed in the South, and that neither he nor "bad men" in the North need fear them. "No doubt American Horse had heard of the whisky ring, of the District of Columbia ring, Jim Blaine and the Mulligan letters, Belknap and the trading posts," the *Picayune* wrote, referring to a few of the numerous Republican scandals that had emerged recently. "If the Government was really anxious to punish wickedness, why should it not begin like charity, at home? Why should it expose men to the fatigues of long, weary marches to reach a few underfed savages, while there are whole coveys of plump sinners right within its reach?"[49]

Politicians are usually plump targets for humorists, and the newspapers of 1876 often mocked them for their position on the military or Indian policy. Pithy barbs got across a newspaper's opinion better than a long-winded editorial and showed readers that its party and candidates were superior to those of the opposing side. As Sitting Bull was the most popular butt of jokes about Indians, Grant was the most frequent target of political humor. The *Austin Democratic Statesman* implied that the failed Sioux campaign would be the Republicans' undoing: "Sitting Bull's star is still in the ascendant, and the constellation of Taurus, shining so brilliantly when we cast the *horror*scope of Grant's administration, portends its final eclipse." The *New Orleans Picayune* wrote, "If Grant would make Sioux-table movement he might keep the red skin within their own reservations." The *St. Louis Dispatch* opined that "our Indian policy is either Sioux-icidal or Sioux-perfluous."[50]

Some newspapers mocked Grant's drinking. The *Corpus Christi Gazette* wrote that General Terry "is now between the Little and the Big Horn of a dilemma. That's nothing. Grant has been all around many a big horn and hasn't yet come to the dilemma." The *Louisville Courier-Journal* mocked the president's alleged connection to the scandal involving the stealing of whiskey tax revenue: "If Grant really wants to end this Indian war, he ought to send one or two of his whiskey-ring friends against Sitting Bull. If they could obtain a victory of him in no other way, they could very easily swindle him out of it."[51]

Newspapers also mocked the president's family. The *Courier-Journal* quoted a *Toledo Blade* piece ridiculing Grant's brother Orvil, who was mentioned in scandals involving Indian post traderships: "We have not yet heard of any applications for the Little Horn post-traderships. It is to be hoped that brother Orvill will take that Post himself. However the post of danger is the post of honor, and that sort of post Brother Orvill has always religiously shunned."[52]

Grant's son Fred came in for more abuse because he was in the army and had been recently promoted but was not serving at the front. The *Picayune* wrote that "a Washington paper remarks that Lieut. Fred Grant has been promoted but not yet ordered to the Yellowstone. His scalp is too precious to the owner." A few weeks later the paper denied a report that Fred Grant would be sent to the front. "Oh, no, indeed. He goes to Texas. It would never do to bring our Freddie within the possible reach of Sitting Bull."[53]

But southern papers were not the only ones who ridiculed the president's son. The *Chicago Times* wrote sarcastically about Fred Grant's military service: "To see Lieut. Grant walking down State Street switching a 25 cent cane, fighting Indians, and saving his country, is one of the noblest and nobbiest sights under the sun." Also in Illinois, the Democratic *Quincy Herald* similarly wrote that "the country can rejoice that Fred is safe" although hundreds of "heroes" fell at the Little Bighorn.[54]

Other Republican politicians were mocked as well. The *New York Herald* made light of the intraparty battle for the presidential nomination between New York senator Roscoe Conkling and Secretary of the Treasury Benjamin Bristow, who had led the prosecution of the whiskey ring: "Red Cloud Conkling, the great chief of the republican Sioux, has been in a temper with The-Man-Who-Is-Not-Afraid-of-Whiskey, Bristow, chief of the reform band. It was the latter chief who put his coup stick on Red Cloud at Cincinnati, and although the blow was not fatal it was disabling. But Red Cloud crippled is more than a match for most of the chiefs in full health."[55]

Giving Republican politicians Indian names was a frequent gag for Democratic newspapers, particularly the *Louisville Courier-Journal,* which regularly referred to Republican Indiana senator Oliver Morton as "Sitting Bull" Morton. In September the paper wrote that "Sitting Bull Morton says he has 'a conscience.' It would cost more to keep six harlots than to keep his conscience." A brief joke on the same page noted that Benjamin Harrison, the Republican nominee for Indiana governor, was a lineal descendent of Pocahontas. "Hence his intimacy with Sitting Bull." A week later the paper regretted the harsh language: "On one or two occasions we have spoken of Indiana's chief bloody shirtist—and her chief dirty shirtist, too, in point of fact—as Sitting Bull Morton. This was probably too severe; but of course we did it with the understanding that we are to apologize to Sitting Bull the first opportunity."[56]

Newspapers of both parties ridiculed the peace policy of supplying the hostile Indians with food, clothing, and weapons through the reservation system. The Republican *Chicago Tribune,* which argued in favor of the government granting pensions to the widows of enlisted men as well as Libbie Custer, wrote facetiously that the government, since it supplied the tribes with food and weapons, should also "pension the Indian widows, and present Sitting Bull with a sword and the freedom of the whole Indian country." The Democratic *New York Herald* wrote tongue in cheek that taxpayers would be glad to know that Sitting Bull's tribe had been freshly supplied with guns, powder, and blankets at the Indian agency—the blankets stamped "U.S." A few weeks later it sarcastically criticized Grant's former interior secretary, Columbus Delano, for leaving Sitting Bull "short of ammunition" and forcing him to use bows and arrows: "We owe the fact that the Indians were well armed and supplied to that provident statesman. He should not abandon Sitting Bull in this time of his need. We have no doubt Delano could take a cargo of powder into the Sioux country by the way of Canada. Sitting Bull is anxious to hear from him."[57]

The *St. Louis Dispatch* joked that the Grant administration should send whiskey distillers to the reservation and wrote: "Is it not about time to establish another Sunday-school among the Sioux? How would it be, as the weather grows warm, for the ladies to send them a few hundred linen dusters—the overcoats sent last fall are badly worn, and are besides out of season." In another issue the *Dispatch* published a variation of the popular barb about Indian traderships in the war zone: "We have not heard of any applications for the Little Horn post-tradership. It is going dirt cheap."[58]

The *Picayune* urged Grant to call for volunteers from Louisiana to fight in the war: "We will guarantee he can get the most bloodthirsty from the ranks of the carpet-baggers, who are already on the ground. By this means he can save money on the transportation item, and so fulfill the Republican hobby of retrenchment. We make this as a suggestion, simply; some one else can make the motion." But later in the month it noted that Sgt. Gilbert Bates, a Wisconsin Union veteran who had carried an American flag across the South in 1868 to show that the former Confederates were patriotic, had not volunteered to march to the Little Bighorn. This joke supported the Democratic idea that troops were not needed in South, which was peaceful, but in the West.[59]

Republican newspapers made fun of the Democratic position about troop deployments and often tied their barbs to the Hamburg Massacre.

The *New York Times* imagined that Democrats who called reports of the massacre an exaggeration might also start defending the Indians in the same fashion in order to make political points:

> It is possible that some political advocate of the chivalric virtues of Sitting Bull might declare that he was weary of hearing these everlasting stories of Sioux outrages; and he might sneer at "the bloody shirt" in the faces of gentlemen who represented the peaceful and serene Sioux country. . . . These apologists for the Indian warrior might even make it a point in appropriation bills that none of the money to be expended should be used to oppress the Sioux, and the reports of bloody doings on the Big Horn might be set down to the fraudulent outcome of "the outrage mill." . . . If the exigencies of a Presidential canvass required it, there are undoubtedly many friends of Col. M. C. Butler who would be swift to declare on the floor of Congress that Sitting Bull was a high-toned, chivalric gentleman, who would not hurt a fly.[60]

The *New York Herald,* although not a Republican paper, was horrified by the Hamburg Massacre and mocked southerners over it. In a brief headlined "The Right Man in the Right Place," the *Herald* joked that Sitting Bull would run for mayor of Hamburg. A few days later it wrote that Sitting Bull was "gratified" by the Hamburg riot. "It shows that Sioux civilization and Sioux tactics are spreading. Sitting Bull thinks all the prisoners, and not just four, should have been shot; but still he is not exacting. He knows it requires time to educate a community up to the Sioux standard."[61]

Papers of both parties also ridiculed the Democratic position on reducing the size of the army. The *New York Herald* mocked House Speaker and Pennsylvania Democrat Samuel J. Randall: "Mr. Randall ought to be satisfied. Sitting Bull has helped him to cut down the army." Others repeated the gag that Sitting Bull was a member of the Democratic Party. The *Newton Kansan*, for example, wrote that "Sitting Bull is the Democratic candidate for Congress in the Little Big Horn district. He is in favor of a reduction in the army." The *St. Louis Dispatch* similarly reported that "Maj. Gen. Sedentary Bull is talked of for Congress from the Sioux District. It is rumored that Crook and Terry will not vote for him." The *Bismarck Tribune* ran a satirical biography of Sitting Bull, claiming, "politically, he is a Tilden man," but he has no stance on one of the campaign issues—hard money versus soft money. He doesn't care, "as the traders take either in pay for war material." The Democratic *New Orleans Picayune* felt compelled to respond to the frequent joke about Sitting Bull's politics: "'If you live another month,' says the Detroit Free Press, 'you will hear that Sitting Bull and Gov. Tilden have been in secret correspondence. The Republican papers hold back the news to make the effect more tremendous.'"[62]

Ridiculing rival newspapers over their coverage, politics, and accuracy was in fact standard fare for journalists' humor columns in 1876, and many editors took shots at each other over their Little Bighorn coverage. Many of the western papers criticized the ignorance of easterners. The *Rocky Mountain News,* for example, took issue with unnamed "fighting editors of eastern newspapers" who were criticizing Crook for moving too slow. "But the same bloodthirsty editors wouldn't venture within 175 miles of the Indian country, during the war, even if they knew they could get a fat sutlership." The *Bismarck Tribune* teased the editor of an anonymous "country newspaper" for calling Terry's command "the Sioux City expedition of the Black Hills." The *Tribune* was certainly testy about geography. It also chastised the *Stillwater Lumberman* for reporting that the battle had taken place in the Black Hills, which the *Tribune* noted are 400 miles east of the Little Bighorn.[63]

The *New York Herald* mocked newspapers that mistakenly referred to Father De Smet, the famous priest who had befriended Sitting Bull, as "the old blackguard" when his real nickname, according to the *Herald,* was "the old black gown." In fact, the *Herald* was probably not completely accurate, either. Sitting Bull biographer Robert Utley uses the translation "black robe." At any rate, the *Herald* concluded that journalistic mistakes could not destroy the work of that "great, good man."[64]

The great Indian leader's name was used by the *Picayune* to slam a Yankee paper: "The Northern papers call the *New York Times* the Sitting Bull of the political campaign." The *Picayune* also made a joke based on the fact that the reporter killed at the Little Bighorn, Mark Kellogg, had the same last name as the Republican carpetbagger governor of Louisiana, William Pitt Kellogg: "William Pitt, however, was not so patriotic as to have allowed himself to be caught with the lamented Custer. Who can seize an eel by the tail!"[65]

Chicago had one of the most competitive newspaper markets in the country, and the papers' coverage there reflected that by mocking the quality of each other's stories. The *Chicago Times*, for example, regularly accused the *Chicago Inter-Ocean* of combining wire reports with letters from army officers to make it seem to the reader that it had a reporter at the front. According to the *Times,* the *Inter-Ocean* had "the only living correspondent who can at once pick up daily city hall items and send special telegrams from Crook."[66]

The *Inter-Ocean* and other Chicago papers retaliated by ridiculing the *Times* for its self-importance and braggadocio about its war correspondent's reports from Crook's column. The *Inter-Ocean* compared the reports of the correspondent, John F. Finerty, with Crook's dispatches and wrote tongue in cheek that Crook should be kicked out of the service for neglecting to mention Finerty's heroism. "Were it not for the fact that the gallant young fellow wields a quill almost as well as he handles the sword and the carbine, and that he has an organ as fearless in the cause of truth as he is blood-thirsty in the pursuit of Indians, the world would have remained forever in ignorance of his furious charges, his hair-breadth escapes, and his bullet-riddled horses," the *Inter-Ocean* wrote sarcastically. "Through the medium of the *Times*, however, and despite the foolish jealousy of Crook, we know who the real hero of the battle of the Rosebud is, and what he did for his country on that field of carnage." If only Finerty had been with Custer, the *Inter-Ocean* lamented, the Little Bighorn might have turned out differently. The *Chicago Daily News* echoed the *Inter-Ocean,* writing that according to the *Times* Finerty was "the bravest man on the frontier."[67]

Reporters, on the other hand, sometimes made fun of themselves. Phocion Howard of the *Chicago Tribune,* describing his train trip to the frontier, wrote that the railroad conductors teased him by calling him "Standing Bull." When he got to the front, he poked fun at himself for staying behind when the troops he was accompanying attacked a village:

O'Kelly, the New York Herald correspondent, seized his repeating rifle and went on shore with the first detachment, but your correspondent, like Martha, chose the better (and more safe) part, and remained at his post (the safest one on the boat) on top of the pilot-house. His judgment and discretion were profitable in the end, for while O'Kelly was trudging through the sagebrush, your correspondent quietly slipped on shore under cover of Long John Campbell, and led the van in rifling the deserted Indian camp. I captured the high-muck-a-muck's primitive war outfit and enough red flannel medicine bags to last the Whisky Ring as long as it quarters in the Cook County Jail.[68]

Everything, it seems, was fair game for mockery. Everything except the death of Custer and his men. Jokes that directly mocked Custer—like the one that titles this chapter—were published infrequently in 1876. In one rare example, the *Rocky Mountain Herald* wrote: "There is a mooted question just now which has the most 'scalps'—Gen. Grant or Gen. Sitting Bull. There will yet arise a lively discussion to know which of 'em it was got Custer's scalp."[69]

A few papers joked about public reaction to Custer's death, especially the poems written about battle that were published in some newspapers. *The Louisville Sunday Review* wrote that "Custer would have cursed his fate if he had lived to see the poems on his death. This is a bull, but not a Sitting Bull." Denver's *Rocky Mountain Herald* similarly wrote that "Custer, after all, is better off than the most of us, as the fortunes of war saved him from the awful fate of having to read the poems written on the massacre."[70]

Many newspapers, of course, wrote lengthy profiles about Custer or amusing episodes from his life, including his boyhood and his years as a student at West Point. For example, the *New York Times* published a story from an Ohio school principal who said Custer's teachers grew to love him despite his "waywardness" on occasion in the classroom:

> "When taken to task for misconduct, he would usually say: 'I know it was wrong, but I could not help it.'
> 'Could not help it?'
> 'No, Sir. I wanted to do it.'
> 'But could you not restrain your impulses?'
> 'Don't know, Sir—never tried.'
> 'But don't you think you ought to try?'
> 'What if I could; but I don't feel like trying.'
> His logic was overwhelming—at least his teacher had to accept it as such."[71]

A man who had been two years behind Custer at West Point wrote a moving tribute that the *Louisville Courier-Journal* deemed important enough to take about a column and a half—a large amount of space for a feature story in that paper. The writer, identified only as J.M.W., recalled that he first met Custer when the future general was leading a group of older cadets to pull a prank on the freshman, who were sleeping in tents. The writer, who was one of the freshman, was startled awake "just in time to look full into the laughing face of Custer." The future hero grabbed the freshman's bottom blanket and drug it and the groggy cadet down the company ground. After the wild ride Custer disappeared, letting the freshman find his way back to his tent in the dark.[72]

≫→

Readers in 1876 no doubt found jokes and stories like these amusing; more than 125 years later, many might find them tedious or contrived. What makes people laugh is a mystery. Carr and Greeves express it well when they write, "As far as we're concerned, there are three enduring mysteries of human existence: sex, death and jokes."[73] Still, one certain purpose for laughter is to reduce fear. Humor can do that by reducing the importance of things that are fearful and awe-inspiring. What was once frightening is familiar and less intimidating when it can be laughed at.[74] The nineteenth-century editors who made jokes about the Sioux war likely helped Americans understand and cope with a tragedy which, when first reported, was so overwhelming as to be almost incomprehensible. The death of the army's most famous Indian fighter and the near destruction of its most famous Indian-fighting unit raised questions about the country's military, government policy, and political leaders. Juxtaposed with the centennial celebration of American successes, the news of the Little Bighorn was jarring, to say the least. Many Americans wondered how the country could deal with the frontier, or any crisis, if the best it had to offer was beaten by what they considered an inferior culture.

The majority of jokes printed in American newspapers helped reduce the size of the threat by mocking it while at the same time usually respecting the dead. Jokes directly ridiculing Custer and his men were rare. Such barbs aimed at the military were reserved for generals and militia who were not at the front, or for politicians who had established a failed Indian policy. Mocking the political leaders focused the public on what needed to be done to win the war and establish a better policy.

Jokes about the fear of scalping and torture could help readers cope with the disastrous news by allowing them to laugh instead of being traumatized by the horror of the mutilations found on the battlefield. Furthermore, jokes about Sitting Bull and the tribes helped readers to put into perspective what seemed like an unwinnable war. Twenty-first-century readers might focus on the stereotypes and racism of some of this humor—and there was surely some of that in these jokes. But when considering this topic, it is important to remember that for the newspaper reader in 1876 the Indians were the enemy in an active war and thus were considered fair game for ridicule. At the same time, in a reflection of the country's conflicting opinions about Indians, whites were sometimes the butt of jokes in which Indians were the heroes. Sitting Bull was sometimes cast as a brilliant leader who could outfight the whites in battle and outnegotiate them at the agencies. John Grass's mischievous gift of a broken musket for the president was repeated as a good joke rather than as an insult.

Were these jokes in poor taste? Standards of what is tasteful and what is crude vary across time and culture. Ted Cohen writes in his philosophical study of humor that there is no rule about when you can joke about death; it is up to the individual. However, Cohen, who writes about Holocaust jokes and others of questionable taste, offers two principles: "One, jokes cannot be the entire human response to death, or to anything else; two, any total response to death that does not include the possibility of jokes is less than a totally human response."[75]

In the aftermath of the Little Bighorn, American journalists reacted in an entirely human way: they reported the tragedy as best they could, and they provided their readers with some humor to help them understand an overwhelming event.

CHAPTER 8

"Duty and Valor"

The Focus of Little Bighorn Coverage

If the press, as so many writers have argued, created the myth of Custer's Last Stand, it did a pretty poor job. The picture of a dashing young general leading his men in a heroic sacrifice against overwhelming odds has not been an enduring image. More than 125 years after the Little Bighorn, Custer and his Last Stand are indeed embedded in American culture—but not infrequently as an example of a disaster brought on by stupidity or arrogance. At other times Custer is recalled as a ridiculous figure to illustrate a situation in which someone is hopelessly outnumbered. And when Custer is placed in the context of his own time, he usually represents the poor treatment of American Indians by white Americans. Many of these uses of the Custer story would likely confuse, surprise, or even repulse the journalists who wrote about the Little Bighorn in 1876.

The use of Custer imagery is certainly widespread. For example, psychologist Kevin Leman titled a chapter of a child-raising book "Where Did They All Come From" to refer to the confusion of parents over the actions of their kids. "These could have been General Custer's last words, but they don't have to be yours," Leman wrote reassuringly about his chapter title.[1] The hip-hop artist Nelly brags in the song "Heart of a Champion" that his "last stance" is like that of "General Custard." The name is presumably misspelled to rhyme with "mustard"—meaning money—which is what the singer has a lot of—and suggests Nelly can "hot dog" like Custer did.[2] Nineteenth-century journalists enjoyed word play and would have appreciated Nelly's lyrics and other Little Bighorn–related puns, which still occasionally appear in modern funny pages, like a drawing of Custer in a booth selling maps of the Little Bighorn with the caption "Custer's Next-to-Last Stand."[3]

Those journalists, who specialized in evocative, even outlandish headlines, would certainly appreciate the ubiquity of the phrase "Last Stand," which has been used in current times to describe every type of crisis from the violent revolution that consumed Libyan dictator Muammar Gaddafi to the more metaphorical challenges that faced Barack Obama and George W. Bush. Many modern references allude to Custer rather than to a last stand. An *Economist* cover features a cartoon of Bush dressed as a cavalry officer leading a charge as an image of what it thought would be a failed surge during the Iraq War.[4] When fired *New York Times* editor Howell Raines wanted to describe the criticism he had received for mistakes at the paper in 2003, he told an interviewer, "I've got more arrows in me than Custer's horse."[5]

Some journalists in 1876 might have laughed at that crack because they did appreciate rough humor, although they usually poked fun at the living or fictitious characters instead of the heroic dead. There is no question, however, that they would be horrified by the modern tendency to ridicule Custer's death as if he had not been a real person. Ban T-shirts, which claims to provide the "most radical political T-shirts on the internet," offers a shirt with a famous Civil War photo of a standing Custer turned on his side to make him look like he's lying down. Custer's image is pierced with ten arrows and appears over the caption "Custer Pwned!!!" which is video gamer slang for "owned"—being beaten in humiliating fashion.[6]

What these varied images have in common is that they have almost nothing in common with the heroic image of Custer most Americans held in 1876. To be sure, many at the time blamed the defeat on his rashness, but he was universally recognized as having earned respect for his years of service—particularly during the Civil War—and for ultimately sacrificing his life for his country. It was that part of the story that the journalists of 1876 did a good job of telling. Critics of Little Bighorn press coverage claim journalists called for the extermination of the Indians, injected politics into the story, and created the myth of the Last Stand based on error-filled reporting. All of the criticisms have some validity but are largely unfair.

It is popular in academic circles to suggest that the United States waged a war of genocide against the Indians. Historian Benjamin Madley claimed in a speech that violence endorsed by the government led to the near disappearance of the tribes. Madley, who specializes in studying genocide, said that if the country was founded on genocide it would have profound implications for the reevaluation of the history of the country, school curricula, and reparations.[7] Popular history, too, beginning with *A Century of Dishonor,* first published in 1881 but still available in bookstores, has emphasized the cruelty of the government and the general population of the United States in their treatment of Indians. *Bury My Heart at Wounded Knee,* another popular book that focused on the Indian side of the story, was reissued in 2011 in a lavish fortieth anniversary edition.[8] On the other hand, opponents of the genocide argument, like historian Guenther Lewy, point out that genocide was never the official policy of the United States. Lewy claims that diseases to which American Indians had no immunity were the main cause of the reduction of the tribes, and those who study the Indian wars must consider the context of the moral standards of the time for waging war.[9]

Whichever side of the argument one endorses, there is no debate that at times the government and the citizens treated the Indians unfairly. How much of this was due to unfair press coverage by the journalists of the day? Scholars who have studied the Little Bighorn generally think the press fanned the flames of public outrage toward the Indians and urged extermination of the tribes. Robert Utley, writing in *Custer and the Great Controversy,* argues that the Indians got little sympathy. Journalism historian William E. Huntzicker asserts that the battle "united the moderate and extremist" in subduing the tribes and notes the use of words like "demons, devils and vampires" to describe the Indians. John Coward, writing in a history of coverage of the Indian wars, notes that some newspapers, particularly in the East, published sympathetic stories about the Indians, but that "the Battle of the Little Bighorn generated some of the most hateful Indian news stories of the century."[10]

It is true that much of the language in the Little Bighorn coverage was extreme by today's standards. Americans living in the politically correct twenty-first century recoil at pejoratives like "savage." Still, it is important to place the emotional language in the context of the times.

Americans in parts of the West were living in an active war zone, and other parts of the country had seen Indian wars within living memory. Even in the settled East, Americans had vivid memories of the horrific casualties and the total war campaigns waged during the Civil War, which was scarcely ten years removed from the Little Bighorn. Indeed, frequent violent episodes in the South like the Hamburg Massacre raised the specter of bloody guerrilla war without end or, in the worst case, a renewal of open rebellion. A population intimately familiar with such things was not squeamish about using strong language in identifying the enemy and urging the strongest measures to deal with them. The press coverage of the Little Bighorn must be seen in the context of the Civil War and Reconstruction, not just in the context of a five-hundred-year interaction between European Americans and Native Americans. To be sure, some newspapers called for the extermination of the "savages," but during the Civil War some newspapers had also called for the extermination of Rebels or Yankees, portraying them as subhuman beasts. In 1876 this threatening language was regularly applied to others besides Indians. The outlaws of the infamous James Gang, led by former Quantrill raider Jesse, were called "savages" in some newspaper copy in 1876. Henry Watterson's *Louisville Courier-Journal* apoplectically castigated the *Cincinnati Commercial* for endorsing the use of federal troops to protect black voters in South Carolina. "They hate us," the paper screamed in an editorial headlined with a straight line to indicate where curse words should go. "Their whole policy is to destroy and exterminate us. All of us feel this, know this."[11]

Such phrasing was hyperbole, especially from a paper run by Watterson, who in his memoir claimed he had many Republican friends and did not let politics interfere with his personal relations.[12] Similarly, much of the "extermination" talk about Indians was also emotional reaction to the horrifying news of Custer's defeat. In San Francisco, the initial *Alta California* Little Bighorn coverage was openly bloodthirsty. "If the Sioux were wiped out now, it would not atone for the harm that Sitting Bull has done," the *California* noted in a front-page comment on July 8, the first day it printed news of the Little Bighorn. "The red devils should be driven to the Reservation on the other side of Jordan." The paper apparently was reflecting the emotions of the city. New Yorkers may have forgotten that a war was going on, but San Franciscans still remembered the Modoc war and closely followed the action on the frontier. The day after first reporting the Little Bighorn, the *California* recommended that citizens organize volunteer units to "make the punishment of these savages swift and sure." The editorial noted that a thousand men could be recruited immediately. "The public demands some participation in avenging the fate of the rash but gallant Custer, and the public is likely to grow impatient over a long campaign like that against the Modocs. In our own city the feeling is very strong, and volunteers will be forthcoming."[13]

Nevertheless, like many papers the *California* softened its stance as the weeks went by. In early August it urged readers to consider the work of E. S. McDonald, an officer who had trained a unit of Indian soldiers and claimed to have civilized them. The *California* noted that McDonald was from San Francisco and was known to everyone in the Bay Area as a serious man: "Now our people know Captain McDonald, know that he is ardent in whatever he undertakes and may be over sanguine. But he certainly has shown the great capacity of the Indians he has drilled and educated, and his views are worthy of deep consideration." The *California,* however, was unsure of the idea of moving the Sioux to the Midwest to learn agriculture. The newspaper noted that a mission in California had mixed results with trying to teach Indians farming: "They were certainly not civilized too much; but something connected with civilization was fatal to them, and they died off rapidly."[14]

The *California,* aside from its first bombastic editorials about the Little Bighorn, was not in favor of the Indians dying off. It argued that the peace policy was unfair to them and would lead to just such an outcome: "They are cheated; allowed to own their own ponies and to acquire the best arms, and to supply themselves with ammunition, and go out upon their real or pretended hunts, thus tempted into making war, or else only murdering the few unprotected whites they may chance to meet on the plains or in the hills, and whenever wearied with such hunting and perhaps short of provisions, allowed to return as before and be rationed. This is extra and unreasonable benevolence which leads the Indian to think himself master, and eventually to lead him to destruction."[15] The best policy toward the Indians, the *California* commented when it learned of a peace commission to the hostiles, "is to whip them after they make war till they sue for peace. Any other management leads them to suppose that war is a game in which they have everything to gain, and nothing to lose."[16]

This is not to say that the *California* and other papers like it were greatly concerned about the plight of the tribes. They were not. Their main concern and sympathy lay with civilians killed by Indians and with the beleaguered frontier army that tried to protect them. The *California* marveled at people like Wendell Phillips, the activist who attacked Sherman by claiming that the general wanted to exterminate the Indians. It compared such thinking to misplaced sympathy toward criminals. Sherman only wanted to keep the Indians on their reservations by taking away their horses, the *California* wrote.

> But probably this same class of impractical humanitarians, and those whose great purpose in Christianizing those fearful, sullen savages, would object to the policy of putting the roaming Indian—the American Bedouin—upon his feet instead of his pony. . . . And the news of the annihilation of the gallant Custer and his heroic band had scarcely been published ere President Grant received a petition from this class or society of Indian admirers, advising him not to make a severe war upon those savages. Could impudence go farther? Should the community respect the petitions or opinions or principles of people who show more sympathy for the murdering Indian than for the poor fellows who lose their lives in defending our frontiers?"[17]

Only a minority of newspapers wanted to wage a war of extermination; most, like the *California,* wanted a severe war—meaning that the army should fight it the way it fought the Civil War. People knew the way to end the horror of war was to fight it without mercy so that victory was quickly achieved and peace restored. The Indians, although almost universally acknowledged to be victims of some level of white chicanery, were seen as the enemy. It was only natural that stories and editorials did not give equal balance to their point of view. But it is important to acknowledge that their side *was* heard. Editorialists routinely acknowledged the guilt of miners invading the Black Hills, the cheating of Indians by government agents, and the overall failure of the government to enforce treaty provisions. When reporters were able to contact Indians who had fought at the battle, they were quick to publish their quotes in the general rush to get a scoop about the battle and Custer's demise. Even the often vilified Sitting Bull was quoted through intermediaries at the reservations. One of the most republished stories in the aftermath of the battle was Sitting Bull's comment to Bear Stands Up that he wanted peace but had been forced into fighting by the whites.[18]

In fact, in their eagerness to get the story and comment on it, the journalists of 1876 were not much different from the twenty-first-century scribes covering the conflicts in Iraq and Afghanistan. It is a useful comparison to examine because the various subsets of the global war on terror actually have parallels with the Indian conflicts. Both eras feature a small (in comparison to the total population), professional, all-volunteer military fighting an unconventional foe in a harsh environment far from the main U.S. population centers. The fighting is ferocious, it is hard for U.S. soldiers to tell civilians from combatants, and in the rare cases when U.S. soldiers are taken prisoner they are often abused by their captors. The similarities are not lost on today's military.

Robert D. Kaplan writes in *Hog Pilots, Blue Water Grunts,* his profile of the twenty-first-century U.S. military, that many soldiers he interviewed "found more benefit in studying the nineteenth-century Indian wars than the two world wars combined" because the former featured mobile small raids rather than massed battles. Kaplan notes that many of the forts of the U.S. Army were located on the Great Plains and were legacies of the Indian wars. In fact, the army "consciously maintained the legacy of the Indian Wars" through names of some of its units. The 4th Battalion of the 23rd Infantry Regiment, for example, are called the Tomahawks, and its three rifle companies are called "Apache," "Black Hawk," and Comanche." Kaplan could have added that many weapons systems, such as the Tomahawk missile and the Apache helicopter, are named after imagery from the Indian wars.[19]

The similarity goes beyond nomenclature. American frontier soldiers experienced feelings of isolation and frequent threats from an elusive foe. Modern U.S. troops have similar feelings fighting from their heavily barricaded outposts, surrounded by what they call "Indian country." Joseph Kearns Goodwin's description of his service in Iraq and Afghanistan sounds like it could have come from one of his frontier forbears when he describes "the intense bonds of friendship the young soldiers formed with one another, immersed as they were in an alien landscape, wholly reliant upon each other, and under constant threat of mortal danger."[20]

When U.S. Army Sgt. James Riley described the feeling of being attacked by hundreds of Iraqi soldiers and insurgents after his maintenance company took a wrong turn into Nasiriyah in the early days of the Iraq War, he used the Little Bighorn for a comparison: "We were like Custer," he recalled, still sounding shocked when he was interviewed upon his release from captivity. "We were surrounded. We had no working weapons. We couldn't even make a bayonet charge—we would have been mowed down. We didn't have a choice, sir."[21]

A detailed study of the press coverage of the fighting in Iraq and Afghanistan would take a lengthy book of its own, but a brief analysis of *Washington Post* press coverage of the battle of Nasiriyah offers a good case study of how modern American journalists report on their country's wars. The battle, which lasted for several days in March 2003, is an apt comparison to the Little Bighorn because it included the destruction of Sergeant Riley's 507th Maintenance Company, a rear-area unit that found itself cut off from the main body of troops. It was one of the worst setbacks for the U.S. military in the first phase of the war and generated a great deal of publicity because the Iraqis distributed video of prisoners from the 507th, including a woman. Another female soldier, Jessica Lynch, was missing and became a household name as the military searched for her.

In covering Nasiriyah, *Washington Post* reporters, like Indian war reporters, relied mainly on official U.S. sources while less frequently reporting comments from Iraqis. Stories about the fighting usually carried an American spin on the news, and, as in the Sioux war coverage, expectation of victory. For example, the initial report of the fighting in Nasiriyah mentioned guerrilla attacks on U.S. troops but quoted officials as "dismissing" their significance and echoed the optimistic tone of officers. The *Post* quoted Gen. Tommy Franks, the overall commander of the invasion: "Our troops are performing as we would expect, magnificently." The story was accompanied by a photo of an Iraqi soldier surrendering to U.S. troops.[22] When it became obvious that the fighting was stiffer than expected, U.S. generals got ample space to explain the situation. A typical *Post* story quoted some anonymous military officials admitting that "they may have underestimated the resolve of Iraqi troops and paramilitary units and overestimated the greeting U.S. troops would receive from the population." The story noted that marines in Nasiriyah engaged in a six-hour battle that ended only when air support arrived. But it concluded that the marines had secured the town and were moving on to Baghdad. Franks was quoted as saying his plan was going as he had expected, but that the speed of the advance meant troops would bypass some hostile units and some "clean-up" operations would continue."[23]

When news broke the next day about the attack on the 507th, in an echo of the shock the press had felt about news of Custer's defeat the *Post* devoted about half of its front page—three stories and two pictures—to the story under a banner headline calling it "the heaviest day of American causalities." One news analysis piece argued that the battle showed that the Iraqis would not necessarily surrender easily or welcome the Americans as liberators.[24] Just as nineteenth-century editors pointed out that the Little Bighorn showed that the country was in for a long Indian war, the modern press jumped on Nasiriyah to argue that Iraq would be a long war.

And as the press after the Little Bighorn reported graphic details about the mutilation of the Seventh Cavalry dead, the *Post* published disturbing details about Iraqi video footage of the American dead from Nasiriyah. "An orderly in blue scrubs could be seen moving the bodies. He smiled briefly at the camera."[25] Another story emphasized the brutality and deceptiveness of the Iraqis and provided more detail of the video: "The gruesome footage provided lingering, close-up images of the dead soldiers lying on the floor. Two of them appeared to have been shot in the head, one directly between his eyes and one in the forehead." The video was apparently of soldiers from the 507th. But Lt. Gen. John Abizaid told reporters that other Americans were killed in the fighting in Nasiriyah when Iraqis pretended to surrender and then opened fire, or when Iraqis in civilian clothes pretended to welcome troops before firing.[26]

The *Post* did not run pictures from the video until it had confirmation that the soldiers' families had been notified that they were prisoners. *Post* executive editor Leonard Downie, Jr., said the paper was "relatively conservative" in running pictures of dead people in any circumstances and tried to be "a good houseguest." But other media ran the images immediately, and Wesley Pruden, editor-in-chief of *Post* cross-town rival the

Washington Times, said his paper ran the images to show "the true face of the enemy, who we're dealing with, that they would take these prisoners and treat them like this."[27]

The images had that effect on some viewers. A *Post* feature on the reaction of family and friends of the dead soldiers included an angry quote from Art Berrera, who ran a surplus store near Fort Bliss, where the 507th was based: "'The Iraqis—we're dealing with a tribal mentality,' he said, nearly spitting out the words."[28]

Two days later, the *Post* editorialized that the Iraqi regime was guilty of war crimes, including broadcasting the video and executing prisoners. The *Post* noted that Iraqis might resent the presence of the Americans. "But the final spasms of brutality by the regime's criminal apparatus ought to reinforce one truth about this war: The end of Saddam Hussein's rule will be a liberation." The *Post* frequently ran editorials supporting the war effort, encouraging the public to be patient despite some bad news like Nasiriyah. The country had faced worse setbacks in previous wars, the *Post* noted, but with modern media coverage Americans "felt the blows almost as they occurred." The military would experience more losses, and each would cause anguish, followed by memorials and eventually monuments. "Ultimately the monument that matters will be victory and a sustained commitment to a rebuilt Iraq—a commitment that will leave Americans safer and the Iraqi people better off."[29]

Stories about combat soldiers were usually sympathetic, and the descriptions of the fighting could have fit in a story about the Little Bighorn campaign. One reporter described the excitement of Pfc. Nick McLaughlin coming under fire for the first time: "It didn't seem real 'til the first round went by my ear," he said. The story related the frustration of fighting the insurgents, who would fire a few shots and disappear. One marine described trying to fight back as "shooting at shadows." Another story sympathetically described marines sweeping a village near Nasiriyah, looking for weapons. They found some in an innocent-looking family home. The story emphasized the dilemma of the troops because the weapons could have been planted by the Iraqi army, or the homeowner could have been an insurgent. "All the Marines are sure of is that there's another house to check, and another after that."[30]

The marines were checking houses, but were the reporters equally careful in checking facts? The knock on the Little Bighorn coverage is that journalists often got facts wrong or printed whatever news they found without verification. It is certainly true that the press made mistakes both big and small, including unverified quotes from Custer and the often gleeful stories about Sitting Bull and Crazy Horse being killed in the battle. But a key difference between the nineteenth-century and twenty-first-century reporters is that those from the earlier era acknowledged upfront that they were reporting rumors or doubtful information and corrected it as soon as they got more details. It was common for the *Chicago Tribune* to publish a paragraph about a report of Crook defeating the Sioux under the cautious headline "A Rumor. Too Good to Be True." Two days later, the *Tribune* reported that it had "partial confirmation" of what it still called a rumor but explained in the headline that "There Must Be Something in It."[31] Such reporting has the advantage of letting the readers know everything the journalists learn but warning them to be skeptical.

Modern journalists, just as hungry for scoops as their forebears, also sometimes report sketchy stories, but with an air of professionalism that does not permit admitting that they could use more verification. The theory of objectivity, which dictates that journalists keep their opinions out of news columns, encourages them to rely on quotes from official sources and not question the information unless another source can be found to make the counterargument. This practice does not necessarily keep errors out of the press but rather lets the press repeat incorrect information from official sources without an indication of doubt in the report. Craig Silverman, a former journalist who has researched media mistakes, acknowledges the accuracy problems of the nineteenth-century press but presents a variety of studies that show modern journalists making errors at a "shocking level." He writes, based on an analysis of these studies, that "close to half of the local news stories in most American papers include at least one error." Furthermore, the number of errors in newspapers and broadcast and online media is "much higher" than the number that are corrected. In other words, modern journalists are not finding, admitting, and correcting the majority of their mistakes.[32]

Certainly the hoary cliché that truth is the first casualty in war applies to the war on terror as well as the Great Sioux War. For example, in the case of Nasiriyah, the *Post* and other news outlets reported that attacks on convoys had led to the marines calling the southern entrances to the city "ambush alley."[33] The dramatic phrase suggests that the marines were surprised by the fierceness of the Iraqis. However, the name was actually developed during planning for the invasion because officers realized the area would be conducive to ambushes.[34]

The story of Jessica Lynch provides one of the best examples of press error in the Iraq War. By March 27 the main fighting in the war had moved well north of Nasiriyah, but the fate of the 507th prisoners and those listed as missing was still in the news. The *Post* published a front-page feature story about Lynch, focusing on her background and why she joined the army.[35] Lynch, an attractive, blond soldier, quickly became a celebrity. When she was rescued, the *Post* reported the story on the front page for three days in row. The first story carried scant details of the rescue but rather focused attention on the jubilant reaction to the news. The next day, however, the *Post* reported details that later turned out to be untrue—that Lynch continued to fire her weapon after she was severely wounded and that, as one official said, "She did not want to be taken alive." (The *Post* repeated the details in at least one subsequent story.) The story also reported that the hospital she was rescued from contained what looked like a torture chamber complete with batteries and metal rods. A later story portrayed an Iraqi as a hero, detailing how he had told U.S. troops where Lynch was being held.[36]

The rescue unit also recovered the remains of several U.S. soldiers, and a few days after Lynch's rescue the Pentagon released the names of eight soldiers killed in the ambush. Lori Piestewa, who was the first American Indian woman killed in combat in the war, received the most coverage, but the *Post* also provided information about the other casualties. One story noted that some of the relatives of the soldiers believed the Iraqis had executed some of the prisoners.[37]

The *Post* devoted about half of the front page and two full inside pages to the 507th soldiers the day it reported that the surviving prisoners were rescued. Riley, the senior soldier present at the time of the surrender, recounted how the soldiers were overwhelmed. As noted earlier, he compared their situation to Custer's Last Stand. The *Post* reported that the Iraqis kicked and beat some of the prisoners, and that some of the prisoners worried they would be killed up until the moment they were rescued.[38]

The next day the *Post* published an Iraqi version of events, quoting doctors and patients at the hospital where Lynch was treated. The story claimed that no Iraqi soldiers were at the hospital when special forces rescued Lynch and quoted an Iraqi doctor who called it "just a drama." The story was published on page 17 as opposed to the front-page coverage devoted to the false narrative about Lynch's ferocious resistance. The doctors who treated Lynch said she had no bullet or stab wounds. "It was a road traffic accident," one doctor said, discounting the earlier stories about her fighting prowess.[39]

Historian Richard S. Lowry, who has written frequently about the Iraq War, criticized the media for overlooking the battle to pursue the Lynch story. "As the days and weeks passed, the news media moved on to Lynch's rescue and then the fall of Baghdad. When the Department of Defense finally sorted things out and released the names of the Marines and soldiers who died that day, the media took very little interest. No one ever realized that that bloody day in Nasiriyah, on March 23rd, was the costliest day of combat for America in the invasion of Iraq."[40]

Modern journalists have faster communication technology, more education, and various professional ethics codes to try to follow, but the bottom line is that the fog of war and their own biases afflict today's coverage no less than they did the coverage in 1876. The difference is that modern journalists for the most part either refuse to acknowledge their bias or claim it has no affect on coverage.

The journalists of 1876 were moving as a profession toward what they called "independence," but like the modern term "objectivity" it was hard to define. However, as one journalism historian noted, just about everyone at the time agreed independence did not mean neutrality.[41] Instead, most papers of the era openly identified with one political party but at the same time claimed to be free to criticize policies and politicians within the party rather than just publish what we would today call talking points. The *St. Louis Globe-Democrat,* for example, editorialized that it did not mind being called a party organ, because it was such a strong believer in Republican principles. The *Globe* would not "withhold our meed of praise, when duly earned by those who are honestly divided from us on organic questions." The *Globe,* like many newspapers, ran a regular house ad stating its party loyalty. But the ad noted the limits to that loyalty: "While the Globe-Democrat will always be in the front to sustain the Republican party and its measures, it will reserve the right, as it is its duty, or the duty of any newspaper, to oppose any measure not in unison with Republican principles, although it may emanate from men acknowledging allegiance to the Republican party."[42]

Honest differences of opinion were expected and accepted, but journalists looked with scorn on those who wishy-washily refused to pick a party. Although its motto was "United We Stand Divided We Fall," the *Kentucky Advocate* urged the opposite of unity in politics. The *Advocate* editorialized that it could not respect an independent because such a person "has no fixed political principles. We honor a Radical who has the manliness to stand up boldly for what he conceives to be right, but may the Good Lord deliver us from a so-called 'independent.'"[43]

The *Hartford Courant* agreed with that sentiment, mocking the *Springfield Republican* when that Massachusetts newspaper praised Tilden:

> Our skillful and independent journal at Springfield is slowly and cautiously making up its mind which of the two presidential candidates it will *not* support with the greatest vigor. The process is psychologically interesting. Yesterday it devoted a couple of columns to a weighing in the hand of the bad traits of Tilden; offering the spectacle of a respectable market woman over her basket of eggs considering which of them are too far gone to offer for sale. So far as we can judge, the *Republican* thinks that Tilden is not a very good egg, but will do well enough for an omelette. . . . We do not say the paper is in the position of one sitting on the fence at the end of the course, ready to help over the rails the candidate who happens to come in first. Our opinion is not as personal as that. Politically, we almost think that if it rains we shall have wet weather, unless, indeed, it happens to be a dry rain.[44]

At the *Louisville Courier-Journal,* Watterson chided the independent voter for being undecided between the Republican and Democratic parties because the voter blamed the Republicans for corruption and the Democrats for starting the Civil War: "Flanked by these two opinions he halts; and, for the time being at least, appears as the ass between the two bundles of hay. Nevertheless, the Independent Voter is a most intelligent and honest animal, to be respected no less for his independence than for his intelligence. Yet, after all, he is not free from the very partisan prejudice which he scorns, for his hesitation is produced solely by prejudice against the Democratic party."[45]

Watterson's sarcastic dissection of the independent voter illustrates the passion of journalists to state their positions openly and vigorously. In his rambling two-volume memoir, published about fifty years after the Little Bighorn, he wrote what seemed to be contradictory thoughts about the best practices of the profession he had served for nearly seventy years. On the one hand, in writing about the election of 1876, he averred that "the soul of journalism is disinterestedness. But neither as a principle nor an asset had this been generally discovered fifty years ago." Yet in describing the three eras of the newspaper business he had experienced, he seemed to long for the previous era of "personal" journalism as opposed to what he called the "timorous, corporation, or family-owned billboard" of the twentieth century: "Neither [the newspaper's] individuality nor its self-exploitation, scarcely its grandiose pretension, remains. There continues to be printed in large type an amount of shallow stuff that would not be missed if it were omitted altogether. But, except as a bulletin of yesterday's doings, limited, the daily newspaper counts for little, the single advantage of the editor—in case there is an editor—that is, one clothed with supervising authority who 'edits'—being that he reaches the public with his lucubrations first, the sanctity that once hedged the editorial 'we' long since departed."[46]

It is clear in Watterson's memoir that his insistence that journalists be disinterested (he also used the term "independent") was something quite different from today's objectivity, in which journalists pretend to be completely impartial and hide their own political views from the public. Watterson meant that journalists should not seek public office, like *New York Sun* editor Whitelaw Reid had done by becoming an ambassador, nor should they take any favors from government. But the public would still want to know something about who ran the paper, Watterson claimed:

The people are already beginning to distinguish between the wholesome and the meretricious in their newspapers. Newspaper owners, likewise, are beginning to realize the value of character. Instances might be cited where the public, discerning some sinister but unseen power behind its press, has slowly yet surely withdrawn its confidence and support.

However impersonal it pretends to be, with whatever of mystery it affects to envelop itself, the public insists upon some visible presence. . . . Thus 'personal journalism' cannot be escaped, and whether the 'one-man power' emanates from the Counting Room or the Editorial Room, as they are called, it must be clear and answerable, responsive to the common weal, and, above all, trustworthy.[47]

That the public does not trust the media today is evident from countless surveys.[48] One of the reasons for the mistrust could be the lack of transparency among today's journalists and the organizations they work for. Few news organizations state that they support one of the major parties, but the public can easily sense which way the organization leans based on not just its editorial page but the tone, placement, and emphasis it gives to specific news stories. The public also suspects that individual journalists are biased, and that bias has been confirmed by both research and the admission of working journalists. Writers on both the left and the right argue that news media are biased against their side.[49] The public, in the digital age, has myriad choices in news from aggregators, blogs, and even Facebook pages. No longer tied to just the mainstream media for news, the public in the early twenty-first century wants news sources that are transparent in their politics. FOXNews.com, the website of an organization often derided for leaning right, in 2010 earned the highest customer satisfaction rating ever for a news site in the ten-year history of the American Customer Satisfaction Index. The report showed that Fox understood how to give the audience what it wants and also, unlike other media companies, how to differentiate its product.[50]

Critics say such companies that cater to an audience based on their political views will lead to poorly informed voters who are ultimately turned off by the partisanship and quit participating in politics. But the transparency and passion of the journalists of 1876 contributed to a robust debate over public policy and an intense interest in politics that twenty-first-century Americans can only dream of emulating. Recall that the turnout for the 1876 election was in fact the *highest ever* in U.S. history. Voting turnout nationwide was an astounding 82 percent, compared to 59 percent in the 2012 election. In seven states it topped 90 percent. Even allowing for some fraudulent ballots, it was an extraordinary turnout.[51] Was the public ill served by the press in an election year? Judging from the Little Bighorn coverage, no. Journalists reported the facts of the battle, as they understood them, and they engaged in a natural debate over who was to blame for the battle. Some of this debate fell along partisan lines, with Democrats viciously criticizing the Grant administration and some, but not all, Republicans defending the administration's policies. There was also, of course, debate about Custer's decisions as well. Many Republicans called him rash, but so too did some Democrats. On all of these positions, reasonable people could disagree because there is no black-and-white answer to the question of who was to blame for the disaster. In fact, as one historian wrote, Custer lost because the Indians won.[52] In such a complex issue, it is simplistic to ascribe the opinions of journalists to reflexive partisanship.

There was, however, general consensus on the war itself. Journalists almost universally acknowledged that the Indians had been wronged in some fashion, but that because the country was at war the army must be supported in its efforts to win and restore peace. The proof of this unity is that the Little Bighorn was not an election issue. It virtually dropped out of the political discussion within a month or so of the news first being reported. The *New York Herald* scored a rare, wide-ranging interview with Grant in September at his Long Branch, New Jersey, summer home. After some small talk, the reporter asked Grant about the progress of the Sioux campaign. Grant apparently did not hear "Sioux" and started talking about what was on his mind—the political campaign. The reporter later returned to the Indian campaign, and Grant indicated that the issue would not be resolved before he left office. "Whether our worthy friend, Sitting Bull, will therefore be ignominiously compelled to raise cattle instead of scalping white soldiers will probably depend either on Governor Hayes or Governor Tilden," the reporter concluded. The normally anti-Grant *Herald* praised Grant's "frankness" in an editorial and noted that his comments on the war would be "read with great interest."[53] But the press and the nominees never made the war a main election issue even though the problem was obviously going to extend to 1877.

In contrast, the Iraq and Afghanistan conflicts have played significant roles in the presidential elections of the early twenty-first century. Part of this difference is due to a difference in national confidence between the two eras. The modern war policy has been fraught with debates on everything from how to treat prisoners to the cause of the war itself. One of the widely recognized heroes of the current war is Pat Tillman, a man who gave up a lucrative professional football career to enlist after 9-11. But a popular book about Tillman portrays him as disillusioned by the Iraq War and disgusted with his fellow recruits, who he found "losers and whiners."[54] Although the United States has been fighting for almost all of this century, and thousands of Americans have sacrificed their lives, some of them winning the nation's highest award in the process, the press tends to focus on negative stories like the Abu Ghraib POW abuse scandal. Heroic stories from the battlefield appear so infrequently in the media that *Armchair General* magazine decided to run a regular feature on medal winners to publicize what it believed the mainstream media were ignoring.[55]

In 1876, by contrast, Americans, including journalists, believed their country was a land of destiny. The United States was filled with people who had suffered greatly during the Civil War. Both sides admired their veterans, and enough time had passed that despite the bitterness of the struggle they could acknowledge the valor of the men who fought against them. Custer, as an example, was widely praised in the South on his death, even though he had played a key role in the defeat of the Army of Northern Virginia.

One of the frequent critiques of press coverage of Custer and the Little Bighorn is that journalists collectively created a myth in great measure by hagiographic stories about the general and his "Last Stand."[56] Such thinking insults the intelligence of nineteenth-century Americans and misunderstands the way journalism works. It is true that the press initially misreported some facts about the Little Bighorn. Some stories reported Custer killing Indians with a sword, some got the topography wrong, others reported exaggerated casualty figures. But the essential story was right from the beginning. A celebrated Civil War hero and all his men were killed by an aboriginal foe in a desolate, uncivilized part of the country. The circumstances were mysterious because there were no white survivors, and the Indians for the most part weren't talking. The hero, Custer, was so well known from his own writings and previous press coverage that the reader could imagine him in action without much help from the reporters. Custer was a *cavalryman* for goodness' sake, riding hell-for-leather toward the enemy, long gold hair and a red tie streaming behind him, giving the enemy a good target and facing death with élan. Whether he wielded a pistol or a saber, whether he was killed early or later in the battle (a question likely never to be answered) are mere details; they do not lessen the mythic nature of the event. The story, as reporters say when they latch onto a good one, writes itself. The journalists did not create a legend, they just reported information as they got it. To be sure, some nineteenth-century reporters used more dramatic language than readers are used to in the modern, sterile newspeak of corporate media, but the story itself was mythic. Popular culture, including poems, songs, biographies, Wild West shows, novels, and, later, movies, embedded Custer's Last Stand in the American psyche, not the working press.

Andrew C. Wheeler, the theater critic quoted at the beginning of this book, recognized in his essay written three days after the Little Bighorn was reported that Custer and the battle would occupy a lasting place in the American imagination. Wheeler noted that Indian warfare had fascinated the public since colonial times and never more so than in 1876, when everyone was "Indian-mad" from reading dime novels. The history of the Indian wars was an "appalling picture of unintentional inhumanity, official imbecility and reckless waste of precious blood" but still fascinating.

> Putting aside the ethics of the case entirely, all the circumstances of a collision of this kind are intensely romantic. They rivet the attention as few other events of our undramatic existence can do. Not alone is the vanity of the civilized man touched by the spectacle of highly organized force grappling with the last vestige of defiant barbarism, but the actual conditions are such as to make the picture vivid, intense and exciting. All the animal powers of courage and endurance are called into action; all the skill and wisdom of the educated man are matched against the cunning of the rude man. The contest has all the elements of wildness, celerity and fierceness that make up a tragedy.[57]

Most people, like Wheeler, were immediately aware that Custer's death would become legendary simply because of the circumstances, but they knew well the difference between reality and romance. After all, they had lived through the brutality of the Civil War. Walt Whitman's tear-jerking eulogy to Custer was widely reprinted in newspapers. But so was a joke that, although it was too bad Custer had been killed by the Indians, at least he didn't have to read the dreadful poetry written about him.[58]

A dark sense of humor has always been common among journalists. It could not be otherwise in a profession that so often deals with the dark side of human nature. Yet journalists, too, recognized right away that Custer's last fight was special. The *New York Herald* started collecting money for a monument fund within a week of the first reports of the battle.

> Long after this generation has passed away, long after every vestige of the merciless Sioux has passed from the continent, long after this Yellowstone country has become the seat of towns and cities and a prosperous civilization, the name of Custer and the story of his deeds will be fresh in men's memories. The story that comes to us today with so much horror, with so much pathos, will become a part of our national life. If as has been said, all the world loves a lover, so we may say that all the world honors a hero. What name is brighter than that of Leonidas [the Spartan leader at Thermopylae], who died as Custer died. The deeds of our young captain and his little band are worthy of as much honor as those of Leonidas, and will be remembered as long, unless we, in our selfishness, allow them to die.[59]

Whether through selfishness or politically correct guilt over the treatment of Indians, Custer in many ways is no longer widely honored in the early twenty-first century, as the "Custer Pwned" T-shirt illustrates. No doubt the *Herald* writer and others would be shocked to see Sitting Bull lionized. The great Sioux leader, who after his surrender made money from whites by selling his autograph, probably would not be surprised by the descendants of pioneering whites wearing his image on their clothing.[60] But he likely would be horrified to see the Indian monument at the Little Bighorn Battlefield that honors his tribe in the same display with their hereditary enemies, the Crows and Arikaras, which to the casual observer implies that they were fighting on the same side. On the other hand, if Sitting Bull, who praised the courage of Custer's men in a newspaper interview, toured the battlefield with the general, the two former enemies might find common ground in their mutual understanding of sacrifice and honor. After all, Custer had written once that, if he were an Indian, he would fight for his freedom rather than go on a reservation.[61]

Certainly both old warriors would feel alienated from twenty-first-century American culture, which has itself gradually become alienated from the military since the unifying experience of World War II. The end of the draft in the waning years of the unpopular Vietnam War has meant fewer Americans have served in the military or even have relatives who have served. That includes the press, where, according to *Time* magazine, service "is virtually unheard of, even after a decade of war"—a fact that angers military families and contributes to errors in coverage.[62] Andrew J. Huebner notes that since World War II through the Vietnam War the image of U.S. soldiers has gradually changed from hero to victim.[63] The emphasis on victimhood has continued through the recent conflicts and is perhaps best illustrated by the media focus on Lynch and Tillman, certainly the most famous veterans of the global war on terror.[64] Both should be praised for their sacrifice and service, but both suffered as victims. Lynch was injured in a truck accident before ever firing her weapon, and Tillman felt betrayed by the government going to war in Iraq under what he considered inappropriate reasons and then died in a friendly-fire accident. Donald Walters, a soldier in Lynch's unit who fought until he could no longer resist, risking his life to save others and then being killed after he was captured, has been largely ignored by the media. No bestselling author has come forward to tell his tale, unlike for Lynch and Tillman.[65]

The nineteenth-century press did a better job of covering heroic deeds, but it still moved on quickly to the more prosaic news of the day—in 1876 the presidential election. Hayes and Tilden and the horse race coverage of the day-to-day campaign got most of the press attention within a month of the Little Bighorn. Yet in the early twenty-first century the election is largely forgotten except when a cliffhanger like the 2000 election prompts the media to scramble for similar historical races as a point of comparison. Custer and the Little Bighorn are the enduring national memory from 1876, which calls into question the old saw that "journalism is the first draft of history." Looking back at 1876, it is clear that history has a different focus from the working press. One wonders what stories the journalists of 2012 are ignoring that will be long remembered after the day-to-day news is forgotten. Certainly they are overlooking the stories of many modern heroes in their relentless coverage of politics, celebrity, and the grotesque.

Why do Custer and the Little Bighorn continue to fascinate? The *New York Herald,* which, like its competitors, would soon move from the Little Bighorn to other stories, had the best analysis. In one editorial urging people to donate to a monument fund, the *Herald* seemed to be speaking not just to people in 1876 but to Americans in the future:

> The underlying thought in this massacre is duty and valor. General Custer sought this duty like a true man and performed it like a brave man. These are qualities we can never honor too much in this hard, mean, money-seeking age. Even those who would criticise the judgment of Custer, or who would think if they had been there they would have done so much better, will not deny him the highest qualities of manhood and soldiership. . . . An example like this of Custer is a legacy to a nation, a rich reward which we should accept with thanks and reverence.[66]

Notes

CHAPTER 1

1. Nym Crinkle, "Custer as an Author," *New York World,* July 9, 1876. Crinkle was Wheeler's pseudonym. Cooper is a reference to James Fenimore Cooper. Beadle's is a popular series of cheap adventure novels.

2. "Generals Kilpatrick and Custer," *Harper's Weekly,* March 19, 1864. Two recent books that make the Gettysburg argument are Tom Carhart, *Lost Triumph: Lee's Real Plan at Gettysburg—and Why It Failed* (New York: G. P. Putnam's Sons, 2005), and Paul D. Walker, *The Cavalry Battle That Saved the Union: Custer vs. Stuart at Gettysburg* (Gretna, La., 2002).

3. A.H.R., letter to the editor, *New York Herald,* July 16, 1876; Philip Hoffman, letter to the editor, *New York Herald,* July 15, 1876; School Girl, letter to the editor, *New York Herald,* July 13, 1876.

4. J.M.W., "Custer," *Louisville Courier-Journal,* July 14, 1876.

5. J. Cutler Andrews, *The North Reports the Civil War* (Pittsburg: University of Pittsburg Press, 1985), 548; James Donovan, *A Terrible Glory: Custer and the Little Bighorn—The Last Great Battle of the American West* (New York: Little, Brown, 2008), 47.

6. J.M.W., "Custer," *Louisville Courier-Journal,* July 14, 1876

7. "The Condensed Age," *Hartford Courant,* September 19, 1876.

8. Samuel Rezneck, "Distress, Relief, and Discontent in the United States during the Depression of 1873–78," *Journal of Political Economy* 58, no. 6 (December 1950): 494–512.

9. Robert W. Rydell, *All the World's a Fair: Visions of Empire at American International Expositions, 1876–1916* (Chicago: University of Chicago Press, 1984), 10.

10. *Prelude to the Century* (Alexandria, Va.: Time-Life Books, 1999), 26, 29.

11. Rydell, *All the World's a Fair,* 24–25.

12. Robert F. Berkhofer, Jr., *The White Man's Indian* (New York: Alfred A. Knopf, 1978), 147.

13. *Hartford Courant,* May 19, 1876.

14. *Centennial Newspaper Exhibition, 1876,* (New York: Geo. P. Rowell, 1876), viii.

15. Ibid., iii–iv.

16. Ted Curtis Smythe, *The Gilded Age Press, 1865–1900* (Westport, Conn.: Praeger, 2003), x, 71–72; Gerald J. Baldasty, *The Commercialization of News in the Nineteenth Century* (Madison: University of Wisconsin Press, 1992), 129.

17. *Centennial Newspaper Exhibition,* viii.

18. Smythe, *Gilded Age Press,* ix.

19. "Telegraphic Progress," *Alta (San Francisco) California,* June 26, 1876.

20. Histories of the battle vary in reporting the exact number of Seventh Cavalry fatalities. Some of the bodies were not identified or were not found. The total depends on whether the historian includes civilians like journalist Mark Kellogg or those who died of wounds after the battle. Jerome A. Greene, a retired research historian for the National Park Service, wrote in his history of the battlefield that 268 soldiers, civilians, and scouts were killed in the battle or died later from their wounds; see Greene, *Stricken Field: The Little Bighorn since 1876* (Norman: University of Oklahoma Press, 2008), 9. See James S. Brust, Brian C. Pohanka, and Sandy Barnard, *Where Custer Fell: Photographs of the Little Bighorn Battlefield Then and Now* (Norman: University of Oklahoma Press, 2005), and John S. Gray, *Centennial Campaign: The Sioux War of 1876* (Norman: University of Oklahoma Press, 1988), for detailed information about casualty figures and where they occurred on the battlefield.

21. Oliver Knight, *Following the Indian Wars: The Story of the Newspaper Correspondents among the Indian Campaigners* (Norman: University of Oklahoma Press, 1960), 195.

22. Robert M. Utley, *Custer and the Great Controversy: The Origin and Development of a Legend* (Lincoln: University of Nebraska Press, 1998), 14.

23. Vine Deloria, Jr., *Custer Died for Your Sins: An Indian Manifesto* (Norman: University of Oklahoma Press, 1988).

24. See the following as examples: Stephen Weir, *History's Worst Decisions: And the People Who Made Them* (New York: Fall River Press, 2009); Ballard C. Campbell, *American Disasters: 201 Calamities That Shook the Nation* (New York: Checkmark Books, 2008); Stuart Flexner and Doris Flexner, *The Pessimists Guide to History* (New York: Quill, 2000); Julian Spilsbury, *Great Military Disasters: A History of Incompetence* (New York: MetroBooks, 2010); Chris McNab, *The World's Worst Military Disasters: Chronicling the Greatest Battlefield Catastrophes of All Time* (New York: Barnes and Noble Books, 2005); Michael E. Haskew, ed., *Great Military Disasters* (Bath, U.K.: 2009); and Steven Eden, *Military Blunders: Wartime Fiascoes from the Roman Age through World War I* (New York: MetroBooks, 1995). At least three of this genre feature Custer on the cover: Saul David, *Military Blunders: The How and Why of Military Failure* (New York: Carroll and Graf, 1998); William R. Forstchen and Bill Fawcett, eds., *It Seemed Like a Good Idea at the Time: A Compendium of Great Historical Fiascoes* (New York: Avon Books, 2000); and Geoffrey Regan, *The Brassey's Book of Military Blunders* (Dulles, Va.: Brassey's, 2000).

25. Robert M. Utley, *Cavalier in Buckskin: George Armstrong Custer and the Western Military Frontier* (Norman: University of Oklahoma Press, 1988), 194–97; Paul L. Hedren, *Great Sioux War Orders of Battle: How the United States Army Waged War on the Northern Plains, 1876–1877* (Norman, Okla.: Arthur H. Clark, 2011), 175. Many historians have made similar arguments. Gray, *Centennial Campaign,* 183, concludes that Custer was hampered by poor intelligence, and that "Custer's decisions, judged in the light of what he knew at the time, instead of by our hindsight, were neither disobedient, rash, nor stupid." Larry Sklenar, *To Hell with Honor: Custer and the Little Bighorn* (Norman: University of Oklahoma Press, 2000), 339–40, concludes that Custer followed standard military doctrine and was "nearly successful."

26. See Michael A. Elliott, *Custerology: The Enduring Legacy of the Indian Wars and George Armstrong Custer* (Chicago: University of Chicago Press, 2007), for a study of Custer enthusiasts.

27. Utley, *Cavalier in Buckskin*,13–15; Louise Barnett, *Touched by Fire: The Life Death, and Mythic Afterlife of George Armstrong Custer* (New York: Henry Holt, 1996), 11.

28. Stephen L. Ambrose, *Crazy Horse and Custer: The Parallel Lives of Two American Warriors* (Garden City, N.Y.: Doubleday, 1975), 99–101, 108.

29. Duane Schultz, *Custer: Lessons in Leadership* (Palgrave MacMillan: Houndmills, U.K., 2010), 13–16.

30. Utley, *Cavalier in Buckskin*, 33.

31. Donovan, *Terrible Glory*, 64–65.

32. Barnett, *Touched by Fire*, 162–63. The *(St. Louis) Missouri Democratic* later merged with the *St. Louis Globe*. Utley, *Cavalier in Buckskin*, 75.

33. Thom Hatch, *The Custer Companion: A Comprehensive Guide to the Life of George Armstrong Custer and the Plains Indian Wars* (Mechanicsburg, Pa.: Stackpole,2002), 81.

34. Donovan, *Terrible Glory*, 68.

35. Ronald H. Nichols, *In Custer's Shadow: Major Marcus Reno* (Norman: University of Oklahoma Press, 2000), 135.

36. Utley, *Cavalier in Buckskin*, 31.

37. Jeffery D. Wert, *Custer: The Controversial Life of George Armstrong Custer* (New York: Simon and Schuster, 1996), 219–20.

38. Hatch, *Custer Companion*, 120, 40–41.

39. Ibid., 205–207.

40. Ibid., 137–38.

41. Donovan, *Terrible Glory*, 121–23.

42. Douglas D. Scott, P. Willey, and Melissa A. Connor, *They Died with Custer: Soldiers' Bones from the Battle of the Little Bighorn* (Norman: University of Oklahoma Press, 1998), 90; Utley, *Cavalier in Buckskin*, 186.

43. Hedren, *Great Sioux War,* 29.

44. Donovan, *Terrible Glory*, 120, 126; Charles Windolph, *I Fought with Custer: The Story of Sergeant Windolph, Last Survivor of the Battle of the Little Big Horn as Told to Frazier and Robert Hunt* (Lincoln: University of Nebraska Press, 1987), 53.

45. John R. Langellier, "Custer: The Making of a Myth," in *Little Bighorn Remembered,* by Herman J. Viola (New York: Times Books, 1999), 197.

46. John H. Monnett, *Where a Hundred Soldiers Were Killed* (Albuquerque: University of New Mexico Press, 2008); Robert M. Utley, *Custer Battlefield: A History and Guide to the Battle of the Little Bighorn* (Washington, D.C.: National Park Service, 1988), 14–15; Donovan, *Terrible Glory*, 27–29.

47. Utley, *Custer Battlefield*, 15, 18.

48. Ibid., 14–20.

49. Robert M. Utley, *The Lance and the Shield: The Life and Times of Sitting Bull* (New York: Ballantine Books, 1994), 112, 116.

50. Donovan, *Terrible Glory*, 33; Utley, *Lance and the Shield,* 116–20.

51. Utley, *Lance and the Shield,* 126.

52. Ibid., 126–29.

53. Utley, *Custer Battlefield,* 27, 32.

54. Ibid., 32; Hatch, *Custer Companion,* 195.

55. Utley, *Custer Battlefield,* 27.

56. Donovan, *Terrible Glory,* 121.

57. Hedren, *Great Sioux War,* 21–29.

58. Ibid., 27, 32.

59. Utley, *Cavalier in Buckskin,* 159–63; Hatch, *Custer Companion,* 171–72.

60. Utley, *Cavalier in Buckskin,* 163; Schultz, *Custer,* 154–57; Donovan, *Terrible Glory,* 115.

61. Utley, *Custer Battlefield,* 33–34; Utley, *Lance and the Shield,* 137–38.

62. Donovan, *Terrible Glory,* 150–53.

63. Hedren, *Great Sioux War,* 53. Donovan, *Terrible Glory,* 153–54. Barnett, *Touched by Fire,* 279, writes that news of the Rosebud would have been "precious intelligence" from Crook. Hedren, *Great Sioux War,* 41, writes that communication between the commands was "seemingly encouraged though not demanded or expected" by Sheridan.

64. Utley, *Custer Battlefield,* 30–34.

65. Utley, *Cavalier in Buckskin,* 174–76.

66. See, for example, Edgar I. Stewart, *Custer's Luck* (Norman: University of Oklahoma, 1989), 248–50, 493. Stewart concludes that Custer "disobeyed the spirit if not the letter of his orders."

67. Utley, *Cavalier in Buckskin,* 175–76.

68. Donovan, *Terrible Glory,* 176–77.

69. Ibid., 183.

70. Don Rickey, Jr., *Forty Miles a Day on Beans and Hay: The Enlisted Soldier Fighting the Indian Wars* (Norman: University of Oklahoma Press, 1973), 70.

71. Utley, *Custer Battlefield,* 43–44; Donovan, *Terrible Glory,* 196.

72. Utley, *Custer Battlefield,* 47.

73. Donovan, *Terrible Glory,* 193–94.

74. Utley, *Custer Battlefield,* 48.

75. Ibid., 52–53. As with casualty figures, historians have reported different numbers for the various units. The most widely accepted number for fatalities on the Custer portion of the battlefield is 210. The discrepancy between Utley's estimate that Custer had about 225 men but 210 were killed can be explained by the fact that some men were sent back to Reno as messengers or straggled from Custer's column; see Gray, *Centennial Campaign,* 296; Brust et al., *Where Custer Fell,* 7, 30.

76. Utley, *Custer Battlefield,* 53.

77. Donovan, *Terrible Glory,* 215.

78. Utley, *Custer Battlefield,* 53–57.

79. Donovan, *Terrible Glory,* 229.

80. Utley, *Custer Battlefield,* 56.

81. Ibid., 69.

82. Brust et al., *Where Custer Fell,* 45; Stewart, *Custer's Luck,* 393–95.

83. Brust et al., *Where Custer Fell,* 47; Donovan, *Terrible Glory,* 386. A total of twenty-four medals of honor were awarded for actions in the siege, the most in any battle until Iwo Jima.

84. Donovan, *Terrible Glory,* 260.

85. Ibid., 225–26, 250–51.

86. Ibid., 252, 266–67, 276; Utley, *Cavalier in Buckskin,* 187, 190–91.

87. Utley, *Cavalier in Buckskin,* 189–90; Donovan, 275–77.

88. Evan S. Connell, *Son of the Morning Star* (New York: Promontory Press, 1993), 373–74.

89. Ambrose, *Crazy Horse and Custer,* 443–44.

90. Utley, *Custer Battlefield,* 72.

91. Brust et al., *Where Custer Fell,* 112, 115–16.

92. Donovan, *Terrible Glory,* 308; Brust et al., *Where Custer Fell,* 103.

93. Donovan, *Terrible Glory,* 309; Hatch, *Custer Companion,* 130–33; Connell, *Son of the Morning Star,* 386–99.

94. Connell, *Son of the Morning Star,* 409–10.

95. Donovan, *Terrible Glory,* 307.

96. Wert, *Custer,* 355.

CHAPTER 2

1. "The News from the Frontier—A Centennial War," *New York Herald,* June 25, 1876.

2. "Another Indian Raid," *New York World,* May 12, 1876.

3. *New York World,* May 29, 1876.

4. William E. Huntzicker, "The Frontier Press, 1800–1900," in *The Media in America: A History,* ed. Wm. David Sloan and James D. Starrt (Northport, Ala.: Vision Press, 2002), 186; Utley, *Cavalier in Buckskin,* 150–51.

5. Royal Cortissoz, *The Life of Whitelaw Reid,* vol. 1 (New York: Charles Scribner's Sons, 1921), 312; Donovan, *Terrible Glory,* 112, 166.

6. John F. Finerty, *War-Path and Bivouac; or, The Conquest of the Sioux* (Norman: University of Oklahoma Press, 1994), 4.

7. Sandy Barnard, *I Go with Custer: The Life and Death of Reporter Mark Kellogg* (Bismarck, N.Dak.: Bismarck Tribune, 1996), 89–90, 101–102.

8. Ibid., 109.

9. Knight, *Following the Indian Wars,* 217.

10. Ibid., 201–204.

11. "Going to the War," *New York Herald,* June 9, 1876.

12. "The Indian War," *New York Herald,* June 19, 1876.

13. "The Indian War," *New York Herald,* June 24, 1876.

14. "The News from the Frontier—A Centennial War," *New York Herald,* June 25, 1876; "After Sitting Bull," *New York Herald,* June 28, 1876.

15. "The Fight with the Sioux," *New York World,* June 25, 1876; "Up the Big Horn," *New York World,* June 27, 1876.

16. "General Crook's Fight" and "Germany," *Hartford Daily Courant,* June 24, 1876; "Border Battles" and "War on the Mosquitoes," *St. Louis Globe-Democrat,* June 24, 1876.

17. Utley, *Custer and the Great Controversy,* 32–34; Knight, *Following the Indian Wars,* 213–14.

18. Knight, *Following the Indian Wars,* 213.

19. W. A. Graham, *The Custer Myth: A Sourcebook of Custeriana* (Mechanicsburg, Pa.: Stackpole, 1995), 351.

20. Utley, *Custer and the Great Controversy,* 43.

21. "The Indian War," *Baltimore American and Commercial Advertiser,* July 6, 1876.

22. *Centennial Newspaper Exhibition,* 192.

23. "Custer's Defeat," *Baltimore American and Commercial Advertiser,* July 6, 1876.

24. *New York Times,* June 26, 1876.

25. "An Indian Victory, *New York Times,* July 7, 1876. Gen. E. R. S. Canby and the Rev. E. Thomas were murdered by the Modocs during peace negotiations between that tribe and the U.S. government.

26. "Hays Editor 'Scoops the World' on the Story of Custer Massacre," *Hays (Kans.) Daily News,* November 11, 1929. See also James E. Mueller, "Little Bighorn Coverage in Kansas Newspapers: Last Stand for a Partisan Press," in *Custer and His Times,* vol. 4, ed. John P. Hart (LaGrange Park, Ill.: Little Big Horn Associates).

27. "Hays Editor 'Scoops the World' on the Story of Custer Massacre," *Hays (Kans.) Daily News,* November 11, 1929; Mueller, "Little Bighorn Coverage in Kansas Newspapers," 6.

28. "Horrible!" *Leavenworth Daily Times,* July 7, 1876; Mueller, "Little Bighorn Coverage in Kansas Newspapers."

29. "The Indian War," *Hartford Daily Courant,* July 6, 1876; "Terrible Slaughter!" *Flemensburg (Ky.) Democrat,* July 13, 1876.

30. "A Bloody Battle," *New York Herald,* July 6, 1876.

31. "The Indian War," *Galveston (Tex.) News,* July 7, 1876; "Custer Killed," *New York World,* July 6, 1876; "Custer," *Louisville Courier-Journal,* July 7, 1876.

32. "The Indian War," *Louisville Commercial,* July 6, 1876; "Latest Telegraph," *New Orleans Picayune,* July 7, 1876.

33. "Butchered Boys," *Chicago Times,* July 6, 1876; "Custer Slain," *Chicago Daily News,* July 6, 1876.

34. Utley, *Custer and the Great Controversy,* 36–37.

35. "The Massacre," *New York Herald,* July 7, 1876.

36. *St. Louis Globe-Democrat,* July 7, 1876; "The Tomahawk," *St. Louis Globe-Democrat,* July 7, 1876.

37. "The Tomahawk," *St. Louis Globe-Democrat,* July 7, 1876.

38. Utley, *Lance and the Shield,* 19.

39. "Gen. Custer and His Santee Scouts," *Galveston News,* July 16, 1876; Justin E. Walsh, *To Print the News and Raise Hell!* (Chapel Hill: University of North Carolina Press, 1968), 176.

40. "Custer's Death," *New York Herald,* July 8, 1876.

41. Knight, *Following the Indian Wars,* 216.

42. Hatch, *Custer Companion,* 229–30.

43. "Custer's Death," *New York Herald,* July 8, 1876. The casualty figure of 115 was either a typo or a mistake. More than two hundred were killed with Custer.

44. Utley, *Custer Battlefield,* 72.

45. Brust et al., *Where Custer Fell,* 75.

46. "Washington," *New York Herald,* July 8, 1876.

47. "The Latest News," *New York Herald,* July 9, 1876.

48. "The Sioux War," *New York Herald,* July 9, 1876.

49. "The Terrible Sioux," *New York Herald,* July 11, 1876.

50. *Dallas Daily Herald,* July 19, 1876.

51. "The Indian War," *New York World,* July 13, 1876.

52. "An Officer's Diary," *New York Herald,* July 13, 1876.

53. "The Indian Campaign," *New York Herald,* July 14, 1876.

54. W. A. Graham, *The Story of the Little Big Horn* (New York: Bonanza Books, 1959), 162–67.

55. "Sitting Bull Reported Dead," *Baltimore American and Commercial Advertiser,* July 15, 1876.

56. "The Indian War," *New York Herald,* July 15 1876.

57. "Sitting Bull's Death Confirmed," *Baltimore American and Commercial Advertiser,* July 21, 1876; "Nine Sioux Chiefs Killed," *Baltimore American and Commercial Advertiser,* July 24, 1876.

58. *Dallas Daily Herald,* July 26, 1876.

59. "The Indian War," *New York Herald,* July 14, 1876.

60. "The Agency Indians," *Baltimore American and Commercial Advertiser,* July 15, 1876.

61. "At an End," *St. Louis Globe-Democrat,* August 28, 1876.

62. *New York World,* September 21, 1876.

CHAPTER 3

1. "Military Views," *St. Louis Globe-Democrat,* July 7, 1876.

2. "Custer's Battle," *St. Louis Globe-Democrat,* July 15, 1876.

3. Utley, *Cavalier in Buckskin,* 110.

4. Smythe, *Gilded Age Press,* 25, 72.

5. "The Slaughter Near the Little Horn River—Death of General Custer," *New York Herald,* July 7, 1876.

6. "General Custer," *New York Herald,* July 14, 1876.

7. "The Dead Cavalryman," *New York Herald,* July 10, 1876; "Reminiscences," *Chicago Tribune,* July 7, 1876.

8. "The Dead Cavalryman," *New York Herald,* July 10, 1876.

9. "General Custer," *New York Herald,* July 14, 1876.

10. "A Poet's Tribute to Custer," *New York Herald,* July 14, 187.

11. *Indianapolis Journal* cited in "A Prediction by Custer," *New York Herald,* 14 July 1876.

12. "Honors to Custer Memory," *New York Herald,* July 8, 1876; "To the Memory of Custer," *New York Herald,* July 11, 1876; "The Monument to Custer," *New York Herald,* July 15, 1876.

13. "The Fighting Custer," *New York Herald,* July 16, 1876.

14. *Louisville Courier-Journal,* July 11, 1876.

15. *Dallas Daily Herald,* July 13, 1876.

16. "The Fall of Custer," *Galveston News,* July 19, 1876.

17. *Raleigh News* cited in "Custer and the South," *New York World,* July 22, 1876.

18. "The Death of Custer," *New Orleans Picayune,* July 7, 1876.

19. *Atlanta Constitution,* July 8, 1876.

20. "A Southern Movement," *New York Herald,* July 23, 1876.

21. Ibid.

22. *Owensboro (Ky.) Examiner,* July 28, 1876; "The Gallant Custar," *Leavenworth (Kans.) Daily Appeal,* July 13, 1876.

23. "The Custer Massacre," *(Springfield) Illinois Daily State Register,* July 7, 1876. See also James E. Mueller, "Little Bighorn Coverage in the Illinois Press," in *Custer and His Times,* vol. 5, ed. John P. Hart (Cordova, Tenn.: Little Big Horn Associates).

24. "The Indian War" and "Who Killed Custer?" *Chicago Daily News,* July 7, 1876.

25. *New York World,* July 6, 1876; "The Custer Disaster," *New York World,* July 7, 1876.

26. "The Question of Responsibility," *New York World,* July 8, 1876.

27. "Defeat and Death" and "A Terrible Blunder,"*Chicago Times,* July 7, 1876.

28. "Too Much Courage," *Chicago Times,* July 10, 1876; Mueller, "Little Bighorn Coverage in the Illinois Press."

29. "Indians!" *Chicago Times,* July 22, 1876.

30. "The Little-Horn Massacre," *Chicago Tribune,* July 7, 1876,

31. Curtis, "The Custer Tragedy," *Chicago Inter-Ocean,* July 10, 1876; Mueller, "Little Bighorn Coverage in the Illinois Press."

32. "The Indian Massacre of Custer," *Galena (Ill.) Gazette,* July 14, 1876; "The Indians, *Ottawa (Ill.) Republican,* July 13, 1876.

33. *Chanute (Kans.) Times,* July 13, 1876; "A Frightful Disaster," *(Topeka) Commonwealth,* July 7, 1876. The "one-to-five" theory was the idea that one Southern soldier was equal to five Yankees because of his superior fighting ability.

34. *New York Times,* July 9, 1876.

35. "The Indian War," *Hartford Daily Courant,* July 7, 1876; *Hartford Daily Courant,* July 28, 1876.

36. *Baltimore American and Commercial Advertiser,* July 7, 1876, and July 8, 1876.

37. Mueller, "Little Bighorn Coverage in Kansas Newspapers," 267.

38. "Custer's Fatal Campaign," *Bloomington (Ill.) Pantagraph,* July 11, 1876.

39. "The Montana Slaughter," *New York Tribune,* July 7, 1876; "Soldiers and Their Critics," *New York Tribune,* July 11, 1876.

40. "The Custar Massacre," *Laramie (Wyo.) Daily Sentinel,* July 7, 1876.

41. "Custer Vindicated," *Helena (Mont.) Daily Herald,* July 20, 1876.

42. "Massacred," *Bismarck (Dak.) Weekly Tribune,* July 12, 1876.

43. "The Custer Massacre," *Rocky Mountain (Denver) Herald,* July 15, 1876.

44. "Extermination the Only Remedy," *Rocky Mountain (Denver) News,* July 8, 1876.

45. "The Quaker Policy," *Rocky Mountain (Denver) Herald,* August 5, 1876.

46. "Extermination the Only Remedy," *Rocky Mountain (Denver) News,* July 8, 1876.

47. Mueller, "Little Bighorn Coverage in Kansas Newspapers," 261.

48. *New York Tribune,* July 8, 1876; "Our Incomprehensible Indian Policy," *New York Tribune,* July 17, 1876.

49. "The Little-Horn Massacre," *Chicago Tribune,* July 7, 1876; "A Short War," *St. Louis Globe-Democrat,* July 10, 1876.

50. "Grant's Indian Policy," *Leavenworth (Kans.) Daily Times,* July 14, 1876; *(Topeka, Kans.) Commonwealth,* July 12, 1876.

51. "The President and the Press," *Chicago Inter-Ocean,* July 14, 1876; Mueller, "Little Bighorn Coverage in the Illinois Press," 235.

52. "Gen. Grant's Peace Policy," *New York Times,* July 30, 1876.

53. "The Indian Problem," *Baltimore American and Commercial Advertiser,* July 8, 1876.

54. *Oskaloosa (Kans.) Independent,* July 8, 1876; *Washington (Kans.) Republican,* July 21, 1876; Mueller, "Little Bighorn Coverage in Kansas Newspaper," 265.

55. *San Antonio Republican,* July 15, 1876.

56. *Woodford (Ky.) Weekly,* July 14, 1876.

57. *Dallas Daily Herald,* July 7, 1876, and July 15, 1876.

58. *Fort Worth Daily Democrat,* July 7, 1876, and July 9, 1876.

59. "From Washington," *(San Marcos) West Texas Free Press,* July 22, 1876.

60. *(Atlanta) Constitution,* July 7, 1876, and July 8, 1876.

61. *Mayfield (Ky.) Monitor,* July 22, 1876; "Minor Editorials," *Owensboro (Ky.) Examiner,* July 21, 1876; James E. Mueller, "Kentucky Press Coverage of the Little Bighorn: Detached Partisanship," *Greasy Grass* 21 (May, 2005).

62. "A Gentleman and a Hero," *Louisville Courier-Journal,* July 8, 1876; *Louisville Courier-Journal,* July 21, 1876.

63. *Hartford Daily Courant,* July 15, 1876.

64. *Galveston News,* July 20, 1876.

65. *Louisville Courier-Journal,* July 15, 1876.

66. "Indian War," *Dallas Daily Herald,* July 7, 1876, and July 8, 1876. The editorial refers to Indiana U.S. senator Oliver P. Morton; secretary to Grant, Orville Babcock; and Maine congressman James G. Blaine.

67. "Custar's Murder," *Dallas Daily Herald,* July 9, 1876.

CHAPTER 4

1. Hayes also shared a carriage with Custer at a reunion of the Army of the Cumberland; see Thomas Henry Looker to Rutherford B. Hayes, September 6, 1876, Thomas Henry Looker Papers, Rutherford B. Hayes Presidential Center, Fremont, Ohio (hereafter Hayes Papers). Looker did not specify the date of the reunion.

2. Charles Richard Williams, ed., *Diary and Letters of Rutherford Birchard Hayes, Nineteenth President of the United States*, Vol. 3: *1865–1881* (Columbus: Ohio State Archaeological and Historical Society, 1924), 250.

3. Lawrence A. Frost, *General Custer's Libbie* (Seattle: Superior, 1976), 206.

4. H. Capehart to Rutherford B. Hayes, July 7, 1876, Hayes Papers.

5. P. W. Hitchcock letter to Rutherford B. Hayes, July 10, 1876, Hayes Papers.

6. B. F. Potts to Rutherford B. Hayes, July 5, 1876, Hayes Papers.

7. W. G. Deshler to Rutherford B. Hayes, Aug. 5, 1876, Hayes Papers.

8. J. M. Bulkley to Rutherford B. Hayes, July 21, 1876, Hayes Papers.

9. J. M. Bulkley to Rutherford B. Hayes, August 27, 1876, Hayes Papers.

10. John Woolley and Gerhard Peters, "Voter Turnout in Presidential Elections: 1828–2008," American Presidency Project, www.presidency.ucsb.edu/data/turnout.php.

11. Michael F. Holt, *By One Vote: The Disputed Presidential Election of 1876* (Lawrence: University of Kansas Press, 2008), xi.

12. Ibid., xiii; H. J. Eckenrode, *Rutherford B. Hayes: Statesman of Reunion* (New York: Dodd, Mead, 1930), 141.

13. Lloyd Robinson, *The Stolen Election: Hayes Versus Tilden—1876* (New York: Forge, 2001), 109–10.

14. Keith Ian Polakoff, *The Politics of Inertia: The Election of 1876 and the End of Reconstruction* (Baton Rouge: Louisiana State University Press, 1973), 178.

15. Kerwin Swint, *Mudslingers: The Twenty-Five Dirtiest Political Campaigns of All Time* (New York: Sterling/Union Square Press, 2008), 79.

16. Evan Cornog and Richard Whelan, *Hats in the Ring: An Illustrated History of American Presidential Campaigns* (New York: Random House, 2000), 127–28.

17. Roy Morris, Jr., *Fraud of the Century: Rutherford B. Hayes, Samuel Tilden, and the Stolen Election of 1876* (New York: Simon and Schuster, 2003), 110.

18. Utley, *Custer and the Great Controversy*, 39, 41–42.

19. Brian W. Dippie, "The Southern Response to Custer's Last Stand," in *The Great Sioux War 1876–77*, ed. Paul L. Hedren (Helena: Montana Historical Society Press, 1991), 234.

20. Brian W. Dippie, *Custer's Last Stand: The Anatomy of an American Myth* (Lincoln: University of Nebraska Press, 1994), 11.

21. Polakoff, *Politics of Inertia*, 6–7.

22. Robinson, *Stolen Election*, 81.

23. Mark Wahlgren Summers, *The Press Gang: Newspapers and Politics, 1865–1878* (Chapel Hill: University of North Carolina Press, 1994), 300; *Hartford Daily Courant*, May 30, 1876.

24. Robinson, *Stolen Election*, 65.

25. Alexander Clarence Flick, *Samuel Jones Tilden: A Study in Political Sagacity* (New York: Dodd, Mead, 1939), 282.

26. Summers, *Press Gang*, 301–302.

27. Swint, *Mudslingers*, 81.

28. Summers, *Press Gang*, 303–304.

29. Wm. D. Howells, *Sketch of the Life and Character of Rutherford B. Hayes* (New York: Hurd and Houghton, 1876), 163; Polakoff, *Politics of Inertia*, 36.

30. Polakoff, *Politics of Inertia*, 115.

31. "The Campaign and Its Character," *Bismarck (Dak.) Tribune*, July 5, 1876.

32. "Address of Theodore M. Pomeroy," *New York Times*, June 15, 1876.

33. "The Republican Platform," *New York Times*, June 16, 1876.

34. "Gen. Terry's Expedition" and "Governed Too Much," *New York Times*, June 18, 1876.

35. "The Unwashed and Their Allies," *New York Times*, June 27, 1876.

36. "The Cincinnati Platform," *New York World*, June 16, 1876; "The Indian Battle," *New York Herald*, June 16, 1876; "The Power of the West," *New York Herald*, June 17, 1876.

37. "Hayes and Wheeler," *New York Herald*, June 18, 1876.

38. "After the Battle," *Hartford Daily Courant*, June 19, 1876.

39. "Governor Hayes at Home," *Hartford Daily Courant*, June 26, 1876.

40. *Hartford Daily Courant*, June 26, 1876.

41. "The Centennial Canvas—The Position of Hayes and Tilden—Is It to Be the Black Flag?" *New York Herald*, July 3, 1876.

42. "The War with the Sioux," *New York Herald*, July 3, 1876.

43. "Now for St. Louis," *Louisville Courier-Journal*, June 17, 1876.

44. "A Scrap of a War Record" and "Civil Service Planks," *Louisville Courier-Journal*, June 26, 1876.

45. "What Will St. Louis Do?" and "The Indian Bureau and the War Department," *Louisville Courier-Journal*, June 27, 1876.

46. "Tilden's Generals" and "A Winter Campaign," *St. Louis Globe-Democrat*, October 21, 1876.

47. "Assassination in Politics," *Alta (San Francisco) California*, June 14, 1876.

48. "Blaine and Hayes," *Alta (San Francisco) California*, June 17, 1876; "The National Republican Platform," *Alta (San Francisco) California*, June 16, 1876.

49. "Another Indian Raid," *New York World*, May 12, 1876. Also, former Republican senator Carl Schurz called the Democratic campaign for reform "a demand for a new deal of the spoils"; see "Carl Schurz," *St. Louis Globe-Democrat*, September 1, 1876.

50. "Our Victory Must Be Complete," *New York World*, May 27, 1876.

51. "A Word or Two with the Convention," *New York World*, June 27, 1876.

52. "The Campaign," *Louisville Courier-Journal*, July 25, 1876.

53. "Reno on the Custer Massacre" and "Tilden and Hendricks," *New York World*, August 5, 1876.

54. "What the Democratic House Has Done," August 24, 1876.

55. "Soldiers and Their Critics," *New York World,* July 11, 1876.

56. "Politics Run Mad," *New York Times,* July 8, 1876.

57. "The Custer Disaster," *New York World,* July 7, 1876.

58. "Politics Run Mad," *New York Times,* July 8, 1876; "Mr. Tilden's Methods," *New York Times,* July 8, 1876.

59. "Gen. Hayes' Letter of Acceptance," *New York Times,* July 10, 1876.

60. "Gen. Grant's Peace Policy," "Some Points of Contrast," and "Democratic Burdens," *New York Times,* July 30, 1876.

61. "The 'Factory System' for the Indians," *New York Times,* August 14, 1876.

62. C.M., "The War with the Indians," *New York Times,* August 27, 1876.

63. "The Black Hills Country," *New York Times,* October 29, 1876.

64. "Editorial Notes," *Alta (San Francisco) California,* June 22, 1876.

65. "Niggardly Policy," *Alta (San Francisco) California,* August 1, 1876.

66. "The Nation and Its Parties," *Missoulian* (Missoula, Mont.), August 9, 1876; *Alta (San Francisco) California,* July 13, 1876.

67. "Indian Cheek," *Alta (San Francisco) California,* August 8, 1876.

68. "Our Indian Policy," *Alta (San Francisco) California,* October 8, 1876.

69. Ibid.; "Reform in Earnest" and "The Resumption Repeal," *Alta (San Francisco) California,* August 5, 1876.

70. "Hayes' Letter," *Alta (San Francisco) California,* July 11, 1876; C.A.W., "Governor Hayes," *Alta (San Francisco) California,* September 18, 1876.

71. *St. Louis Dispatch,* September 11, 1876.

72. "The Sioux Negotiations," *St. Louis Dispatch,* September 11, 1876.

73. "A Sham Issue," *St. Louis Dispatch,* September 20, 1876; "Business vs. Politics," *St. Louis Dispatch,* September 25, 1876.

74. "The Great Issues," *St. Louis Dispatch,* September 8, 1876; "The Bloody Shirt," *St. Louis Dispatch,* September 22, 1876.

75. "The Indian Problem," *Louisville Courier-Journal,* July 12, 1876; editorial, *Louisville Courier-Journal,* July 21, 1876.

76. "Little Horn River Massacre," *New Orleans Picayune,* July 8, 1876.

77. *Woodford (Ky.) Weekly,* July 14, 1876.

78. *Fort Worth Daily Democrat,* July 15, 1876.

79. "The Latest News from the Front," *Louisville Courier-Journal,* September 19, 1876.

80. "Reform," *New Orleans Picayune,* September 23, 1876; "Louisiana First," *New Orleans Picayune,* June 16, 1876.

81. "Reconciliation," *News Orleans Picayune,* August 1, 1876.

82. "Business in Politics," *New Orleans Picayune,* July 20, 1876.

83. "An Indian Victory," *Emporia (Kans.) News,* July 14, 1876; "The Custer Massacre—Must the Responsibility Rest on the Living or the Dead?" *New York Herald,* October 2, 1876.

84. Saxon, "Our Washington Letter," *Bozeman (Mont.) Avant Courier,* August 18, 1876.

85. "Recruiting for the Cavalry," *New York Herald,* August 27, 1876.

86. Hugh J. Reilly, *The Frontier Newspaper and the Coverage of the Plains Indian Wars* (Santa Barbara, Calif.: Praeger, 2010), 41. Reilly states that Little Bighorn coverage faded quickly from Montana newspapers and that editors in other parts of the country kept the story alive. "Subjects for Dime Novels," *St. Louis Globe-Democrat,* August 6, 1876.

87. "The Indian Question—Impending Battle on the Rosebud," *New York Herald,* August 7, 1876.

88. "For the Removal of Custer," *Alta (San Francisco) California,* September 8, 1876.

89. "Logan's Logic," *St. Louis Globe-Democrat,* September 16, 1876.

90. "Pulitzer," *Louisville Courier-Journal,* September 4, 1876.

91. "Tilden and the Next Rebellion," *Alta (San Francisco) California,* November 5, 1876.

CHAPTER 5

1. "A Mistake," *Chicago Tribune,* August 12, 1876.

2. Walter Allen, *Governor Chamberlain's Administration in South Carolina: A Chapter of Reconstruction in the Southern States* (New York: G. P. Putnam's Sons, 1888), 312.

3. Ibid., 319, 320, 348.

4. Joel Williamson, *After Slavery: The Negro in South Carolina during Reconstruction, 1861–1877* (Chapel Hill: University of North Carolina Press, 1965), 268–69.

5. Daniel E. Sutherland, *A Savage Conflict: The Decisive Role of Guerillas in the American Civil War* (Chapel Hill: University of North Carolina Press, 2009), 34, 39.

6. "The War in the West" and "War in South Carolina," *Hartford Daily Courant,* July 10, 1876; *Hartford Daily Courant,* July 17, 1876.

7. "Too Old to Learn," *Hartford Daily Courant,* July 20, 1876.

8. "The Hamburg Massacre," *Hartford Daily Courant,* August 9, 1876.

9. B., "The National Capital," *Hartford Daily Courant,* August 16, 1876; *Hartford Daily Courant,* August 17, 1876.

10. F. H. Little, "Another Southern Outrage," *Hartford Daily Courant,* September 26, 1876; "The Indian War," *Hartford Daily Courant,* September 26, 1876.

11. "The Indian War," *Hartford Daily Courant,* September 22, 1876; *Hartford Daily Courant,* September 23, 1876.

12. "An Election War," *Hartford Daily Courant,* October 18, 1876.

13. "One Week More," *Hartford Daily Courant,* October 30, 1876; "Reasons Why," *Hartford Daily Courant,* November 4, 1876.

14. "Gen. Custer's Last Fight" and "Trouble in Hamburg," *New York Times,* July 9, 1876; "The Disturbance at Hamburg" and "The Indian War," *New York Times,* July 10, 1876.

15. "The Old Rebel Spirit," *New York Times,* July 14, 1876; editorial, *New York Times,* July 14, 1876. Thomas A. Hendricks was the Democratic nominee for vice president.

16. "Democratic Campaigning," *New York Times,* July 17, 1876; "Notes of the Campaign," *New York Times,* July 19, 1876.

17. "The Old Rebel Spirit," *(Lawrence, Kans.) Republican Journal,* July 28, 1876.

18. Life, "Washington Letter," *Chanute (Kans.) Times,* July 27, 1876.

19. "Fiendish Massacre," *Atchison (Kans.) Daily Champion,* July 19, 1876; "The South Carolina Massacre," *Chicago Tribune,* July 17, 1876. Part of the article was reprinted without attribution under the headline "Fiendish Massacre" in the July 20, 1876, edition of the *Newton Kansan.*

20. *Chicago Inter-Ocean,* July 18, 1876.

21. "The Hamburg Massacre," *Burlington (Kans.) Weekly Patriot,* July 26, 1876.

22. "The Hamburg Horror Again" and "Southern Tildenism," *(Springfield) Illinois Daily State Journal,* July 20, 1876.

23. "Fiendish Massacre," *Washington (Kans.) Republican,* July 21, 1876.

24. "The White League," *St. Louis Globe-Democrat,* July 14, 1876; *St. Louis Globe-Democrat,* July 15, 1876.

25. "South Carolina Troubles," *St. Louis Globe-Democrat,* July 18, 1876; *St. Louis Globe-Democrat,* July 19, 1876, *St. Louis Globe-Democrat,* July 26, 1876; *Chicago Inter-Ocean,* July 12, 1876.

26. "Troops in the South," *(Springfield) Illinois Daily State Journal,* July 11, 1876.

27. "The Bloody Shirt," *St. Louis Globe-Democrat,* August 9, 1876.

28. "Troops," *St. Louis Globe-Democrat,* October 20, 1876.

29. *St. Louis Dispatch,* July 14, 1876, and July 15, 1876.

30. "Two Rousing Republican Meetings," *Monroe (Mich.) Commercial,* September 21, 1876; "The Hamburg Murders," *Monroe (Mich.) Commercial,* July 27, 1876.

31. *York (Neb.) Republican,* August 10, 1876.

32. *Alta (San Francisco) California,* July 14, 1876; "Congress" and "Unreconstructed Rebels," *Alta (San Francisco) California,* July 16, 1876.

33. "Editorial Notes," *Alta (San Francisco) California,* July 20, 1876.

34. "Six Negroes and One White Man," *Alta (San Francisco) California,* July 21, 1876.

35. "Fiendish Massacre," *Atchison (Kans.) Daily Champion,* July 19, 1876.

36. "The Death of Custer," *New Orleans Picayune,* July 7, 1876.

37. *New Orleans Picayune,* July 8, 1876.

38. "Serious Trouble in Hamburg, S.C." and "Further Particulars of the Riot," *New Orleans Picayune,* July 10, 1876.

39. C.M'K., "The Hamburg Butchery," *New Orleans Picayune,* July 16, 1876; "Latest Telegraph," *New Orleans Picayune,* July 19, 1876.

40. "The Hamburg Riot," *New Orleans Picayune,* July 20, 1876.

41. "Gov. Chamberlain's Request," *New Orleans Picayune,* July 21, 1876.

42. *Atlanta Constitution,* July 9, 1876.

43. Ibid.; "Peace Reigns in Hamburg" and "The Hamburg Fight," *Atlanta Constitution,* July 11, 1876.

44. *Atlanta Constitution,* July 12, 1876, and July 13, 1876.

45. "Shall the South Elect Hayes?" *Atlanta Constitution,* July 13, 1876.

46. Kennesaw, "The Hamburg Inquest," *Atlanta Constitution*, July 19, 1876.

47. *Atlanta Constitution*, July 18, 1876.

48. "The Hamburg Riot," *Louisville Courier-Journal*, July 17, 1876.

49. *Louisville Courier-Journal*, July 22, 1876.

50. *Louisville Courier-Journal*, August 4, 1876.

51. "A Grim Joke," *Louisville Courier-Journal*, August 18, 1876.

52. "The Bayonet in the South," *Louisville Courier-Journal*, August 21, 1876. The editorial referred to Massachusetts senator George S. Boutwell, Zachariah Chandler, chairman of the Republican National Committee, and Indiana senator Oliver Morton.

53. *Louisville Courier-Journal*, September 14, 1876.

54. "Soldiers for the South," *New York World*, August 25, 1876.

55. *New York World*, September 15, 1876.

56. *New York World*, September 27, 1876.

57. "Deeds of Negro Fiends," *New York World*, November 4, 1876; "A Black Reign of Terror," *New York World*, September 27, 1876; "Negro Lawlessness," *New York World*, September 19, 1876; "The Indian War," *New York World*, September 19, 1876.

58. "A Family Fight," *New York World*, August 23, 1876.

59. *New York World*, August 17, 1876.

60. "Bloodshed in the South—How to Elect Hayes and Wheeler," *New York Herald*, July 10, 1876; "How the South Should Punish Outrages," *New York Herald*, July 17, 1876.

61. "The Hamburg Massacre," *New York Herald*, July 18, 1876.

62. "A Bottom Fact in the Southern Question," *New York Herald*, August 14, 1876.

63. "Governor Chamberlain's Letter," *New York Herald*, August 7, 1876; "Employment of Troops in the South—The New Order of the Secretary of War," *New York Herald*, August 18, 1876.

64. "Is It South Carolina or Mexico?" *New York Herald*, October 14, 1876; "The Bayonet," *New York Herald*, October 23, 1876; "The Palmetto State," *New York Herald*, October 25, 1876; "The Enslaved State," *New York Herald*, October 28, 1876.

65. "The Hamburg Massacre," *New York Herald*, July 31, 1876.

66. "The Bloody Shirt," *Laramie (Wyo.) Daily Sentinel*, October 20, 1876.

67. "What History Will Say of Our Period," *Hartford Daily Courant*, September 2, 1876.

CHAPTER 6

1. "The Indian War," *St. Louis Dispatch*, July 10, 1876.

2. "The Little-Horn Massacre," *Chicago Tribune*, July 7, 1876. Sheridan repeatedly denied ever making the remark, but it has been used frequently by historians and activists as a club to beat the frontier army and nineteenth-century Americans. Sheridan was, of course, a man of his time and believed that Indians must be "civilized," yet he still expressed sympathy for their condition on reservations. See Paul Andrew Hutton, *Phil Sheridan and His Army* (Norman: University of Oklahoma Press, 1999), 180–86,

and Roy Morris, Jr., *Sheridan: The Life and Wars of General Phil Sheridan* (New York: Vintage Books, 1993), 376.

3. Marc H. Abrams, *Sioux War Dispatches: Reports from the Field, 1876–1877* (Yardley, Pa.: Westholme, 2012), 186.

4. "Indians!" *Chicago Times,* July 22, 1876.

5. Walsh, *To Print the News,* 61–63. Walsh notes that Storey was writing sympathetic editorials about Indians almost thirty years before Helen Hunt Jackson wrote her seminal book *A Century of Dishonor.* One example of the pejorative headlines is "The Red Fiends," *Chicago Times,* July 9, 1876.

6. John Coward, "The Indian Wars," in *The Greenwood Library of American War Reporting,* Vol. 4: *The Indian Wars and the Spanish-American War,* ed. David Copeland (Westport, Conn.: Greenwood Press, 2005), 16–17. See also Roger L. Nichols, "Printer's Ink and Red Skins: Western Newspapermen and the Indians," *Kansas Quarterly* 3, no. 4 (Fall 1971): 82–88.

7. Sutherland, *Savage Conflict,* 175, 247, 258.

8. Andrew S. Coopersmith, *Fighting Words: An Illustrated History of Newspaper Accounts of the Civil War* (New York: New Press, 2004), 279.

9. Coward, "Indian Wars," 57.

10. "The Indian Question," *St. Louis Dispatch,* August 2, 1876; *St. Louis Globe-Democrat,* July 18, 1876.

11. "Washington," *New York Herald,* July 8, 1876.

12. "How to Avenge Custer," *Peoria (Ill.) Daily Transcript,* July 10, 1876; "The Indians," *Ottawa (Ill.) Republican,* July 13, 1876.

13. "If Trained Indian Fighters Are Called For," *Galveston (Tex.) News,* July 8, 1876.

14. "Little Horn River Massacre," *New Orleans Picayune,* July 8, 1876. The quote refers to Secretary of the Interior Columbus Delano.

15. "Our Trouble with the Sioux," *(Topeka, Kans.) Commonwealth,* July 20, 1876; "The Indian War" and "Shall We Have a Black Hills Brigade," *Black Hills (Dak.) Pioneer,* July 22, 1876.

16. "Now It's Business" and "What Will Be Done about It?" *Bismarck (Dak.) Weekly Tribune,* July 12, 1876.

17. "The Indian Business" and "The Indian War of Races," *Omaha (Neb.) Weekly Herald,* July 14, 1876.

18. "The Sioux War," *(Missoula, Mont.) Missoulian,* July 26, 1876.

19. Coward, "Indian Wars," 18.

20. "Damaging Rumors," *Laramie (Wyo.) Sentinel,* July 14, 1876; "Indian Scares," *Laramie (Wyo.) Sentinel,* July 15, 1876.

21. Paul L. Hedren, ed., *Ho! For the Black Hills: Captain Jack Crawford Reports the Black Hills Gold Rush and Great Sioux War* (Pierre: South Dakota State Historical Society Press, 2012), 119.

22. "The Custer Disaster," *New York World,* July 7, 1876; "First Exterminate the Agents," *New York World,* July 14, 1876; editorial, *New York World,* July 16, 1876.

23. Wendell Phillips, "The Indian Question," *New York Herald,* July 19, 1876.

24. "The Indian Question—Wendell Phillips to General Sherman," *New York Herald,* July 19, 1876.

25. "The Indian Question—Do We Understand Our Foes?" *New York Herald,* July 30, 1876.

26. "What Is an Indian?" *Chicago Times,* July 23, 1876.

27. "Disarm the Indians," *Chicago Inter-Ocean,* July 7, 1876.

28. "The Indian Question," *New Orleans Picayune,* August 5, 1876.

29. "Across the Yellowstone," *New Orleans Picayune,* August 30, 1876.

30. "The 'Factory System' for the Indians," *New York Times,* August 14, 1876.

31. "Our Indian Policy," *Burlington (Kans.) Weekly Patriot,* July 19, 1876. Citizenship was granted to all American Indians under the Indian Citizenship Act, which was passed by Congress in 1924.

32. "The Indian War," *Hartford Daily Courant,* July 7, 1876.

33. "Gen. Grant's Peace Policy," *New York Times,* July 30, 1876; "The 'Factory System' for the Indians," *New York Times,* August 14, 1876.

34. "Whites Defeated by Indians," *Transylvania (Richmond, Ky.) Presbyterian,* July 14, 1876.

35. "Where Does the Responsibility Rest?" *Owensboro (Ky.) Examiner,* July 14, 1876.

36. *Louisville Courier-Journal,* July 10, 1876; "The True Issue," *Louisville Courier-Journal,* July 12, 1876.

37. *Louisville Courier-Journal,* July 14, 1876.

38. *Louisville Courier-Journal,* July 30, 1876, and July 27, 1876.

39. *Baltimore American and Commercial Advertiser,* July 11, 1876.

40. "The Indian War," *Hartford Daily Courant,* July 7, 1876; *Hartford Daily Courant,* July 12, 1876.

41. *Hartford Daily Courant,* July 25, 1876.

42. "Our Red Enigma," *Hartford Daily Courant,* August 1, 1876.

43. John M. Coward, *The Newspaper Indian: Native American Identity in the Press, 1820–90* (Urbana: University of Illinois Press, 1999), 153–54, 190; *Hartford Daily Courant,* July 15, 1876.

44. "Sitting Bull's Bloody Career," *Baltimore American and Commercial Advertiser,* July 8, 1876; "Causes of the War," *Baltimore American and Commercial Advertiser,* July 10, 1876.

45. "The Indian War," *Baltimore American and Commercial Advertiser,* July 10, 1876.

46. *Rocky Mountain (Denver) News,* July 8, 1876; Coward, "Indian Wars," 190.

47. ". . . Battle with the Indians," *St. Louis Dispatch,* July 7, 1876; "Modern Warfare," *St. Louis Dispatch,* August 8, 1876.

48. "The Late Butchery," *St. Louis Globe-Democrat,* July 21, 1876.

49. "Washington," *Louisville Courier-Journal,* July 15, 1876.

50. "Moving on the Sioux," *New York Herald,* August 19, 1876.

51. "The Indian Commission," *Hartford Daily Courant,* September 27, 1876.

52. *St. Louis Globe-Democrat,* September 27, 1876.

53. "Sitting Bull's Autobiography," *New York Herald,* July 9, 1876; "Sitting Bull," *New York Herald,* July 12, 1876; "The Life of a Savage," *New York Herald,* July 9, 1876.

54. "Crook and the Indians," *Baltimore American and Commercial Advertiser,* July 17, 1876.

55. *Baltimore American and Commercial Advertiser,* July 24, 1876.

56 "The News," *Baltimore American and Commercial Advertiser,* July 12, 1876.

57. "Indian Names," *Baltimore American and Commercial Advertiser,* July 22, 1876; Utley, *Lance and the Shield,* 14–15; Kingsley M. Bray, *Crazy Horse: A Lakota Life* (Norman: University of Oklahoma Press, 2006), 57–59.

58. "Mark Twain on the Indians," *(Danville) Kentucky Advocate,* July 28, 1876.

CHAPTER 7

1. "Thanksgiving," *Laramie (Wyo.) Daily Sentinel,* July 8, 1876.

2. *Rocky Mountain (Denver) News,* July 11, 1876.

3. *Louisville Courier-Journal,* July 18, 1876.

4. Deuceace, "Humorists," *St. Louis Globe-Democrat,* August 20, 1876.

5. James R. Aswell, ed., *Native American Humor* (New York: Harper and Brothers, 1947), xii. The book title refers to humor native to the United States, not to the humor of American Indians.

6. Michael West, *Transcendental Wordplay: America's Romantic Punsters and the Search for the Language of Nature* (Athens: Ohio University Press, 2000), 13.

7. Deuceace, "Humorists," *St. Louis Globe-Democrat,* August 20, 1876.

8. "Chips," *Hartford Daily Courant,* August 16, 1876.

9. Samuel S. Cox, *Why We Laugh* (Bronx, New York: Benjamin Blom, 1969), 97–101, quotes from 53–54. This was first published in 1876.

10. Barry J. Blake, *Playing with Words: Humour in the English Language* (Oakville, Conn.: Equinox, 2007), 32.

11. Jimmy Carr and Lucy Greeves, *Only Joking: What's So Funny about Making People Laugh?* (New York: Gotham Books, 2006), 172–73. The latter joke is so widely known among comedians that it was the subject of a 2005 film—*The Aristocrats*— which featured famous and not-so-famous comedians recounting their versions of the joke.

12. John C. Meyer, "Humor as a Double-Edged Sword: Four Functions of Humor in Communication," *Communication Theory* 10, no. 3 (August 2000), 310.

13. Ibid., 312–15.

14. Coward, "Indian Wars," 209.

15. *Louisville Courier-Journal,* July 11, 1876; *Rocky Mountain (Denver) Herald,* July 22, 1876.

16. "Currency," *Louisville Sunday Review,* July 23, 1876; *New York Herald,* July 12, 1876.

17. *Rocky Mountain (Denver) Herald,* August 12, 1876.

18. *St. Louis Dispatch,* July 15, 1876.

19. *Owensboro (Ky.) Examiner,* July 14, 1876.

20. *Louisville Courier-Journal,* July 14, 1876.

21. *Bozeman (Mont.) Avant Courier,* July 28, 1876; "Personal Intelligence," *New York Herald,* August 14, 1876.

22. *New York Herald,* July 11, 1876, and July 26, 1876.

23. Bismark, Jr., "Sitting Bulls True Pedigree," *Bismarck (Dak.) Tribune,* August 30, 1876.

24. Reilly, *Frontier Newspaper,* 130, notes that the story of Sitting Bull attending West Point as a youth nicknamed Bison was reported in several frontier newspapers. "A Wisconsin Fish Story," *Hartford Daily Courant,* August 11, 1876.

25. "Sitting Bull," *Hartford Daily Courant,* August 11, 1876.

26. "The Youth of Sitting Bull," *Bismarck (Dak.) Tribune,* October 26, 1876.

27. *Bismarck (Dak.) Tribune,* August 16, 1876.

28. *Rocky Mountain (Denver) Herald,* August 19, 1876; *Rocky Mountain (Denver) News,* August 1, 1876.

29. *Chicago Tribune,* July 10, 1876; *Chicago Times,* July 18, 1876.

30. "Sioux Servants," *New York Times,* September 9, 1876.

31. "Currency," *Louisville Sunday Review,* July 23, 1876; *St. Louis Dispatch,* July 11, 1876; *Louisville Courier-Journal,* July 26, 1876, and September 27, 1876.

32. "General and Personal," *St. Louis Globe-Democrat,* September 9, 1876; *Bozeman (Mont.) Avant Courier,* July 28, 1876.

33. *Louisville Courier-Journal,* September 27, 1876; *New York Herald,* July 27, 1876; "Loathe the Poor Indian," *Williamstown (Ky.) Sentinel,* July 5, 1876.

34. "Novel Missile," *Clark County (Ky.) Democrat,* July 1876; *Louisville Courier-Journal,* July 14, 1876.

35. "The Sioux War," *New York Herald,* August 24, 1876.

36. "Scared Already," *(Lawrence, Kans.) Republican Daily Journal,* July 8, 1876.

37. *New York Times,* August 3, 1876; Phocion, "The Indians," *Chicago Tribune,* August 15, 1876.

38. "Small Talk," *Louisville Courier-Journal,* July 13, 1876.

39. *New Orleans Picayune,* August 18, 1876; *Vicksburg Herald* as quoted in the *New York Times,* August 1, 1876; "Texas Facts & Fancies," *Austin Daily Democratic Statesman,* July 14, 1876.

40. *Leavenworth (Kans.) Daily Appeal,* July 31, 1876; *(Missoula, Mont.) Missoulian,* August 16, 1876; *Bismarck (Dak.) Tribune,* August 9, 1876. On "banditti," see Eric Foner, *Reconstruction: America's Unfinished Revolution 1863–1877* (New York: Harper and Row, 1989), 554.

41. *Rocky Mountain (Denver) Herald,* July 15, 1876; *Bismarck (Dak.) Tribune,* November 1, 1876; *(Missoula, Mont.) Missoulian,* August 16, 1876.

42. *Louisville Courier-Journal,* August 29, 1876.

43. *Louisville Courier-Journal,* September 7, 1876.

44. *Louisville Courier-Journal,* September 21, 1876.

45. *St. Louis Globe-Democrat,* September 1, 1876.

46. *New York Herald,* July 11, 1876; *Louisville Courier-Journal,* September 27, 1876, and September 25, 1876.

47. *Cheyenne Leader* cited in *Rocky Mountain (Denver) News,* July 19, 1876; *Bismarck (Dak.) Tribune,* September 20, 1876.

48. *Louisville Courier-Journal,* September 27, 1876.

49. "Some Indian Talk," *New Orleans Picayune,* September 23, 1876. The Republican *New York Times* also reported the incident on September 23 but identified the chief as Young-Man-Afraid-of-His-Horses.

50. "Texas Facts & Fancies," *Austin Daily Democratic Statesman,* July 15, 1876; *New Orleans Picayune,* September 2, 1876; *St. Louis Dispatch,* July 14, 1876.

51. *Corpus Christi (Tex.) Gazette,* July 19, 1876; *Louisville Courier-Journal,* July 21, 1876.

52. *Louisville Courier-Journal,* July 21, 1876.

53. *New Orleans Picayune,* July 25, 1876, and August 13, 1876.

54. *Chicago Times,* July 18, 1876; *Quincy (Ill.) Herald,* July 13, 1876.

55. *New York Herald,* August 14, 1876.

56. *Louisville Courier-Journal,* September 8, 1876, and September 16, 1876.

57. *Chicago Tribune,* July 17, 1876; "News for Taxpayers," *New York Herald,* July 15, 1876; *New York Herald,* August 6, 1876.

58. *St. Louis Dispatch,* July 8, 1876, and July 11, 1876.

59. *New Orleans Picayune,* August 19, 1876, and July 25, 1876.

60. "The Last Indian Struggle," *New York Times,* August 25, 1876.

61. *New York Herald,* July 10, 1876; "Sioux Civilization," *New York Herald,* July 15, 1876.

62. *New York Herald,* July 12, 1876; *Newton Kansan,* July 20, 1876; *St. Louis Dispatch,* July 14, 1876; Bismark, Jr., "Sitting Bulls True Pedigree," *Bismarck (Dak.) Tribune,* August 30, 1876; *New Orleans Picayune,* August 20, 1876.

63. *Rocky Mountain (Denver) News,* July 22, 1876; *Bismarck (Dak.) Tribune,* August 2, 1876, and July 19, 1876.

64. *New York Herald,* July 26, 1876; Utley, *Lance and the Shield,* 76.

65. *New Orleans Picayune,* August 8, 1876, and July 17, 1876.

66. *Chicago Times,* July 18, 1876.

67. "Envy and Jealousy," *Chicago Inter-Ocean,* July 17, 1876; *Chicago Daily News,* July 26, 1876.

68. "Sitting Bull," *Chicago Tribune,* July 15, 1876; Phocion, "Indians," *Chicago Tribune,* August 11, 1876. Long John is a brand of Scotch whiskey.

69. *Rocky Mountain (Denver) Herald,* July 29, 1876. See Brian W. Dippie in collaboration with John M. Carroll, *Bards of the Little Big Horn* (Bryan, Tex.: Guidon Press, 1978), for a collection of many of these poems.

70. "Currency," *Louisville Sunday Review,* July 23, 1876; *Rocky Mountain (Denver) Herald,* August 12, 1876.

71. "Custer as a Boy," *New York Times,* July 29, 1876.

72. "Custer," *Louisville Courier-Journal,* July 14, 1876.

73. Carr and Greeves, *Only Joking,* 3.

74. Arthur Asa Berger, *Blind Men and Elephants: Perspectives on Humor* (New Brunswick, N.J.: Transaction, 1995), 160.

75. Ted Cohen, *Jokes: Philosophical Thoughts on Joking Matters* (Chicago: University of Chicago Press, 1999), 70.

CHAPTER 8

1. Kevin Leman, *Have a New Kid by Friday* (Grand Rapids, Mich.: Revell, 2008), 11.

2. Cornell Haynes, Jr., "Heart of a Champion," AZLyrics, www.azlyrics.com/lyrics/nelly/heartofachampion.html.

3. Dan Piraro, "Custer's Next-to-Last-Stand," Cartoonist Group, www.cartoonistgroup.com/store/add.php?iid=73712.

4. Fareed Zakaria, "What If He Doesn't Go: Gaddafi's Last Stand," *Time,* April 4, 2011; "His Last Stand," *Newsmax,* January 2011; "Bush's Last Stand," *U.S. News and World Report,* May 14, 2007; "Baghdad or Bust," *Economist,* January 13, 2007.

5. Howell Raines, "An Hour with Howell Raines about His Controversial Resignation from the 'New York Times,'" interview by Charlie Rose, *Current Affairs,* July 11, 2003, http://www.charlierose.com/view/interview/1889.

6. "Custer Pwned. Native American Video Gaming T-shirt," Ban T-shirts, www.bant-shirts.com/custer-pwn3d-t-shirt.htm. The company also sells a T-shirt featuring a photo of Sitting Bull over the caption "Hero."

7. Shana Friedman, *Tufts Daily,* November 21, 2011, www.tuftsdaily.com/news/dartmouth-professor-defines-actions-against-native-americans-as-genocide-1.2675514. For Benjamin L. Madley, see UCLA Department of History, www.history.ucla.edu/people/faculty/faculty-1/faculty-1?lid=7219.

8. Helen Jackson, *A Century of Dishonor: A Sketch of the United States Government's Dealings with Some of the Indian Tribes* (New York: Indian Head Books, 1994); Dee Brown, *Bury My Heart at Wounded Knee: An Indian History of the American West* (New York: Sterling Innovation, 2009).

9. Guenter Lewy, "Were American Indians the Victims of Genocide?" George Mason University History News Network, January 22, 2007, http://hnn.us/articles/7302.html.

10. Utley, *Custer and the Great Controversy,* 39–41; Huntzicker, "Frontier Press," 188; Coward, "Indian Wars," 15, 187.

11. "The Organ of the ____!" *Louisville Courier-Journal,* October 23, 1876. William C. Quantrill was a notorious guerrilla leader whose outfit sacked Lawrence, Kansas, in 1863.

12. Henry Watterson, *"Marse Henry": An Autobiography* (New York: George H. Doran, 1919).

13. "Brevities," *Alta (San Francisco) California,* July 8, 1876; "Reinforcements of Volunteers," *Alta (San Francisco) California,* July 9, 1876.

14. "Capt. McDonald and the Indians," *Alta (San Francisco) California,* August 2, 1876; "What to Do with the Sioux," *Alta (San Francisco) California,* August 23, 1876.

15. "Indian Cheek," *Alta (San Francisco) California,* August 8, 1876.

16. *Alta (San Francisco) California,* August 30, 1876.

17. "False Sympathies," *Alta (San Francisco) California,* July 24, 1876.

18. See, for example, "Washington," *Louisville Courier-Journal,* July 15, 1876.

19. Robert D. Kaplan, *Hog Pilots, Blue Water Grunts* (New York: Random House, 2007), 9, 290, 234–35.

20. Joseph Kearns Goodwin, "Bonds of Friendship on an Emotional Journey," *Nieman Reports* 71 (Fall, 2010), 66.

21. Peter Baker, "Days of Darkness, with Death Outside the Door," *Washington (D.C.) Post,* April 14, 2003.

22. Rajiv Chandrasekaran and Peter Baker, "Bridges Seized: More Airstrikes Pound Capital," *Washington (D.C.) Post,* March 23, 2003.

23. Rajiv Chandrasekaran and Peter Baker, "Republican Guard Is Target of Bombing," *Washington (D.C.) Post,* March 25, 2003.

24. Thomas E. Ricks, "U.S. Losses Expose Risks; Raise Doubts about Strategy," *Washington (D.C.) Post,* March 24, 2003.

25. Bradley Graham and Jonathan Weisman, "Display of Five POWs Draws Firm Rebuke," *Washington (D.C.) Post,* March 24, 2003.

26. Susan B. Glasser and Rajiv Chandrasekaran, "16 May Be Dead, Five Others Are Taken Prisoner," *Washington (D.C.) Post,* March 24, 2003.

27. Howard Kurtz, "Too Painful to Publish?" *Washington (D.C.) Post,* March 25, 2003.

28. Lee Hockstader, "Texas Base Stunned to See POWs," *Washington (D.C.) Post,* March 25, 2003.

29. "War Crimes," *Washington (D.C.) Post,* March 27, 2003; "Grievous Losses," *Washington (D.C.) Post,* March 24, 2003; "Perseverance," *Washington (D.C.) Post,* March 30, 2003; "Saving Civilians," *Washington (D.C.) Post,* April 1, 2003.

30. Jonathan Finer, "One Shot, and War Becomes Real," *Washington (D.C.) Post,* March 27, 2003; Jonathan Finer, "U.S. Mounts House-to-House Sweeps," *Washington (D.C.) Post,* March 30, 2003.

31. "The Indians," *Chicago Tribune,* August 14, 1876, and August 16, 1876.

32. Craig Silverman, *Regret the Error: How Media Mistakes Pollute the Press and Imperil Free Speech* (New York: Union Square Press, 2007), 42, 70, 86.

33. Rajiv Chandrasekaran and Peter Baker, "Massive Bombs Strike Baghdad; Iraq Says Market Blast Kills 58," *Washington (D.C.) Post,* March 29, 2003.

34. John Keegan, *The Iraq War* (New York: Alfred A. Knopf, 2004), 149.

35. Tamara Jones, "Hope in a Hollow for a Girl Who Dreamed," *Washington (D.C.) Post,* March 26, 2003.

36. Vernon Loeb and Dana Priest, "Missing Soldier Rescued," *Washington (D.C.) Post,* April 2, 2003; Susan Schmidt and Vernon Loeb, "She Was Fighting to the Death," *Washington (D.C.) Post,* April 3, 2003. See Ian Shapira, "Rescued POW Lynch Arrives in Washington," *Washington (D.C.) Post,* April 13, 2003, as an example of repeating the incorrect details; Peter Baker, "Iraqi Man Risked All to Help Free American Soldier," *Washington (D.C.) Post,* April 4, 2003.

37. Lee Hockstader, "Somber Epilogue to Daring Rescue," *Washington (D.C.) Post,* April 6, 2003.

38. Peter Baker, "Days of Darkness, with Death Outside the Door," *Washington (D.C.) Post,* April 14, 2003.

39. Keith Richburg, "Iraqis Say Lynch Raid Faced No Resistance," *Washington (D.C.) Post,* April 15, 2003.

40. Richard S. Lowry, "Nasiriyah revisited," Op-For, March 22, 2010, http://op-for.com/2010/03/nasiriyah_revisited.html.

41. Ted Curtis Smythe and Paulette D. Kilmer, "The Press and Industrial America, 1865–1883," in *The Media in America: A History,* ed. Wm. David Sloan and James D. Starrt (Northport, Ala.: Vision Press, 2002), 205.

42. *St. Louis Globe-Democrat,* July 7, 1876; "St. Louis Globe-Democrat," *St. Louis Globe-Democrat,* June 26, 1876.

43. *(Danville) Kentucky Advocate,* July 28, 1876.

44. *Hartford Daily Courant,* July 20, 1876.

45. "The Independent Voter," *Louisville Courier-Journal,* August 23, 1876.

46. Watterson, *"Marse Henry,"* 268, 224–25.

47. Ibid., 234–35.

48. James E. Mueller, "Journalistic Objectivity: Time to Abandon It?" *Phi Kappa Phi Forum,* Winter/Spring 2007, 15–16. For a recent poll on confidence in public institutions, including media, see Jeffrey M. Jones, "Americans Most Confident in Military, Least in Congress," Gallup Politics, June 23, 2011, www.gallup.com/poll/148163/Americans-Confident-Military-Least-Congress.aspx.

49. Tim Groseclose, *Left Turn: How Liberal Media Bias Distorts the American Mind* (New York: St. Martin's Press, 2011), 99–110. Groseclose, a UCLA political science professor, cites numerous surveys to illustrate media bias and constructs quantitative tools to measure such bias. Eric Alterman, *What Liberal Media? The Truth about Bias and the News* (New York: Basic Books, 2003), argues that the conservative media control much of the public political debate.

50. Jon Gingerich, "Fox Takes Historic 'Customer Satisfaction' Rating," *O'Dwyers,* August 2010, 9.

51. Holt, *By One Vote,* 167. Michael P. McDonald, "2012 General Election Turnout Rates," *United States Elections Project,* http://elections. gmu.edu/Turnout_html.

52. Utley, *Cavalier in Buckskin,* 194.

53. "President Grant" and "Grant's Plain Talk," *New York Herald,* September 2, 1876.

54. Jon Krakauer, *Where Men Win Glory: The Odyssey of Pat Tillman* (New York: Anchor Books, 2010), 167, 263.

55. Jerry D. Morelock, "No Wars without Heroes," *Armchair General,* July 2006, 8.

56. Richard Slotkin, *The Fatal Environment: The Myth of the Frontier in the Age of Industrialization, 1800–1900* (Norman: University of Oklahoma Press, 1998), 476; Bruce A. Rosenberg, *Custer and the Epic of Defeat* (University Park: Pennsylvania State University Press, 1974), 5.

57. Nym Crinkle, "Custer as an Author," *New York World,* July 9, 1876.

58. Dippie, *Bards of the Little Big Horn,* 22; "Currency," *Louisville Sunday Review,* July 23, 1876.

59. "A Monument to Custer," *New York Herald,* July 12, 1876.

60. Utley, *Lance and the Shield,* 239.

61. Graham, *Custer Myth,* 71; Utley, *Cavalier in Buckskin,* 149.

62. Mark Thompson, "The Other 1%," *Time,* November 21, 2011, 39.

63. Andrew J. Huebner, *The Warrior Image: Soldiers in American Culture from the Second World War to the Vietnam Era* (Chapel Hill: University of North Carolina Press, 2008), 275–78.

64. James E. Mueller, "Victims, Villains and Heroes: Comparing Newspaper Coverage of World War II and the Iraq War," *Southwestern Mass Communication Journal* 21, no. 2 (Spring 2006): 71–83. While the present volume was in production, more books about the global war on terror were published, including Dakota Meyer and Bing West, *Into the Fire: A Firsthand Account of the Most Extraordinary Battle in the Afghan War* (New York: Random House, 2012). It is the account of the fight in which Meyer won the Medal of Honor. Doubtlessly, more such memoirs will be published in the years ahead. But the fact remains that the earliest and most widely celebrated veterans of the war were largely portrayed by the press as victims.

65. Richard S. Lowry, *Marines in the Garden of Eden: The True Story of Seven Bloody Days in Iraq* (New York: Berkley Caliber, 2007), 134–35, writes that the "details of Walters' horrible ordeal" will never be known. Krakauer's book about Tillman and Rick Bragg, *I'm a Soldier, Too: The Jessica Lynch Story* (New York: Knopf, 2003), are best-selling biographies.

66. "A Monument to Custer," *New York Herald,* July 12, 1876.

Bibliography

MANUSCRIPT COLLECTIONS

Rutherford B. Hayes Presidential Center, Fremont, Ohio.
    Rutherford B. Hayes Papers.
    Thomas Henry Looker Papers.

BOOKS AND ARTICLES

Abrams, Marc H. *Sioux War Dispatches: Reports from the Field, 1876–1877.* Yardley, Pa.: Westholme, 2012.

Allen, Walter. *Governor Chamberlain's Administration in South Carolina: A Chapter of Reconstruction in the Southern States.* New York: G. P. Putnam's Sons, 1888.

Alterman, Eric. *What Liberal Media? The Truth about Bias and the News.* New York: Basic Books, 2003.

Ambrose, Stephen L. *Crazy Horse and Custer: The Parallel Lives of Two American Warriors.* Garden City, N.Y.: Doubleday, 1975.

Andrews, J. Cutler. *The North Reports the Civil War.* Pittsburgh: University of Pittsburg Press, 1985.

Aswell, James R., ed. *Native American Humor.* New York: Harper and Brothers, 1947.

Baldasty, Gerald J. *The Commercialization of News in the Nineteenth Century.* Madison: University of Wisconsin Press, 1992.

Barnard, Sandy. *I Go with Custer: The Life and Death of Reporter Mark Kellogg.* Bismarck, N.D.: Bismarck Tribune, 1996.

Barnett, Louise. *Touched by Fire: The Life Death, and Mythic Afterlife of George Armstrong Custer.* New York: Henry Holt, 1996.

Berger, Arthur Asa. *Blind Men and Elephants: Perspectives on Humor.* News Brunswick, N.J.: Transaction, 1995.

Berkhofer, Robert F., Jr., *The White Man's Indian.* New York: Alfred A. Knopf, 1978.

Blake, Barry J. *Playing with Words: Humour in the English Language.* Oakville, Conn.: Equinox, 2007.

Bragg, Rick. *I'm a Soldier, Too: The Jessica Lynch Story.* New York: Knopf, 2003.

Bray, Kingsley M. *Crazy Horse: A Lakota Life.* Norman: University of Oklahoma Press, 2006.

Brown, Dee. *Bury My Heart at Wounded Knee: An Indian History of the American West.* New York: Sterling Innovation, 2009.

Brust, James S., Brian C. Pohanka, and Sandy Barnard. *Where Custer Fell: Photographs of the Little Bighorn Battlefield Then and Now*. Norman: University of Oklahoma Press, 2005.

Campbell, Ballard C. *American Disasters: 201 Calamities That Shook the Nation*. New York: Checkmark Books, 2008.

Carhart, Tom. *Lost Triumph: Lee's Real Plan at Gettysburg—and Why It Failed*. New York: G. P. Putnam's Sons, 2005.

Carr, Jimmy, and Lucy Greeves. *Only Joking: What's So Funny about Making People Laugh?* New York: Gotham Books, 2006.

Centennial Newspaper Exhibition, 1876. New York: Geo. P. Rowell, 1876.

Clark, Thomas D. *A History of Kentucky*. New York: Prentice-Hall, 1937.

Cohen, Ted. *Jokes: Philosophical Thoughts on Joking Matters*. Chicago: University of Chicago Press, 1999.

Connell, Evan S. *Son of the Morning Star*. New York: Promontory Press, 1993.

Coopersmith, Andrew S. *Fighting Words: An Illustrated History of Newspaper Accounts of the Civil War*. New York: New Press, 2004.

Copeland, David, ed. *The Indian Wars and the Spanish-American War*. Vol. 4 of *The Greenwood Library of American War Reporting*. Westport, Conn.: Greenwood Press, 2005.

Cornog, Evan, and Richard Whelan. *Hats in the Ring: An Illustrated History of American Presidential Campaigns*. New York: Random House, 2000.

Cortissoz, Royal. *The Life of Whitelaw Reid,* vol. 1. New York: Charles Scribner's Sons, 1921.

Coward, John. "The Indian Wars." In *The Greenwood Library of American War Reporting,* Vol. 4: *The Indian Wars and the Spanish-American War,* ed. David Copeland, 1–309. Westport, Conn.: Greenwood Press, 2005.

———. *The Newspaper Indian: Native American Identity in the Press, 1820–90*. Urbana, Ill.: University of Illinois Press, 1999.

Cox, Samuel S. *Why We Laugh*. Bronx, N.Y.: Benjamin Blom, 1969.

David, Saul. *Military Blunders: The How and Why of Military Failure*. New York: Carroll and Graf, 1998.

Deloria, Vine, Jr. *Custer Died for Your Sins: An Indian Manifesto*. Norman: University of Oklahoma Press, 1988.

Dippie, Brian W. *Custer's Last Stand: The Anatomy of an American Myth*. Lincoln: University of Nebraska Press, 1994.

———. "The Southern Response to Custer's Last Stand." In *The Great Sioux War 1876–77,* ed. Paul L. Hedren. Helena, Mont.: Montana Historical Society Press, 1991.

Dippie, Brian W., with John M. Carroll. *Bards of the Little Big Horn*. Bryan, Tex.: Guidon Press, 1978.

Donovan, James. *A Terrible Glory: Custer and the Little Bighorn: The Last Great Battle of the American West*. New York: Little, Brown, 2008.

Eckenrode, H. J. *Rutherford B. Hayes: Statesman of Reunion*. New York: Dodd, Mead, 1930.

Eden, Steven. *Military Blunders: Wartime Fiascoes from the Roman Age through World War I.* New York: MetroBooks, 1995.

Elliott, Michael A. *Custerology: The Enduring Legacy of the Indian Wars and George Armstrong Custer.* Chicago: University of Chicago Press, 2007.

Finerty, John F. *War-Path and Bivouac; or; The Conquest of the Sioux.* Norman: University of Oklahoma Press, 1994.

Flexner, Stuart, and Doris Flexner. *The Pessimists Guide to History.* New York: Quill, 2000.

Flick, Alexander Clarence. *Samuel Jones Tilden: A Study in Political Sagacity.* New York: Dodd, Mead, 1939.

Foner, Eric. *Reconstruction: America's Unfinished Revolution 1863–1877.* New York: Harper and Row, 1989.

Forstchen, William R., and Bill Fawcett, eds. *It Seemed Like a Good Idea at the Time: A Compendium of Great Historical Fiascoes.* New York: Avon Books, 2000.

Friedman, Shana. "Dartmouth Professor Defines Actions against Native Americans as Genocide." *Tufts Daily,* November 21, 2011. www.tuftsdaily.com/news/dartmouth -professor-defines-actions-against-native-americans-as-genocide-1.2675514.

Frost, Lawrence A. *General Custer's Libbie.* Seattle: Superior, 1976.

Gingerich, Jon. "Fox Takes Historic 'Customer Satisfaction' Rating." *O'Dwyers,* August 2010, 9.

Goodwin, Joseph Kearns. "Bonds of Friendship on an Emotional Journey." *Nieman Reports* 71 (Fall 2010): 66–67.

Graham, W. A. *The Custer Myth: A Sourcebook of Custeriana.* Mechanicsburg, Pa.: Stackpole, 1995.

———. *The Story of the Little Big Horn.* New York: Bonanza Books, 1959.

Gray, John S. *Centennial Campaign: The Sioux War of 1876.* Norman: University of Oklahoma Press, 1988.

Greene, Jerome A. *Stricken Field: The Little Bighorn since 1876.* Norman: University of Oklahoma Press, 2008.

Groseclose, Tim. *Left Turn: How Liberal Media Bias Distorts the American Mind.* New York: St. Martin's Press, 2011.

Haskew, Michael E., ed. *Great Military Disasters.* Bath, U.K.: 2009.

Hatch, Thom. *The Custer Companion: A Comprehensive Guide to the Life of George Armstrong Custer and the Plains Indian Wars.* Mechanicsburg, Pa.: Stackpole, 2002.

Hedren, Paul L. *Great Sioux War Orders of Battle: How the United States Army Waged War on the Northern Plains, 1876–1877.* Norman, Okla.: Arthur H. Clark, 2011.

———, ed. *Ho! For the Black Hills: Captain Jack Crawford Reports the Black Hills Gold Rush and Great Sioux War.* Pierre: South Dakota State Historical Society Press, 2012.

Holt, Michael F. *By One Vote: The Disputed Presidential Election of 1876.* Lawrence: University of Kansas Press, 2008.

Howells, Wm. D. *Sketch of the Life and Character of Rutherford B. Hayes.* New York: Hurd and Houghton, 1876.

Huebner, Andrew J. *The Warrior Image: Soldiers in American Culture from the Second World War to the Vietnam Era.* Chapel Hill: University of North Carolina Press, 2008.

Huntzicker, William E. "The Frontier Press, 1800–1900." In *The Media in America: A History,* ed. Wm. David Sloan and James D. Starrt, 175–98. Northport, Ala.: Vision Press, 2002.

Hutton, Paul Andrew. *Phil Sheridan and His Army.* Norman: University of Oklahoma Press, 1999.

Jackson, Helen. *A Century of Dishonor: A Sketch of the United States Government's Dealings with Some of the Indian Tribes.* New York: Indian Head Books, 1994.

Jones, Jeffrey M. "Americans Most Confident in Military, Least in Congress." Gallup Politics, June 23, 2011. www.gallup.com/poll/148163/Americans-Confident -Military-Least-Congress.aspx.

Kaplan, Robert D. *Hog Pilots, Blue Water Grunts.* New York: Random House, 2007.

Keegan, John. *The Iraq War.* New York: Alfred A. Knopf, 2004.

Knight, Oliver. *Following the Indian Wars: The Story of the Newspaper Correspondents among the Indian Campaigners.* Norman: University of Oklahoma Press, 1960.

Krakauer, Jon. *Where Men Win Glory: The Odyssey of Pat Tillman.* New York: Anchor Books, 2010.

Langellier, John R. "Custer: The Making of a Myth." In *Little Bighorn Remembered,* by Herman J. Viola, 186–219. New York: Times Books, 1999.

Leman, Kevin. *Have a New Kid by Friday.* Grand Rapids, Mich.: Revell, 2008.

Lewy, Guenter. "Were American Indians the Victims of Genocide?" George Mason University History News Network, January 22, 2007. http://hnn.us/articles/7302 .html.

Lowry, Richard S. *Marines in the Garden of Eden: The True Story of Seven Bloody Days in Iraq.* New York: Berkley Caliber, 2007.

———. "Nasiriyah Revisited." Op-For, March 22, 2010. http://op-for.com/2010/03 /nasiriyah_revisited.html.

McDonald, Michael P. "2012 General Election Turnout Rates," *United States Elections Project,* http://elections. gmu.edu/Turnout_html.

McNab, Chris. *The World's Worst Military Disasters: Chronicling the Greatest Battlefield Catastrophes of All Time.* New York: Barnes and Noble Books, 2005.

Meyer, Dakota, and Bing West. *Into the Fire: A Firsthand Account of the Most Extraordinary Battle in the Afghan War.* New York: Random House, 2012.

Meyer, John C. "Humor as a Double-Edged Sword: Four Functions of Humor in Communication." *Communication Theory* 10, no. 3 (August 2000): 310–31.

Monnett, John H. *Where a Hundred Soldiers Were Killed.* Albuquerque: University of New Mexico Press, 2008.

Morelock, Jerry D. "No Wars without Heroes." *Armchair General,* July 2006, 8.

Morris, Roy, Jr. *Fraud of the Century: Rutherford B. Hayes, Samuel Tilden, and the Stolen Election of 1876.* New York: Simon and Schuster, 2003.

———. *Sheridan: The Life and Wars of General Phil Sheridan.* New York: Vintage Books, 1993.

Mueller, James. E. "Journalistic Objectivity: Time to Abandon It?" *Phi Kappa Phi Forum,* Winter/Spring 2007, 14–18.

———. "Kentucky Press Coverage of the Little Bighorn: Detached Partisanship," *Greasy Grass* 21 (May 2005): 15–23.

———. "Little Bighorn Coverage in Kansas Newspapers: Last Stand for a Partisan Press." In *Custer and His Times,* vol. 4, ed. John P. Hart, 251–74. LaGrange Park, Ill.: Little Big Horn Associates, 2002.

———. "Little Bighorn Coverage in the Illinois Press." In *Custer and His Times,* vol. 5, ed. John P. Hart, 208–47. Cordova, Tenn.: Little Big Horn Associates, 2008.

———. "Victims, Villains and Heroes: Comparing Newspaper Coverage of World War II and the Iraq War." *Southwestern Mass Communication Journal* 21, no. 2 (Spring 2006): 71–83.

Nichols, Roger L. "Printer's Ink and Red Skins: Western Newspapermen and the Indians." *Kansas Quarterly* 3, no. 4 (Fall 1971): 82–88.

Nichols, Ronald H. *In Custer's Shadow: Major Marcus Reno.* Norman: University of Oklahoma Press, 2000.

Polakoff, Keith Ian. *The Politics of Inertia: The Election of 1876 and the End of Reconstruction.* Baton Rouge: Louisiana State University Press, 1973.

Prelude to the Century. Alexandria, Va.: Time-Life Books, 1999.

Regan, Geoffrey. *The Brassey's Book of Military Blunders.* Dulles, Va.: Brassey's, 2000.

Reilly, Hugh J. *The Frontier Newspaper and the Coverage of the Plains Indian Wars.* Santa Barbara, Calif.: Praeger, 2010.

Reynolds, Quentin. *Custer's Last Stand.* New York: Random House, 1951.

Rezneck, Samuel. "Distress, Relief, and Discontent in the United States during the Depression of 1873–78." *Journal of Political Economy* 58, no. 6 (December 1950): 494–512.

Rickey, Don, Jr. *Forty Miles a Day on Beans and Hay: The Enlisted Soldier Fighting the Indian Wars.* Norman: University of Oklahoma Press, 1973.

Robinson, Lloyd. *The Stolen Election: Hayes versus Tilden—1876.* New York: Forge, 2001.

Rosenberg, Bruce A. *Custer and the Epic of Defeat.* University Park: Pennsylvania State University Press, 1974.

Rydell, Robert. W. *All the World's a Fair: Visions of Empire at American International Expositions, 1876–1916.* Chicago: University of Chicago Press, 1984.

Schultz, Duane. *Custer: Lessons in Leadership.* Palgrave MacMillan: Houndmills, U.K., 2010.

Scott, Douglas D., P. Willey, and Melissa A. Connor. *They Died with Custer: Soldiers' Bones from the Battle of the Little Bighorn.* Norman: University of Oklahoma Press, 1998.

Silverman, Craig. *Regret the Error: How Media Mistakes Pollute the Press and Imperil Free Speech.* New York: Union Square Press, 2007.

Sklenar, Larry. *To Hell with Honor: Custer and the Little Bighorn.* Norman: University of Oklahoma Press, 2000.

Sloan, Wm. David, and James D. Starrt, eds. *The Media in America: A History.* Northport, Ala.: Vision Press, 1999.

Slotkin, Richard. *The Fatal Environment: The Myth of the Frontier in the Age of Industrialization, 1800–1890*. Norman: University of Oklahoma Press, 1998.

Smythe, Ted Curtis. *The Gilded Age Press, 1865–1900*. Westport, Conn.: Praeger, 2003.

Smythe, Ted Curtis, and Paulette D. Kilmer. "The Press and Industrial America, 1865–1883." In *The Media in America: A History*, ed. Wm. David Sloan and James D. Starrt, 199–222. Northport, Ala.: Vision Press, 2002.

Spilsbury, Julian. *Great Military Disasters: A History of Incompetence*. New York: MetroBooks, 2010.

Stewart, Edgar I. *Custer's Luck*. Norman: University of Oklahoma Press, 1980.

Summers, Mark Wahlgren. *The Press Gang: Newspapers and Politics 1865–1878*. Chapel Hill: University of North Carolina Press, 1994.

Sutherland, Daniel E. *A Savage Conflict: The Decisive Role of Guerillas in the American Civil War*. Chapel Hill: University of North Carolina Press, 2009.

Swint, Kerwin. *Mudslingers: The Twenty-Five Dirtiest Political Campaigns of All Time*. New York: Sterling/Union Square Press, 2008.

Thompson, Mark. "The Other 1%." *Time,* November 21, 2011, 34–39.

Utley, Robert M. *Cavalier in Buckskin: George Armstrong Custer and the Western Military Frontier*. Norman: University of Oklahoma Press, 1988.

———. *Custer and the Great Controversy: The Origin and Development of a Legend*. Lincoln: University of Nebraska Press, 1998.

———. *Custer Battlefield: A History and Guide to the Battle of the Little Bighorn*. Washington, D.C.: National Park Service, 1988.

———. *The Lance and the Shield: The Life and Times of Sitting Bull*. New York: Ballantine Books, 1994.

Viola, Herman J. *Little Bighorn Remembered*. New York: Times Books, 1999.

Walker, Paul D. *The Cavalry Battle That Saved the Union: Custer vs. Stuart at Gettysburg*. Gretna, La.: Pelican, 2002.

Walsh, Justin E. *To Print the News and Raise Hell!* Chapel Hill: University of North Carolina Press, 1968.

Watterson, Henry. *"Marse Henry": An Autobiography*. New York: George H. Doran, 1919.

Weir, Stephen. *History's Worst Decisions and the People Who Made Them*. New York: Fall River Press, 2009.

Wert, Jeffery. *Custer: The Controversial Life of George Armstrong Custer*. New York: Simon and Schuster, 1996.

West, Michael. *Transcendental Wordplay: America's Romantic Punsters and the Search for the Language of Nature*. Athens: Ohio University Press, 2000.

Williams, Charles Richard, ed. *Diary and Letters of Rutherford Birchard Hayes, Nineteenth President of the United States*, Vol. 3: *1865–1881*. Columbus: Ohio State Archaeological and Historical Society, 1924.

Williamson, Joel. *After Slavery: The Negro in South Carolina during Reconstruction, 1861–1877*. Chapel Hill: University of North Carolina Press, 1965.

Windolph, Charles. *I Fought with Custer: The Story of Sergeant Windolph, Last Survivor of the Battle of the Little Big Horn as Told to Frazier and Robert Hunt.* Lincoln: University of Nebraska Press, 1987.

Woolley, John, and Gerhard Peters. "Voter Turnout in Presidential Elections: 1828–2008." American Presidency Project. www.presidency.ucsb.edu/data/turnout.php.

NEWSPAPERS

Alta (San Francisco) California, 1876.

Atchison (Kans.) Daily Champion, 1876.

(Atlanta) Constitution, 1876.

Austin Daily Democratic Statesman, 1876.

Baltimore American and Commercial Advertiser, 1876.

Bismarck (Dak.) Tribune, 1876.

Black Hills (Dak.) Pioneer, 1876.

Bloomington (Ill.) Pantagraph, 1876.

Bozeman (Mont.) Avant Courier, 1876.

Burlington (Kans.) Weekly Patriot, 1876.

Chanute (Kans.) Times, 1876.

Chicago Daily News, 1876.

Chicago Inter-Ocean, 1876.

Chicago Times, 1876.

Chicago Tribune, 1876.

Clark County (Ky.) Democrat, 1876.

Corpus Christi (Tex.) Gazette, 1876.

Dallas Daily Herald, 1876.

(Danville) Kentucky Advocate, 1876.

Emporia (Kans.) News, 1876.

Fort Worth Daily Democrat, 1876.

Galena (Ill.) Gazette, 1876.

Galveston (Tex.) News, 1876.

Hartford Daily Courant, 1876.

Hays (Kans.) Daily News, 1929.

Helena (Mont.) Daily Herald, 1876.

Laramie (Wyo.) Daily Sentinel, 1876.

(Lawrence, Kans.) Republican Daily Journal, 1876.

Leavenworth (Kans.) Daily Appeal, 1876.

Leavenworth (Kans.) Daily Times, 1876.

Louisville Commercial, 1876.

Louisville Courier-Journal, 1876.

Louisville Sunday Review, 1876.

Mayfield (Ky.) Monitor, 1876.

(Missoula, Mont.) Missoulian, 1876.

Monroe (Mich.) Commercial, 1876.

New Orleans Picayune, 1876.

New York Daily Graphic, 1876.

New York Herald, 1876.

New York Times, 1876.

New York Tribune, 1876.

New York World, 1876.

Omaha (Neb.) Weekly Herald, 1876.

Oskaloosa (Kans.) Independent, 1876.

Ottawa (Ill.) Republican, 1876.

Owensboro (Ky.) Examiner, 1876.

Peoria (Ill.) Daily Transcript, 1876.

Quincy (Ill.) Herald, 1876.

(Richmond, Ky.) Transylvania Presbyterian, 1876.

Rocky Mountain (Denver) Herald, 1876.

Rocky Mountain (Denver) News, 1876.

San Antonio Republican, 1876.

(San Marcos) West Texas Free Press, 1876.

(Springfield) Illinois Daily State Journal, 1876.

St. Louis Dispatch, 1876.

St. Louis Globe-Democrat, 1876.

(Topeka, Kans.) Commonwealth, 1876.

Washington (D.C.) Post, 2003.

Washington (Kans.) Republican, 1876.

Williamstown (Ky.) Sentinel, 1876.

Woodford (Ky.) Weekly, 1876.

York (Neb.) Republican, 1876.

Index

References to illustrations are in italic type.

Abizaid, John, 201
Abrams, Marc H., 146
Abu Ghraib POW abuse scandal, 210
Allison, William B. (senator), 18
Allison commission, 18
Alta California: bloodthirsty reaction to news of defeat, 196–97; on Crédit Mobilier stock-influencing scandal, 92–93; Democratic House attacked in, 98, 131, 132; Hamburg took backseat to Sioux war, 131–32; on a resurgence of the Civil War, 107–108; solution to Indian Problem suggested by, 197–98; on telegraph's significance, 10; war news equal to election news in, 97–98
American Customer Satisfaction Index, 208
American Horse (Sioux chief), 125, 183
Apache helicopter, 199
Armchair General magazine, 210
Army and Navy Journal, 94
Assessing blame for defeat, 55–78; blame game ignored by Far West, 70; and Custer's hometown of Monroe, Mich., 60–61; Democratic House of Representatives attacked, 73–74; Democratic papers reluctant to blame Custer, 63–67; and Denver twist, 70–71; eastern Republican editors critical of Custer, 67–68; Grant accused of conspiracy to kill Custer, 74–76; New England critical

of Custer, 68–69; *New York Herald's* emotional defense of Custer, 57–58; *New York Tribune* deferred criticism, 71–72; papers in defense of Grant, 72–73; partisanship and assessment of blame, 55–56; peace policy criticized by Republican papers, 71; poetry in praise of Custer, 58–59; politics reflected in, 78; Reconstruction troops in South criticized, 76–78; Republicans in defense of Custer, 69; small-town Republicans of Illinois and Kansas cite Custer's incaution, 67; southern newspapers prominent Custer defenders, 61–63
Aswell, James R., 170
Atchison Daily Champion, on Hamburg Massacre, 127, 132
Atlanta Constitution, Little Bighorn compared to great battles of history, 62
Austin Daily Democratic Statesman: and joke on Grant Administration, 184; Little Bighorn downplayed by, 37; and Phil Sheridan as target of joke, 180–81

Baltimore American and Commercial Advertiser: accurate report of Little Bighorn story, 37–38; Custer's overconfidence blamed by, 68; Democrats accused of wanting to shrink army by, 73; fair treatment

Baltimore American and Commercial Advertiser (continued)
of Indians urged by, 161, 163; and false report on Sitting Bull's death, 52; modified peace policy called for by, 167

Baltimore Gazette, on Sitting Bull at West Point, 175–76

"Bayonet" rule in the South, 124–25

Bear Stands Up, 53, 165, 199

Belknap, William, 20, 86

Belmont, August, 57

Benham, D. W., 36

Bennett, James Gordon, Jr., 34, 40, 42, 57. See also *New York Herald*

Benteen, Frederick: anti-Custer faction led by, 13; command taken by after Reno's retreat, 26–27; comment on finding Custer's body, 30; ordered to front by Cooke, 15; three companies assigned to, 24; unmentioned in Brisbin's account, 48

Bismarck Tribune (N.Dak.): attack on Democrats as party of rebellion, 87; call for all-out war against Indians tempered, 151–52; criticized papers for errors in geography, 188; and Crook as target of joke, 181; in defense of Custer, 70; on John Grass's teasing of army officers, 183; Kellogg assigned to cover Custer by, 33; Kellogg's stories published by, 34; on scalping by whites, 176–77; on Sitting Bull, 175; on Sitting Bull as "a Tilden man," 187–88. See also Lounsberry, C. A.

Blackburn, J. C. S., and Grant "conspiracy" to kill Custer, 74

Black Hills: and Black Hills Brigade recommended, 151; and botched negotiations for, 18, 31, 160, 198–99; Custer's 1874 survey of, 15, 17, 66–67; and fear of Indians by miners, 34, 80; gold discovered in, 9; and gold rush, 17, 21, 152; *New York Times* on miners and, 88; Sitting Bull's promise to defend, 53, 165; stories over sale of, 165

Black Hills Pioneer (Deadwood City, Dakota Ter.), local volunteers called for to fight Sioux, 151

Blaine, James G., 89, 92–93, 95, 183

Blake, Barry, on current tasteless humor, 172

Blame, assessing. *See* Assessing blame for defeat

Bloody Knife, 24, 25

"Bloody shirt" issue: campaign defended by politicians, 101; countered by Democrats in defense of Custer, 84; and Hamburg Massacre, 136, 137–38, 187; as ineffective because of voters' disgust with war, 93, 127; and Lamar, 129–130; and Morton, 123, 185; Republicans determined to win election with, 7, 82; and Rynd, 130–31; takes voters' minds off hard economic times, 86

Bloomington Pantagraph, Custer defended by, 69

Boston Journal, accused of advocating mob law in Hamburg, 138

Bozeman, Mont. Ter., 36

Bozeman Avant Courier: and play on words, 178; and Sitting Bull jokes, 174–76

Bozeman Times, first newspaper to report Little Bighorn, 36, 37

Bozeman Trail, 16

Braddock, Edward, 180

Bradley, James H., 28

Brisbin, James ("Grasshopper Jim"), on description of battlefields, 46

Bristow, Benjamin, 185

Buchanan, James, 107

Bulkley, J. M., 81

Burlington Weekly Patriot: on Hamburg Massacre, 128; radical solution of making Indians citizens, 158

Bury My Heart at Wounded Knee (Brown), 195

Butler, M. C., and Hamburg Massacre, 122–23

Butler massacre. *See* Hamburg Massacre

Calhoun, James (brother-in-law of Custer), 14–15, 29, 47, 60

Calhoun, Mrs. James (Margaret "Maggie" Custer) (sister), 14, 47, 48

Cameron, James, 49

Campaign of 1876. *See* Presidential campaign of 1876

Capehart, H., 80

Carnahan, John M., 41

Carr, Jimmy, 172, 191, 232n11

Casualties at Little Bighorn, 37–38, 48–49, 52, 141, 216n20

Centennial Exhibition in Philadelphia.: featured prominently in press, 34; occurring as Custer and men were being killed, 8–10, *113*

Century of Dishonor, A (Jackson), 195

Chamberlain, D. H.: on Hamburg Massacre, 122; and request for federal troops, 130, 134–35, 137–38, 143; urged to push investigation of Hamburg massacre, 143

Chanute Times, Custer's overconfidence blamed by, 67

Chaplin, Charlie, 172

Charge of the Light Brigade, The (Tennyson), 55

Cheyennes, Custer's campaign against, 5

Chicago Daily News: Custer blamed by, 64; and the Little Bighorn headlines, 41

Chicago Inter-Ocean: Custer's overconfidence blamed by, 66; in defense of Grant's policies, 73; gun

control as answer to Indian Problem, 156–57; on Hamburg Massacre, 128

Chicago Times: Fred Grant's military service mocked by, 185; and the Little Bighorn headlines, 41; story evolved as details emerged, 65–66; on talents of Indians, 155–56

Chicago Tribune: abandoning peace policy recommended by, 146; both praise and blame for Custer, 66; Grant as "invisible man" in condemning peace policy, 72; on Hamburg Massacre, 121; joking on pensioning Indian widows, 186; and reporters mocked for baldness, 177

Civil service reform, 73, 80, 83, 86, 92, 99

Civil War: attitudes of extermination as continuation of, 148–49; and Custer, 4–5, 6; Hamburg Massacre seen as resurgence of, 108, 123, 135, 141; Tilden attacked over records in, 92

Clark County Democrat, and Indian courage mocked by, 179

Conkling, Roscoe, 89, 185

Conventions, political, 38, 79, 84, 86–89, 97

Cooke, William W., 14, 15, 29, 52

Cox, Samuel, on tasteless humor of the nineteenth century, 171–72

Crawford, John Wallace ("Captain Jack"), 153

Crazy Horse: Ambrose biography of, 28; assault on village of, 32; false story of death, 52–53, 203; and Little Big Man, 18; naming of, 168

Crittenden, Thomas L., 40

Crook, George: background of, 18–19; photo of, *111*; and Rosebud battle, 21–22, 218n63; as target of jokes, 181

Crow agency, 17, 21

Curley (scout), 48, 50

Current events of 1876, 83

Curtis, William, 66

Custer, Boston (brother), 47, 60

Custer, Elizabeth "Libbie" Bacon (wife), 12

Custer, Emmanuel (father), 60

Custer, George Armstrong: accused of abandoning Elliott at Washita, 27, 30; attitude change before battle, 24; background of, 11–12; body found after death, 29–30; character of, 60–61, 63, 66–67, 190; Civil War record of, 4–5, 6; clothing of, 5, 79; controversy over blame for defeat, 11, 216n24; court-martialing of, 13; death compared to biblical story of David, 63; death predicted by Lt. Wallace, 24; and 1873 expedition, 17; frontier reputation of, 3–6; hometown honors for, 60; known as "Hard Ass" by subordinates, 23; legacy of, 106–107, 190, 212–13, 214; and nepotism, 14; photo of, 111; plan of attack a mystery, 25, 27; postwar service of, 13; profiles often politicized, 68–69; Sitting Bull's account of death, 28; and supposed last words before fight, 50–51; and testimony in corruption hearings, 20; tribute to from J.M.W., 190; widespread imagery of, 193–94

Custer, Margaret "Maggie" (sister). See Calhoun, Mrs. James

Custer, Tom (brother), 14, 29, 60

Custer and the Great Controversy (Utley), 84, 195

"Custer Controversy," 11, 216n24

Custer Died for Your Sins (Deloria), 11

Custer National Monument Association, 59, 81

Custer's Last Stand, 3–30; Benteen ordered to Little Bighorn with packs, 25–26; Benteen's inaction controversial, 26; and Benteen's words on seeing Custer's body, 30; Benteen took command to supervise defense, 26; and bodies found, 29; casualties from, 37–38, 48–49, 52, 141; and Centennial Exhibition in Philadelphia (May1876), 8; and communication failure on Rosebud battle, 21–22; and the "Custer Controversy," 11–12; Custer's death uncertain, 27–28; and Custer's dismissal and reinstatement, 19–20; Custer's frontier reputation, 3–6; Custer's men driven hard for thirty miles to Sun Dance site, 23; Custer's plan a mystery, 27; and Custer's top subordinates, 13–15; declining coverage at end of election cycle, 97; and descriptions of Custer's body, 29–30; and factors leading up to Little Bighorn, 17–18; and fifteen-day mission planned by Custer, 23; and Fort Laramie Treaty of 1868, 16; front-page news of, 11; and Little Bighorn River battlefield, 10–11; and lone-survivor myth, 28–29; night march planned by Custer with unusual manner, 23–24; Reno ordered by Custer to chase Indians, 25; and Reno scouting mission, 22; and reservation deadline of Jan. 31, 1876, 18; and retreat by Reno as Indians attacked, 25; Seventh Cavalry divided into four commands, 24; and Seventh Cavalry ready for Little Bighorn campaign, 19; and Sheridan's plan for war on tribes, 18–19; Sitting Bull's account of Custer's death, 28; and Sitting Bull's vision of invincibility, 21; and Terry's controversial orders to Custer, 22–23; and testing of Sheridan's plan, 19–20. See also Custer, George Armstrong

"Custer's Luck," 12, 50–51, 67, 218n66

Daily Constitution (Atlanta): arguing with northern papers on Hamburg, 136; Hamburg given equal billing with Big Horn, 134–35

Dallas Daily Herald: on Custer and Rosser, 61–62; on Custer's "last words," 51; on "deaths" of Sitting Bull and Crazy Horse, 52–53; on Grant "conspiracy" to kill Custer, 74–75; on lack of troops to blame for Custer's demise, 77–78

Davis, Jefferson, 50

Delano, Columbus, 186

Deloria, Vine, 11

Deshler, W. G., 80–81

De Smet, Father, 188

Detroit Free Press, 147, 160, 188

Dime novels, 3–4, 211

Downie, Leonard, Jr., 201

Downing, J. H., 39

Elliott, Joel, 13, 27

Ellis County Star (Hays, Kans.), and the Little Bighorn story, 39

Fariah, Major, 63

Far West (riverboat), 22, 36, 41, 51, 176

Ferry, Thomas W., 81

Fetterman, William J., 16, 17

Finerty, John F., 33

Fisk, Andrew, 36

Flemensburg Democrat (Ky.), and the Little Bighorn headlines, 40

Fletcher, Thomas, 45

Focus of Little Bighorn coverage, 193–214; Americans in 1876 felt country land of destiny, 210; Civil War and Reconstruction as context for, 196; criticisms of coverage have some validity, 194; and Custer imagery examples, 193–94; and Custer seen as hero in 1876, 194; and descriptions of fighting in Iraq much like Little Bighorn, 200–202; emotional reaction to Custer's defeat, 196–97; essential story correct from beginning, 210–11; and failure of agriculture for Indians, 197; and Grant interview after nomination, 209; journalists admitted getting facts wrong, 202–203, 210; Little Bighorn nonissue in campaign, 209; minority in favor of exterminating Indians, 198; modern journalists making errors at "shocking level," 203–204; and parallels between 1876 and twenty-first century conflicts, 199–200; and party loyalty of newspapers, 205–206; press fanned flames of outrage against Indians, 195; tone of coverage softened over time, 197; Wheeler on romantic nature of Indian warfare, 211–12. *See also* Iraq and Afghanistan conflicts

Fort Abraham Lincoln, 8, 19, 20, 22

Fort Ellis, 18, 19, 20, 22, 36

Fort Fetterman, 20, 21, 32

Fort Hays, Kans., 39

Fort Laramie Treaty of 1868, 16, 17, 18

Fort Phil Kearny, 16, 19

Fort Worth Daily Democrat, Grant attacked by, 75, 102

FOXNews.com, 208

Franks, Tommy, 200–201

Fraud of the Century (Morris), 83–84

Galena Gazette (Ill.), Custer blamed by, 67

Galveston News: and the Little Bighorn headlines, 40; in praise of Custer, 62; on public's interest in anything about Custer, 45; Reconstruction troops criticized by, 76–77; regiment of Texans offered to avenge Custer, 150

"Gary Owen" (regiment's anthem), 14

Gatling guns (defined), 19

Gerard, Fred, 24

Gibbon, John: background of, 19; battlefield describes as "horrible" by officer with, 51; column delayed until April, 20, 22; and failure to help Custer, 22; and *New York Times* theory of loss, 67–68; and parade before Terry and, 23; and possible foreshadowing of disaster, 47

"Golden-Haired Leader" (poem), 59

Gold rush, 9, 17, 21, 59, 159

Goodwin, Joseph Kearns, 199

Gottfried, Gilbert, 172

Grand Custer Memorial Ball, 62–63

Grant, Fred (son), 13, 24, 137, 184–85

Grant, Orvil (brother), 20, 184

Grant, Ulysses S.: attacked by *New York Times*, 95; blame for defeat placed on by Democratic newspapers, 56, 102; criticized for small army, 132–33; Custer ordered to withdraw from campaign by, 20; and decision to go to war, 18; and family mocked in press, 184–85; and hard war tactics, 148–49; interview after nomination, 209; as "invisible man" in Republican criticisms of peace policy, 70–72; Philadelphia Centennial Exhibition opened by, 8; scandals in administration of, 82, 96, 102; and southern "conspiracy theory," 74–76, 139; as target of political humor, 184; at Union Army reunion in Toledo in 1873, 79

Grass, John, 182–83, 192

Great Sioux Reservation, establishment of, 16–17

Great Sioux War coverage: and election, 97; ignored by press, 8, 34; as issue in West rather than the East, 97; as nonissue to average person, 104–105; planned by Sheridan, 18–19; regional

view of, 106; and troop competency, 19. *See also* Presidential campaign of 1876

Greeves, Lucy, 172, 191

Guilded Age, 9

Halstead, Murat, 86

Hamburg, S.C., center of "black power," 122, 133–34

Hamburg Massacre, 121–145; black men killed seen as victims, 145; called a "civil war" by *Daily Constitution* of Atlanta, 135; casualties from, 123; comparison of coverage with that of Little Bighorn, 121, 125, 144; and Custer's hometown of Monroe, Mich., 130–31; Democrats criticized over, 125, 127, 132; and effect on election, 128, 142; Hamburg described as "haven for criminals," 133–34; and *Hartford Daily Courant's* stories on, 123–25; inquest covered by *Daily Constitution* of Atlanta, 137; and Ku Klux Klan revival feared, 122; memories of Civil War evoked by, 107–108, 123; and *New York Times*, 126; photo of, *118*; and trial delay, 139; on West Coast, 131

Harper's Weekly, Custer on cover of, 4

Harrison, Benjamin, 101, 185

Harte, Bret, 171

Hartford Daily Courant: on the "condensed age," 7; on Custer's recklessness, 68; on Hamburg Massacre, 123–24; Indian side of story told by, 159; and jokes, 171, 175–76, 233n24; on lawless miners to blame for Little Bighorn, 161; on the Little Bighorn story, 39; on the Rosebud battle, 35; on Tilden's campaign techniques, 85; on Tilden's neglect of Hamburg Massacre, 124; on treaty system, 161–62

Hayes, Rutherford B.: background
of, 81–82; campaign tactics of, 86;
and Custer, 79, 224n1; fundraising
for Custer monument rejected by,
81; and Hamburg Massacre, 123;
and interview after nomination,
89, 100; Little Bighorn nonissue in
campaign of, 80–82, 96; mocked as
"the Great Unknown" in press, 91;
photo of, *119*; popularity of, 90; as
reformer distancing himself from
Grant scandals, 102; Republican
presidential nominee in 1876, 79, 86;
and "Scalpers" club, 90–91; a uniting
force in Republican party, 91; war
not mentioned in letter of acceptance
by, 100
Helena Daily Herald, 36–37, 41, 52, 70
Hendricks, Thomas, 99
Herendeen, George: fanciful account of
battle, 48; on mutilations, 48–49
Hiawatha (Longfellow), 158
Hitchcock, P. W., 80
Hog Pilots, Blue Water Grunts (Kaplan),
199
Hooker, Joseph, 92
Hope, James Barron, 59
Howard, Phocion, 177, 189–190
Humor and the Little Bighorn,
169–192; as aid in coping with
tragedy, 191–92; American humor as
source of pride, 170; common ways
of analyzing humor, 173; and cruel
and tasteless humor, 132, 171–72;
and Democratic position on army
reduction ridiculed, 187–88; generals
butt of many jokes, 180–83; and
Hamburg Massacre, 186–87; jokes
common soon after event, 172–73;
jokes mocking Custer infrequent,
190; joking widespread in aftermath
of Custer's death, 169–170; and
Mark Twain satire, 168; and the

military and government, 179; and
mocking of Indians, 178–79, 185–87;
nineteenth century filled with robust
humor, 170–71, 230n5; politicians
as targets, 184–85; and principles
for determining good taste, 192; and
reporters mocking themselves, 189–
190; and ridiculing rival newspapers
over coverage, 188–89; and scalping
as humorous, 176–78; and Sitting
Bull jokes, 174–75, 181–82, 184; and
tributes to Custer, 190–91

Illinois Daily State Journal, 128, 129
Indianapolis Journal, 59
Indian Bureau: and arms given to
Indians by, 76; corruption in, 80,
91–92, 94, 96, 99, 100, 106; and
Hayes, 107; and inadequate rations
to Indians by, 160; transfer to War
Department recommended, 71, 97,
103; and Universal Peace Union, 167;
warriors estimated in battle by, 19
Indian policy: both Hayes and Tilden
favored reform of, 104; criticisms
of in press, 71–72, 93, 94, 98–99;
election linked to war, 97; on Hayes
failure to mention, 89, 90, 91–92;
linked to election, 93; little mention
in western papers, 98; and Reno,
94; Tilden promoted as best to solve
Indian problem, 102; unmentioned
as link to election by press, 88, 94,
95–96, 104
Indians in Little Bighorn coverage,
147; attitudes toward Indians in
nineteenth century, 146–48; and
Christianity as common theme,
159–162; citizenship for Indians
advocated, 158, 231n31; and
condemnation of false reports on
Indian raids, 153; extermination
policy favored by many, 149–151;

Indians in Little Bighorn (continued)
and Indian culture not understood
by journalists, 167; Indian raids
referred to in press as massacres, 148;
and Indian side of story told, 164,
165; majority opinion was that of
forcing Indians onto reservations,
155; and organized support for
peace policy, 167; solutions offered
for "Indian Problem," 155–58; and
"tough love" policy of many, 152;
and wide disagreement among
editors on the "Indian Problem,"
147–48, 159. See also Sitting Bull
Indian war legacy in military of twenty-
first century, 199–200
Iraq and Afghanistan conflicts: Iraq
War compared with Little Bighorn,
200–202; medal winners ignored
by media, 210; significant roles in
presidential elections, 209

Johnston, Joseph E., 58
Jumping Bull, 21

Kaplan, Robert D., 199
Keller, J. D., 45
Kellogg, Mark, 47–48, 49, 87, 188;
Bismarck Tribune as employer of, 87;
and death of, 36; and joke on, 188;
last dispatch of, 41; only reporter
accompanying Custer, 33–34; profile
printed in New York Herald, 49;
upbeat attitude of, 47–48
Kellogg, William Pitt, 188
Keogh, Myles, 14, 29
Kimball, James C., 166
Ku Klux Klan, 7, 122

Lamar, Lucious Q. C., 129–30
Laramie Daily Sentinel: on false reports of
Indian raids, 153; horror expressed at
Hamburg atrocities, 144; jokes day

after Custer's death, 169; speculation
deemed useless by, 70
Last Stand Hill, 28, 29
Leavenworth Daily Appeal: and Phil
Sheridan as target of joke, 181; in
praise of Custer, 63–64
Leavenworth Daily Times, in defense of
Grant's policies, 72
Lee, Fitzhugh, 167
Lincoln, Abraham, 50, 89, 90, 123, 148
Little Bighorn, Battle of: cause of, 16;
comparison of coverage with that
of Hamburg Massacre, 144; front-
page news, 11; Hamburg Massacre
seen as more important than, 121;
Indians seen as enemy combatants,
145; mutilations reported, 29, 48–49,
51–52; news values of in 1876, 105;
number killed in, 10–11, 216n20. See
also Custer's Last Stand
Little Bighorn coverage. See Focus of
Little Bighorn coverage
Little Big Man (film), 51
Logan, John A., 107
Lone-survivor myth, 28–29
Longfellow, Henry Wadsworth, 158
Louisville Courier-Journal: and Crook
and Terry as targets of joke, 181–82;
on Custer's image after defeat, 6; in
defense of Custer, 61; on delay of
Hamburg trial, 139; fair treatment
of Indians urged by, 160–61; and
Grant "conspiracy" to kill Custer,
76, 139; Grant's decision to send
troops to S.C. mocked by, 138–39;
on Hamburg as favorite material
for Republicans, 137–38; on Hayes
as dark horse, 91; on House bill
enlarging army, 139; independent
voter chided by, 206–207; Indian
names assigned to politicians by,
185; and joke on Grant's alleged
connection to scandal, 184; and

the Little Bighorn headline, 40; local angle on Little Bighorn, 40; and mocking of Indian names, 178; northern newspapers criticized for hypocrisy, 138; Pulitzer's call for reform in, 107; Reconstruction troops criticized by, 77; and scalping jokes, 178; on Spotted Tail's criticism of Grant, 183; on starving Indians as cause for war, 160; in support of Tilden, 94–95; and tasteless jokes after Custer's death, 170; Tilden as promoted as best to solve Indian problem, 102

Louisville Sunday Review: on Custer poems, 190; and Sitting Bull jokes, 174; and Sitting Bull referred to for depilatory, 178

Lounsberry, C. A.: call for all-out war against Indians tempered, 151–52; and fit of newswriting on July 5, 41–42, 46; Kellogg's boss at Bismarck Tribune, 33; and stories based on Kellogg's notes, 34; Terry praised by, 70

Lynch, Jessica, 200, 204–205, 213

Martin, John (aka Giovanni Martini), 15, 51

Mayfield Monitor, and Grant "conspiracy" to kill Custer, 75

McCausland, John, 58

McClellan, George, 92

McDonald, E. S., 197

McDougall, Thomas, 24

McDowell, Irvin, 12

McIntosh, Donald, 47

McLaughlin, Nick, 201–202

Meade, George Gordon, 6

Medals of honor awarded, 26, 219n83

Media of today, public distrust of, 208

Medicine Cloud, 165

Meyer, John C., 173

Milburn, Charles Emmett ("Dashing Charlie"), 164–65

Missoulian (Mont.): and Phil Sheridan as target of joke, 181; Tilden praised by, 98; unconditional surrender by Indians urged by, 152

Missouri Democrat, 13

Mitchell, Thomas J., 165

Moffit, Captain, 63

Monroe (Mich.) Commercial, on Hamburg as "political massacre" in Tilden's interest, 130–31

Monroe, Mich. (Custer's hometown), 11–12, 60–61, 130–31

Morris, Roy, 83–84

Morton, Oliver P., 123, 185

Mutilation of Little Bighorn victims reported, 29, 48–49, 51–52

My Life on the Plains (Custer), 3, 5

Naming practices, Indian, 167–68

Nasiriya, battle of (Iraq) compared with Little Bighorn, 200–202

New Orleans Picayune: assertion that federal troops not needed in South, 134, 186; and call for troops to be sent from South to Indian war, 132; on Custer's gallantry, 62; Grant blamed for Little Bighorn by, 102; and "The Hamburg Butchery," 133; and joke on Grant Administration, 184; and joke on Louisiana governor with name of Kellogg, 188; and the Little Bighorn story, 40–41; and local issues (e.g., race relations) as predominant, 103–104; and Phil Sheridan as target of joke, 180; and response to Sitting Bull-Tilden jokes, 188; in support of peace negotiations with Indians, 157–58; on training Indians to be farmers, 157; war of extermination recommended by, 150–51

Newspapers, growth of, 9–10, *112*

Newton Kansan: peace policy criticized by, 71; on Sitting Bull as Democratic candidate for Congress, 187

New York Herald: and accuracy of report, 49–50; army's Crow allies mocked by, 179; criticized papers for misnaming Father De Smet, 188; and drawings from Sitting Bull's autobiography, 166; emotional editorials on Little Bighorn, 57–59; end to Sioux war urged by, 106; Hamburg seen as emblematic of key issues in country, 143; ignored by press, 35; and Indian hygiene mocked by, 179; joking on U.S. supplying Indians with ammunition, 186; joking that Sitting Bull helped cut army, 187; and Kellogg, 33, 34; and the Little Bighorn headlines, 40; main significance of Hamburg was on election, 142; on mercy for Indians by forcing onto reservations, 155; and mistaken Sitting Bull story, 76; misuse of federal troops charged by, 143; and mocking of Indian women, 178–79; on need for troops in civil matters, 142; on personal loss felt by public, 44; and poetry in praise of Custer, 59; Republican platform criticized by, 88; Republican politicians mocked by, 185; on Rosebud battle, 31; second-day story on Little Bighorn, 42; short-lived feeling of national unity after Tilden nomination, 91; and Sitting Bull's quote via Medicine Cloud, 165; solicitations for monument by, 5, 62–63, 212; southerners mocked over Hamburg Massacre in, 187; and sympathy for southern blacks, 142; Terry's official report published by, 50; on tragic romance of battle,

45–49; troop order seen as joke, 142–43

New York Times: on adaptation of Indians to white civilization, 158; and charges against Democrats, 187; and charges against Tilden, 85; Custer blamed by, 67–68; in defense of Grant's policies, 73; on Indian maids and scalping, 177–78; Indian side of story told by, 159; and jokes of jumpiness of soldiers after Little Bighorn, 180; and the Little Bighorn story, 38–39; partisan press chastised by, 95; and profiles on Custer, 190; on Republican platform, 87–88; Sioux war in 1857 described as war of extermination by, 149

New York Tribune, 32–33; declared battle as unexplainable, 69; Indian policy criticized after nine days, 71–72; politicizing Little Bighorn questioned by, 94–95; and Sioux War coverage, 32–33

New York World: on abandonment of peace policy, 153–54; on another Little Bighorn if troops sent to South, 140; and Belmont, 57; chastised for partisanship by *Times*, 95; on Custer's "frontier skill," 35; and Indian policy linked to election by, 93; and the Little Bighorn headlines, 40; little coverage of Sioux war in, 31–32; potential Civil War in South topped Sioux war in, 141; and Rain-in-the-Face anecdote, 51; schizophrenic attitude toward southern violence, 141; on South Carolina in state of anarchy, 140–41; story evolved as details emerged, 64–65

Norton, W. H., 36

Omaha Herald, "cruel rigorous war" urged by, 152

"One-to-five" theory applied to Custer's loss, 67, 222n33

Oskaloosa Independent (Republican), Democrats in Congress condemned by, 73–74

Ottawa Republican: Custer blamed by, 67; on extermination of Indians, 150

Owensboro Examiner (Ky.), 172; and Custer's death as "Sioux-icide," 172; on Custer's performance at Little Bighorn, 63; and Grant "conspiracy" to kill Custer, 75–76; on treating Indians in civilized, Christian manner, 160

Panic of 1873, 7, 17, 80

Partisanship of press in 1876, 56–57, 205–206

Peoria Daily Transcript, on avenging Custer with frontiersmen, 150

Peyton, George L., 63

Phillips, Wendell, *114*, 154–55, 167, 198

Piestewa, Lori, 204

Pomeroy, Theodore M., 87

Potts, Benjamin F., 80–81

Presidential campaign of 1876, 79–120; and apathy of public toward, 100; as closest presidential campaign in U.S. history, 82; and election day as nerve-wracking, 126; and Hamburg overshadowed Little Bighorn during, 143; Hayes as Republican nominee, 79, 86; issues in, 82–83; Little Bighorn ignored by Hayes campaign, 80–82; ranks as one of dirtiest campaigns of all time, 83; and Republican platform, 87–88; and role of Little Bighorn unclear in, 82–85, 105–108; Tilden as Democratic nominee, 80, 85–86; Union Army reunion in Toledo, 79, 224n1; and voter intimidation, 130; and voter turnout in 1876 compared with that

of 2012, 208; and war less important until Custer's death, 87–97; war not linked to election after mid-July, 97–105. *See also* Little Bighorn, Battle of

Press coverage of Sioux war, 31–54; concern in 1876 with other news, 34; and coverage of the Little Bighorn, 36–37; and Custer as "good copy," 6; Custer's clothing noted by, 5; and detailed reports followed bare, 40–41; and Kansans' disbelief in the Little Bighorn story, 39; little coverage given until Little Bighorn, 31–32; and report of Sheridan's avoidance of press, 49–50; the Rosebud largely ignored by, 35; as side issue in election year, 94; and skepticism of first stories, 38. *See also* Little Bighorn, Battle of

Printer's Ink, 9

Pruden, Wesley, 201–202

Pulitzer, Joseph, 107

Quincy Herald, Fred Grant's military service mocked by, 185

Railroads, and Fort Laramie Treaty, 17

Rain-in-the-Face, 29, 51, 106, 155

Randall, Samuel J., *117*, 187

Rau, Charles, 8

Reconstruction: and Custer, 61; favored press topic in 1876, 34; going poorly in South, 7; and Hamburg Massacre, 121; and Hayes, 100; and importance of corruption, 105; more important to press than frontier wars, 32; Republican policies unpopular, 80; troops stationed in South politicized, 76–78

Red Cloud, 16, 18, 62, 76, 185

Reed, Autie (Custer's nephew), 47, 60

Reid, Whitelaw, 32, 69, 207

Reno, Marcus: account of battle, 94; background of, 13–14; Brisbin's description of battlefield, 47; Indian policy questioned by, 94; lionized in headlines on Little Bighorn, 40–41, 46; and plan of attack, 38–39, 44, 55–56; portrayed by Brisbane as in command, 48; retreat of without Custer's support, 25–26; and scouting mission, 22, 23; and stories of Indians led by whites, 50; three companies assigned to, 24

Republican Daily Journal (Kans.), militiamen mocked by, 179–180

Republican of San Antonio, Tex., Democrats in Congress condemned by, 74

Riley, James, 199, 204

Rivers, Prince, 122, 137

Roberts, Dick, 32–33

Robertson, T. J., 122

Rocky Mountain Herald: and Crook as target of joke, 181; defeat blamed on Custer by (going against party), 70–71

Rocky Mountain News: on "false reports" of scalping, 177; on "fighting editors of eastern newspapers," 188; peace policy criticized by, 71; in praise of Custer (going against party), 70–71

Rogers, S. B., 41

Rosebud, battle of the: body of warrior found from, 24; Brisbin's account of last conference, 47; and Crook as butt of jokes because of, 181; and Crook's botched communication, 21–22, 218n63; and Finerty's heroism, 189; scope thought to be exaggerated, 35, 38; Sherman's reason for Rosebud "detour," 44; and Sitting Bull, 164–65

Rosecrans, William, 92

Rosser, Robert S., 61–62

Rowell, George P., and growth of newspapers, 9–10, 112

Rumors spread in battle stories, 50–53, 164

Rynd, Charles, on Hamburg and bloody shirt, 130–31

Savage Conflict, A (Sutherland), 123

"Scalpers" club, 90–91

Scott, Winfield, 12

Seventh Cavalry: column delayed until April, 20, 22; composition of leaders, 19; Custer in charge of, 8; divided into four commands, 24–25, 218n75; officer corps of, 13–15; and parade before Terry and Gibbon, 23; and Washita victory, 13

Sheridan, Philip H.: Custer favored by, 12; Custer overshadowed by, 3; definition of a "good" Indian by, 146, 229n2; and hard war tactics, 148–49; interview on Little Bighorn, 42; photo of, 111; president of Custer National Monument Association, 81; report of locking himself in room to avoid press, 49–50; as target of jokes, 180; at Union Army reunion in Toledo in 1873, 79; winter campaign of 1876 planned by, 18–19

Sherman, William T.: Custer overshadowed by, 3; Custer's appeal to, 20; interview on Little Bighorn, 42–43; and reason for Rosebud "detour," 44; at Union Army reunion in Toledo in 1873, 79

Sioux War Dispatches (Abrams), 146

Sitting Bull: account of Custer's death told by, 28; confusion with Ogallala of same name, 76; and Crows, 17; fear of, 154; as instigator of Sioux war, 163; interview on Little Bighorn, 53–54; mentioned, 182–87; misleading information on, 45,

52–53, 164; naming of, 168; as object of jokes, 174–75, 181–82, 184; and overconfidence in locating, 35; photo of, *115*; prophecy during Sun Dance ceremony, 21; published drawings of, 166–67; and scalping jokes, 178; and statement to Bear Stands Up that he wanted peace, 165, 199; and village enlargement, 23; as "villain" in Little Bighorn coverage, 162–66

Smith, William Henry, 86

Spotted Tail: admirer of Custer, 62; chief of reservation band, 16; contrasted with Sitting Bull, 162–63; "great speech by" on negotiating peace, 165–66; joke involving, 183; open to sale of Black Hills, 18

St. *Louis Dispatch*: apathy on party of public reported by, 100–101; argument against continuation of peace policy, 149; extermination of Indians recommended by, 146; on folly of sending more troops to South, 130; and joke on Grant's Indian policy, 184; joke on sending whiskey distillers to reservation, 186; on Sitting Bull as Democratic candidate for Congress, 187

St. *Louis Globe-Democrat*: and Crook and Terry as targets of joke, 182–83; defeat blamed on Custer by, 55–56; on disbelief of Little Bighorn in St. Louis, 45; on "Hamburg slaughter" and troop issue, 128–29; headlines for Little Bighorn, 36; Indian policy criticized, 72; joke predicting easy victory, 178; on newspapers trying too hard to be funny, 171; the Rosebud largely ignored by, 35; Spotted Tail's speech mocked by, 16; Tilden supporters attacked over Civil War records, 92

Storey, Wilbur F., 33, 45, 147, 230n5

Sturgis, Samuel D., 14–15, 45, 55

Sun Dance ceremony, 21, 23

Sutherland, Donald A., 123

Taylor, Muggins, 36

Telegraph, importance of, 10

Terry, Alfred H.: ambiguous orders to Custer, 22–23; and campaign of 1876, 19; and Custer's appeal to Grant for reinstatement, 20; dispatch to Sheridan critical of Custer, 36–37, 42; and Great Sioux War, 8; official report published by the *Herald*, 50

Texas Republican, rejoicing at Lincoln's assassination, 148

Tilden, Samuel J.: accused of ignoring Hamburg, 121, 124, 130–31; attacked over Civil War record by press, 92; campaign tactics of, 85–86; charges of being "peace democrat," 91; defeated in close election, 82; Democratic nominee for president in 1876, 80, 85–86; gubernatorial record of, 92; photo of, *120*; short-lived feeling of national unity after Tilden nomination of, 91; and Sitting Bull jokes, 188; and Watterson, 94–95

Tillman, Pat, 210, 213

Tomahawk missile, 199

Topeka Commonwealth: Civil War attitudes compared to Custer's arrogance, 67; and Custer's "one to five" theory to blame, 72, 222n33; in defense of Grant's policies, 72; destroying hostile tribes called for by, 151; and the Little Bighorn story, 39–40

Twain, Mark, 7, 83, 168, 170

Union Army reunion in Toledo, 79, 224n1

Universal Peace Union, 167

Utley, Robert M., 84, 188, 195

Van Buren, Martin, 85

Vicksburg Herald, and Phil Sheridan as target of joke, 180

Vietnam War, 213

Voter turnout in 1876 election, 208

Wallace, George (Lt.), 24

Walters, Donald, 213

Washington Chronicle, on Hamburg Massacre, 136

Washington Post, and battle of Nasiriya (Iraq), 200–202

Washington Republican (Kans.): Democrats in Congress condemned by, 74; on "Fiendish Massacre" in Hamburg, 128

Washita, Battle of, and Custer's victory, 13

Wathena Reporter (Kans.), Custer profile politicized by, 69

Watterson, Henry: as Custer friend, 61; independent voter chided by, 206–207; memoir of, 207–208; publisher of *Louisville Courier-Journal*, 61, 76, 77; as strong Tilden supporter, 94–95

Wayne, Mad Anthony, 41

West Texas Free Press (San Marcos), and Grant "conspiracy" to kill Custer, 75

Wheeler, Andrew C., 3–4, 142, 211–12

Wheeling Register, 63

Whitman, Walt, 211–12

Wild, Edward R., 148

Wooden Leg, 28

Woodford Weekly (Ky.), overthrow of Republican party urged by, 102

Wyandotte Herald (Kans.), and Custer profile, 69

York Republican (Neb.), on Tilden and violence, 131

Young-Man-Afraid-of-His-Horses, 178